A FLOWER FOR THE SEA
A FISH FOR THE SKY

A FLOWER FOR THE SEA
A FISH FOR THE SKY

FRED KELLETT

Dellwood Press

© Fred Kellett 1995
© Cover design Helene Kellett 1995

All rights reserved. No part of this book may be reproduced, stored or introduced into a retrieval system, or transmitted in any form or by any means (electronic, mechanical, photocopying, recording or otherwise) without the prior permission of the publishers or the author.

First published in 1995 by
Dellwood Press
Southwaite,
Carlisle
CA4 0EP

ISBN 0 9526808 0 7

Printed by
Fletcher & Robinson,
Queen Street,
Ulverston
LA12 7AF

To the memory of those men whose war ended at 23.20 hours on the 20th September, 1943.

ERRATA
Illustration - Relative Text
page 143 - page 186
page 186 - page 30

FOREWORD

During the second world war the Royal Navy put flowers on the sea and fish in the sky.

"Flower" class corvettes formed the greater part of the convoy escorts, day in, day out, from early 1941 until the end of the war. 100ft shorter than the Navy's accepted minimum length for an ocean going ship and only just capable of achieving the minimum speed of 16 knots required for an escort vessel, they were considered to be 'an extremely crude means of taking into action an Asdic set, depth charges and a 4in. gun'. Corvettes were built to a sound and simple design which proved to be extremely seaworthy and reliable; they were very boisterous, lively boats but the incessant movement coupled with serious overcrowding made enormous demands on the endurance of their crews.

Due to the priority enjoyed by the RAF over most of the aircraft production in the early years of the war the Barracuda torpedo bomber was not available in any numbers until 1943. It was an ungainly aircraft burdened with a clutter of extraneous gear and, apart from dive-bombing when it had the assistance of gravity, its performance rarely inspired the men who were required to fly it.

This story involves one of the flowers, H.M.S. Polyanthus, and the Barracuda; it is a story of life as it was at the time - seen from the inside - looking out.

ONE

Cleckheaton Feast was the annual holiday for the people of Spen Valley. My earliest memory of the event was of standing on the upper deck of what seemed at the time to be a very large ship and being startled by a great, triumphant blast from its siren; I looked up towards the tall red funnels and another imperious rasping roar tore the air apart for a second time. A warm spray of condensed steam fell from the siren on to my upturned face and baptised me into a fascinating world of ships and the sea.

I was five years old and the ship was the ferry leaving Heysham bound for the Isle of Man.

Cleckheaton sits in that part of the West Riding of Yorkshire where town and city boundaries are lost in a dense urban sprawl. Along with its larger neighbours - Leeds, Bradford, Halifax, Huddersfield, Dewsbury and Wakefield - it was, in 1939, just emerging from the economic depression that had swept the Western World towards the end of the 1920's; a period when skilled and capable men found themselves discarded through no fault of their own and, if they were over thirty, considered too old for re-employment.

My father was one of them.

I was four years old when my parents sank their savings and money borrowed from various sources in a wool and drapery business and moved to Cleckheaton. They gave up a large comfortable house for the cramped accommodation behind a shop which my mother ran while my father tried in vain to find work. From a responsible post in middle-management he was, for many years, forced to surrender his role as bread-winner to his wife. When he finally found regular work it was as a temporary postman and, although he subsequently earned some promotion, it was always on a temporary basis.

I grew up in Cleckheaton: I played football and cricket in its streets, using the same tennis ball for either game; it is where I went to day school and to Sunday school, to the grammar school and to chapel. It witnessed my progress from an only child who was inclined to be soft and sensitive, to a more determined and frequently stubborn youth. It was where my friends lived, it was my home, and in 1939 it was more or less the centre of the world as I knew it.

War was declared on the Sunday of Cleckheaton Feast in 1939.

Arrangements were made with my parents' Accountant for me to be articled to him when I left the grammar school, and so, shortly after my 16th birthday, I had entered the world of accountancy.

Entry to most professions was still subject to the system of articles and parents were required to pay premiums simply to enable their offspring to sit exams. Not only did the system provide a nice lump of cash for the principal, it also provided him with a source of free or very low-paid labour.

I reported for work on the first day and found a senior clerk who had to be obeyed and a fire which had to be lit; the clerk was fine but the fire was a brute. I overcame the problem with the fire when I discovered and removed an empty whisky bottle from beneath the grate. The senior clerk appeared to be a steady, sober type of lad so I awaited the arrival of my new boss with curiosity. In the meantime I was told to wash the windows.

My introduction to the world of accountancy left me with no illusions as to my standing - having been on the top of the heap at school I was now right down at the very bottom again.

It was not a big heap; only one senior articled clerk stood between me and the boss and he was a friendly lad who spared me many of the humiliations frequently inflicted on newcomers. Before the first day was out I had checked pages upon pages of additions, something I was to do for many days thereafter; an occasional break to cross-check entries failed to add any excitement.

My employer had been an outstanding student and became an able and competent accountant. He quickly built up a thriving practice and attracted a number of youths with parents who were prepared to pay good premiums for articles; one or two of the youths proved to be numerate and reliable and with no wages bill to speak of his fortunes multiplied very quickly.

As his personal workload diminished his opportunities to celebrate his good fortune increased. A bad accident some months before I came on the scene left him crippled, reliant on a stout stick and more than ever on the bottle.

In his more sober moments my first employer was a most kind and patient man with very high professional and moral standards. The problems arising from his attempts to mix drink and work were a salutary lesson for a lad undergoing his initiation into the adult world.

My opportunity to find alternative employment came as a direct result of the crisis in Europe which was by then approaching its climax. Territorials in the local Duke of Wellington's Regiment (the Dirty Dukes) were mobilised and the junior clerk in the local office of an international firm of chartered accountants was one of them.

I started work in his place immediately after Cleckheaton Feast in 1939.

With a larger office and more senior clerks to please my life became a long dreary round of additions, followed by more and more additions until my dreams were being interrupted by them. Auditing must be one of the most boring occupations for a junior clerk and even when I was allowed to participate in the more advanced work I found it most unrewarding. Day-dreams made up for the dreams I had lost at night.

Like many of my contemporaries I had attended piano lessons during my school-days and had developed a lively interest in music. An opportunity to take lessons on a pipe-organ provided relief from the boredom of my daily work and a most rewarding leisure interest. It also provided another insight into the world at large when my tutor, a most respectable and highly regarded pillar of society, became over-excited one evening and displayed more interest in other organs. It was my first real encounter with anyone of his type and although I left him in no doubt as to my thoughts, I lost my somewhat naive unquestioning faith in my elders.

During the winter months I also enjoyed the tremendous relief and exercise provided by games of rugby, I hesitate to use the word 'play' in this connection because, yet again, it was an activity that qualified more than most as one of my initiation rites. It was one that I entered into wholeheartedly and without reservation on a sloping field behind the Brown Cow Inn and Whitechapel Church, a field that was a long way from the Rugby Club and any connection with legitimate rugby.

On Saturday afternoons I would join a strangely assorted bunch of creatures wearing colourful, if faded, outfits; their ages would vary between 16 and 46 as would their waist lines. Any cows, sheep or horses that were likely to interfere with our sport were rounded up and herded into the adjoining field and the location and amount of their deposits noted. Such deposits provided opportunities to change the colour of opponents' shirts or faces during the course of the game, always assuming that they were unable to catch you first. There was always a ball in use somewhere or other, a misshapen object long since discarded by the serious players, and likely to be burst before we all trooped off looking and smelling like bags of fertiliser.

The Vicar of Whitechapel was an enthusiastic participant in the sport and on the Saturdays when he had a wedding in the Church the referee would be warned that a player had been delayed. In due course the Vicar would appear and jump over the wall of the churchyard having hastily thrown off his surplice at the first opportunity. That he was always dressed for the game beneath his surplice was beyond question, his claim to have performed the wedding ceremony in rugby boots was doubted.

Third team rugby was a big change from my school rugby but it was great fun and prepared me and many others for the senior games that followed.

Fire-watching duties took over several nights of the week; the duties at the office together with those for my parents' shop involved the discomfort of a night lying on a table top, or at the best, a makeshift campbed but they provided a welcome addition to my income. A couple of incendiaries accidentally fell out of a German plane on its way to Manchester or Liverpool on one of my nights on duty, otherwise firewatching was uneventful.

Bradford was bombed on the first weekend of September, 1940 - it was Cleckheaton Feast again.

As more and more age groups were called up into the Forces the personnel in the office changed and so did the nature of my work. Charity audits became my responsibility; they were accepted as part of a goodwill exercise - the sprats to catch the mackerel - and were another part of my initiation. Time after time I found the figure heads who were accorded all the honour for effort and hard work had contributed little or nothing to the result; a conscientious secretary or clerk was the person who did the work. All too often the beneficiaries of the charities were better off than those who went out to collect on the streets or gave a few odd pence they could ill afford. I learnt that the smallest purse often held the largest heart.

Being a relatively normal person I became increasingly aware of girls during my adolescence, albeit at a distance. I became more aware of Mary at a Christmas party; we had attended the same Sunday school and chapel and shared the same music teacher but our relationship had been very much at a distance. When I walked her home from the party our relationship moved closer - to about arm's-length.

I continued to devote my attention to rugby and music whilst enduring the dull tedium that was auditing; Sundays now held an opportunity for a little shy flirtation with the eyes but it was not until I took out my tennis racquet in early summer that I came within arms-length of Mary again. It never worried us when we had to spend time in the pavilion because of the mixed weather, it enabled us to become far better acquainted and I walked her home more often.

Arm's-length was reduced until it disappeared and goodnight became a kiss and a cuddle.

Our youth created doubts and misgivings in the hearts and minds of our parents who tried to dissuade us from forming too close a friendship. In reality they simply put our feelings for each other to the test and we refused to surrender our friendship to anyone, not even our parents of whom we were extremely fond.

Choir practices at the chapel provided regular opportunities for us to meet; we took part in the traditional performances of the 'Messiah' that were an integral part of the community. The Cleckheaton chapels alone produced four 'Messiahs' each Christmas and great was the rivalry, not all of it friendly.

As my eighteenth birthday drew near my thoughts dwelt more and more on my eventual departure into the armed forces. My preference for the Royal Navy was never in doubt despite my almost complete lack of knowledge of the actual conditions entailed. A former school friend came home on leave resplendent in the uniform of an officer in the RNVR with pilot's wings on his left sleeve, and I contacted the Naval Recruiting Office in Leeds. It was agreed that I would volunteer three or four months before my age group was due for conscription.

Mary and I set out to make the most of the summer of 1941. At Easter we had taken day outings to Bolton Abbey and to the moors. Every alternate Sunday I would play the organ for the services at chapel; on my free Sundays Mary and I would pack our sandwiches and catch the bus to Bradford and then another to Ilkley or Skipton. The Yorkshire dales and moors captured our hearts as we walked the lanes and paths, traced river beds and wandered through woods. It was not unusual for us to cover 10 to 15 miles before catching buses home, tired and happy.

At the junction of the roads to Settle and Grassington near Skipton church, there was a shop which sold hot pork pies containing lovely gravy; they were at their best when eaten as we walked out of the shop and along the road. The butcher's shop is still there and they still sell pies but they will never make a pie to taste as good as the ones we enjoyed in those halcyon days of 1941.

Almost all our spare cash went on these outings, our most expensive day cost us 7/6 and left us with very little spare cash for the following week.

To our great surprise we were able to spend a week at Blackpool with Mary's mother and aunts, and then a weekend at Morecambe where my parents were on holiday. As we walked along the promenade at Morecambe, Mary spotted a small enamel brooch on the ground; it proved to be a replica of the Fleet Air Arm pilots' wings.

It seemed like an omen - we found it on the Sunday morning of Cleckheaton Feast in 1941.

* * * * * *

In November I applied for acceptance for training as a pilot in the Fleet Air Arm and was passed fit for admission into the Royal Navy after a medical examination in Leeds. Shortly afterwards I received instructions to present myself at the Naval Centre in Darlington for a further, stricter medical and interview by a Selection Board.

Not many people were waiting for the early train at Leeds Station on that morning and only two were young enough to be candidates for the Fleet Air Arm. My fellow traveller was an older lad named Bennett, an electrical engineer who had returned from the Argentine at his own expense in order to become a pilot.

At the Naval Centre we discarded our clothes along with another four hopeful volunteers and were put through a rigorous medical examination. Afterwards, we perched on upright chairs ranged along a wall and cautiously eyed one another; the first candidate was called for interview and the room fell silent in the hope that we might overhear the proceedings. He emerged to be greeted with a barrage of questions.

"What happens in there?" "How many are there?" "What are they like?" "What did they ask you?"

He was a confident youth with a public school accent and a condescending manner; his answers were most unhelpful.

"Actually, it was just a formality really. My uncle's a Surgeon Captain and was at prep' school with the Senior Officer; calls him 'Stinker', don't you know."

My turn came. "Have you or your family any connections with the Royal Navy?" I was asked.

"No" I answered. The members of the Board exchanged glances and assumed their impartial expressions.

"Do you think this plane would fly?" asked the lieutenant with wings on his sleeve, as he pointed to a model with an engine on the leading edge of the port wing and an engine on the trailing edge of the starboard wing. I had read of multi-engined planes staggering home with one and two engines damaged.

"I doubt it, sir" I replied and felt I should hedge my bets. "But if anyone built such a plane they would expect it to fly."

A pitying look was my reward.

When all the interviews were complete we were called back in turn and told our fate. The nephew of 'Stinker's' friend and Bennett were recommended for pilot training; the rest of us were offered training as Telegraphist/Air Gunners or 'Y' Scheme entry into the Executive Branch (the deck Navy). I opted for the latter and earned the approval of the Senior Officer. I had yet to learn of the attitude of the traditional officer toward his airborne brother.

Although no one begrudged Bennett his recommendation there was general resentment at the preferment of the other lad; not that any one of us would have failed to make use of a similar advantage. On our way to the station we exchanged impressions of the interviews and agreed that the questions asked by the lieutenant had been ridiculous and particularly inappropriate for youths with no flying knowledge or experience.

"I thought the idea was to train us in such matters" said one.

"Here am I, never been in an aeroplane and I'm asked 'If you have to do a forced landing and you see some cows in a field, how do you know the direction of the wind?'"

"I simply told him I didn't know and asked how I should know," announced Bennett.

"And did he tell you?"

"Apparently cows stand with their backs to the wind ."

"Does the same apply to sea cows?" queried another.

On our journey back to Leeds we took an unusual interest in any fields containing cattle and concluded that Yorkshire was experiencing a plague of whirlwinds that afternoon.

During my last Christmas as a civilian I became increasingly aware of all the familiar faces and places I loved. My future in the Navy offered more interest and excitement than I could find in accountancy but the time had come when reality would replace imagination. As my apprehension grew, my confidence declined; it would be a step into another world, to be faced entirely on my own.

Mary and I said our goodbyes on the Sunday night and I realised how badly I was going to miss her.

"Well you're leaving home now and I feel you'll never come back here to live" was my mother's parting thought as I took my leave of her and walked with my father to the bus terminus.

As I boarded the bus I said goodbye to my father - and to my youth.

TWO

"And this 'ere is a lanyard, it 'as a small loop at this end and a bigger loop with a running knot at the other."

The Chief Petty Officer had reached the end of his introduction to the uniform and equipment which had been issued to us earlier in a very long first day. After outlining its place in the traditions of the Royal Navy and the manner in which it was to be worn he surveyed the faces of the sixty or so men who were in the last throes of civilian life.

"For those of you who feel as bad as you look I draw your attention to the nail above this bed."

He pointed to a sturdy projection on the wall about 8 or 9 feet from the floor.

"If you stand on the bed the small loop on your lanyard can be placed over the nail quite easily and when you've done that you put the big loop round your neck and pull it tight - then all you 'ave to do is jump off the bed."

A few uneasy laughs failed to interrupt a well-established routine.

"Them as don't fancy that will 'ear 'Wakey Wakey' at four bells - that's six o'clock in the morning - and I'm the one who'll be yelling in your ear-'ole. Now get all your 'civvy' gear packed up and ready to send home b'cos you won't be needing it any more; tomorrow I want you to dress up like sailors."

He departed, leaving a bunch of slightly bewildered recruits to cope with a strange new environment where time was expressed in bells and trousers had flaps instead of flies. There was an inescapable finality involved in packing all the civilian clothes and contemplating the new uniforms which replaced them, each item stamped with the name of its owner. All the newly acquired possessions served to emphasise the Navy's complete take over of our lives, particularly that most naval item of all - the hammock, the bed and bedding that would stay with us always.

The long, slow journey from Leeds had taken most of the previous day and the train had been cold. At the entrance to Ipswich station I joined a group of shivering lads gathered round a naval truck; icy winds fresh from the grey North Sea lashed into our faces and warned of the challenges we would face in the days ahead. One by one we clambered up on to the back of the truck and, as it lurched and swayed along the roads to HMS Ganges, we looked out on a flat countryside made dull and uninviting by the dismal weather. I studied the faces of my companions and wondered if they too were experiencing the apprehension and misgivings that were dominating my thoughts. The truck passed through an impressive gateway, flanked by two naval sentries, and stopped. A sailor appeared and smartly removed the pins to release the tailgate; it swung down.

"Out you get and bring your cases with you. Form up in three ranks facing the guardroom."

The response to our first orders in the Royal Navy left a lot to be desired; the efforts of those who obeyed smartly were offset by the uncertainty and indecision of others. The sailor positioned himself in front of the guardroom where he stood stiffly to attention with his arms extended straight down by his side; on his left sleeve the anchor of a leading seaman and three good-conduct stripes testified to his status. Our antics as we formed ranks were met with an impassive gaze.

"Right turn, quick march and for God's sake try and look as tidy as you can."

We turned and faced a ship's mast: it towered up into the sky. As we half walked and half marched to be formally received into the Navy, an anonymous voice observed,

"Everyone has to climb to the top of that before they leave here."

"Keep silence" yelled our escort but the seeds had been sown and my bones were chilled even more by the thoughts of scrambling up and out along those yardarms, way up in the heavens.

HMS Ganges had been one of the Navy's training establishments for boy entrants prior to the outbreak of war, then everything changed and each week brought an influx of new recruits to be trained in things nautical. The course lasted 10 or 12 weeks and covered many things that few of the recruits would ever encounter again in their naval careers and which were sure to have been forgotten if and when they did.

For the first week we were housed in an annexe dormitory and were processed through the induction machinery; dental and medical examinations were followed by vaccinations and jabs that floored some and were scarcely noticed by others. The absence of shore leave in the first week was barely noticed as we faced up to the problems of settling into a new environment. ENSA put on a mid-week show in the canteen and we were urged to join in the chorus of 'The Lights of Home'; it simply fanned the embers of homesickness and as a result the evening was not a success. We retreated to our mess and our beds, our minds preoccupied with thoughts of home.

Despite the tiredness that resulted from early rising, sleep did not come easily. My thoughts were with Mary, we had said our farewells only a few days before; now the real meaning of separation weighed down on me as I wallowed in a sea of nostalgic memories before oblivion eventually came to my rescue.

When all the basic formalities had been completed we were moved into a proper mess in the single-storey barracks which had double bunks ranged along both walls and in two rows down the middle. A couple of long scrubbed tables with matching forms separated the sleeping area from the ablutions beside the entrance. Adjustment to these somewhat austere living conditions was only of minor importance compared with the overwhelming changes to our whole lives.

Language deteriorated quickly. An anxiety to appear as street-wise as the next man frequently turned what should have been everyday conversation into obscene nonsense. Sanity slowly regained control over insecurity but the vocabulary of the vast majority underwent a profound change and the few who resisted the trend were regarded with suspicion.

Broadbent from Lancashire had the bunk above mine; he was short and broad in stature and full of spunk. The rivalry between our respective Counties allowed us to indulge in a constant exchange of insults in a broad dialect that completely baffled many of our neighbours. Our verbal affrays covered a wide range of subjects from cricket to brass bands, anything to provide a diversion from the underlying despondency we were at pains to conceal from each other. Whenever the argument began to go my way, Broadbent would produce his trump card

"Well, who won th' war of th' roses then?"

Weldon, a well-spoken lad in the next bunk, found our conversations quite un-intelligible. He was fascinated by the Chief Petty Officer's habit of smoking his pipe before breakfast and one morning he duly told the Chief that he should wait until he had eaten before lighting his pipe. An astounded Chief was rendered speechless by the innocent, polite and well-meant suggestion whilst we, who were in the immediate vicinity, waited in vain for the storm to break. Finally the Chief broke the silence.

"Any interest in my health is not usually beneficial" he mused. "But old habits die hard, lad. In any case you won't have to worry about me for a week b'cos I'm going on leave tomorrow."

"Where do you live?" asked the solicitous Weldon, with alarming familiarity. The Chief turned away as he answered,

"Elland, in Yorkshire."

"Well I'll go to th' foot of our stairs" cried Broadbent as he turned on me. "As if it isn't bad enough having to put up wi' thee, mi' bloody gaffer's a Yorky an' all."

One of the more self-assured members of our group, Hobbs, came from London's Dockland and occupied a nearby bed. He concentrated much of his spare time on his boots which he treated with frequent and liberal applications of polish and spit. The dull, greasy finish of the leather gradually gave way to a deep glassy polish and earned him many admirers.

"That was a trick I learnt when I was in the army," he boasted. "Didn't like the army much so I deserted and joined this lot instead."

On the parade ground where the majority of our brains were frozen into a numbed stupor, Hobbs displayed a grasp of the commands that suggested his story might well be valid and this gave him a certain prestige in the eyes of several lads. He began to attract a bunch of followers.

Relationships were very superficial. Few of us were inclined to open up too much or invite confidences; in our spare time we did all the sundry jobs our mothers had done for us previously and which we had always taken for granted, darning, mending and washing, known in the navy as 'dhobying'. Some spent hours scrubbing away at their blue collars, anxious to create, by the washed-out look, an image of long service. We wrote our letters home or sat forlornly on our beds polishing, spitting and re-polishing boots with bent heads and gazing through shiny toecaps into our dreams or memories. The appeal of the life we had known and had so recently left behind dominated our thoughts and dulled our enthusiasm as we were being gradually led, chivied, bullied and generally knocked into the mould of an embryo matelot.

Daily perusal of the notice board was an essential routine. Most of the notices concerning sport dealt with cancellations due to the freezing weather. Rugby, which claimed all my sporting enthusiasm in winter; was a permanent casualty of the conditions. It was particularly disappointing for me because a number of New Zealand recruits were in training at the time and the prospects of games of a high standard were anticipated. It was not until a notice appeared asking for entries for the inter-divisional boxing contest that any interest in sport was aroused. Three members of our mess put their names forward; Broadbent in the lightweight division, Kerr, a quiet, reserved and well-spoken Scot, and Hobbs, in the heavyweight division.

Kipling's poem 'If' was painted in large letters on one of the end walls of the gym; I was able to study it more leisurely when I took my seat on the evening of the boxing contests. I felt its message could not have been displayed in a better place as with mounting excitement, I examined the programme along with my messmates for the names of our gladiators. Only two heavyweights were listed, Hobbs and Kerr - our two lads were to fight each other. Broadbent's contest took place fairly early on in the proceedings and our cheers gradually changed from enthusiasm at his non-stop aggression to sympathy for the hiding he was taking; for he faced a most skilful opponent who knew how to deal with a scrapper. Most of Broadbent's attacks were evaded or absorbed on arms and elbows and he only knew one way - to go forward - to attack; the art of defence was not in his book. Even though he had stayed on his feet throughout there was a sense of relief when the contest came to an end. I was upset by the way Broadbent's efforts were dismissed by many of our crowd who were much more concerned with the 'big fight' yet to come.

"At least he did more than all of us here," I found myself arguing as we awaited the clash of the heavyweights, the bout everyone was waiting for.

Hobbs and Kerr certainly filled the ring with a promise of some heavy thumping and Hobbs set out to intimidate and demolish an opponent whom so few fancied or envied. With snorts and grunts he waved his shoulders and elbows around and shot out his arms in the direction of an elusive Kerr who managed to keep well out of harm's way. As the grunting Hobbs rushed towards him yet again, Kerr unexpectedly shot out his left fist which temporarily re-shaped Hobbs' nose and seriously interfered with the aggressive sound effects. Hobbs reacted to this unfriendly gesture by dropping his already suspect guard, Kerr brought over his right hand and deposited Hobbs on his backside where he assumed an expression of absolute amazement and was counted out - Kerr looked very puzzled.

One or two impressions and attitudes were re-arranged that evening, Hobbs lost face and many followers; Kerr never discussed it and Broadbent proved he wasn't a quitter.

Regular sessions of physical training helped in the gradual build up of overall fitness and although swimming was a sport that was encouraged there was little enthusiasm to be found in our mess. Those who could swim were, like myself, capable of meeting the required minimum standard of swimming two lengths of the bath whilst wearing a canvas duck suit but were not, generally speaking, accomplished swimmers.

Drill out on the exposed parade ground probably contributed to the improvement in our physical condition more than any other activity. It was an ordeal in the icy winds; hardly a day passed without someone passing out from the cold, particularly so in the early days shortly after vaccinations. The gunners' mates who were in charge rarely stood still and carried out the drill alongside us in an effort to keep warm. It was even colder out on the river as we struggled to man a whaler and the Chief Petty Officer in charge was driven to the point of despair as one struggling recruit after another failed to control his oar. Eventually, we reached the jetty and scrambled ashore with numbed and frozen limbs, our noses and ears bitten blue by the merciless wind: we were the epitomy of abject misery. My warmest few minutes on an outdoor activity came on the afternoon when the air raid sirens sounded and the ships in the river opened up at enemy planes which had appeared overhead. We were midway through a drill session when the order was given to scatter; it was a situation where I felt speed was of the essence and I hit the ditch at the side of the parade ground as quickly as anyone. As others flung themselves on top of me I was comforted by the thought of the protection they were providing. Fortunately no one was hurt.

Six weeks after we had arrived at Ganges we were each handed a weekend pass and a rail-warrant.

    It had been the longest six weeks of my life - I had felt terribly alone and had been very, very home-sick.

THREE

The railways did not provide a speedy service between Ipswich and Yorkshire. A week-end pass from Ganges was more of a permit to travel than a chance to spend time with family and friends. With so short a time at home I seemed to talk incessantly. Surrounded once more by all the familiar faces and places, the experiences of the previous six weeks, like my uniform, provided me with a sense of achievement. I had so much to tell that I had no time to dwell on the misery which had almost overwhelmed me at times.

Leave was over almost as soon as it began. It was no more than a short break in a long train journey that began with eager anticipation and ended with desolation; a journey which emphasised the irreversible changes in my life I must accept and overcome. There may have been a few recruits who returned from their first week-end leave all bright-eyed and bushy-tailed but I was not one of them, nor was my misery improved by the news that my name was one of a list of six on the notice board. We were instructed to report to the divisional office on the following morning after stand-easy. With nothing to connect the names in any way, there was considerable speculation on the selection of the six and the reason for it.

"You have been chosen for training on RDF which is a top secret development. Your training will take place in the Isle of Man and you will report at this office tomorrow at 08.30 with your kit-bags and hammocks ready to travel. Dismiss."

This was a totally unexpected development which provided a positive distraction from the depression left by my fleeting glimpse of home. Having visited the island twice as a small boy I felt it was a much more inviting prospect than an East Anglia tormented by the wild winds of winter. Even more intriguing was the tantalising top secret training. As with most top secrets there was always someone to provide further information, and we quickly discovered it was a means of detection using radio waves based on the same principles as the equipment used by the RAF but of a much more advanced nature.

All our kit was packed as far as possible that night. I was sorry to be leaving

Broadbent and Weldon behind but pleased to escape from a place which held few happy memories for me.

Someone had decided to make me responsible for the envelope containing all our draft particulars and records, together with a travel warrant for six men, and an itinerary covering stations and train times to ensure our arrival at Fleetwood in time to catch the boat for Douglas.

With our kit-bags and hammocks piled high on a platform truck we headed towards the London train in what amounted to a holiday mood. Authority was left behind, freedom for a few hours lay ahead. By the time we reached London and had found our way to Euston it was decided that refreshment was advisable, the nature and proportions of which varied widely within the party. Two members stayed with the kit whilst the other four refreshed their thirsts or hunger, or both.

Responsibility reared its head when there was no sign of two who had bigger thirsts than the rest of us and I suddenly realised that the envelope and rail warrant made me answerable for them; the sense of freedom I had enjoyed was replaced by mounting apprehension. They arrived shortly before we were due to board the train and announced their intention to stay another day in London. Visions of varying degrees of punishment filled my mind. If the papers I presented failed to reconcile with the bodies nothing could save me; the one who carries the can is the one least capable of defending himself - that much I had learnt already.

"We stick to this itinerary" I said, hoping my nervousness would not betray itself.

"If any of you want to do something else I can't stop you, but remember I have the travel warrant - anyone who is not with me will have a hell of a job getting to the Isle of Man quite apart from explaining a late arrival."

They boarded the train with reluctance; I boarded with relief.

After an uncomfortable overnight journey, we arrived at Fleetwood feeling tired and travel-worn. My first sea voyage had been to the Isle of Man when I was five years old and my first sea voyage in the Royal Navy was aboard an Isle of Man Steam Packet; it rolled and tossed far too much for comfort and a life on the ocean wave lost much of its attraction as we made that crossing to the Isle of Man.

None of our party presented a smart picture when we reported to the Master at Arms office at HMS Valkyrie, a 'ship' consisting of a block of private hotels and boarding houses surrounded by a tall wire fence on the promenade at Douglas. It was distinguished from neighbouring blocks of houses within similar fences by the White Ensign flying from a flag pole in front of the most central house and by the presence of naval personnel. The other blocks housed people interned for the duration of the war, people of alien birth or allegiance who wandered around the compounds with faces emptied of emotion by their

15

hopeless existence.

Along with three of my travelling companions I was directed to a bedroom on the second floor at the back of the house; it contained two beds and a double bunk. In place of the barracks of Ganges we were now housed in a requisitioned private hotel on the promenade at Douglas, and life in the immediate future promised to be far less rigid than it had been previously. Our dining room was in the basement, a large pleasant room facing out into the bay. During our first meal someone queried the room allocation: " How do you get a room at the front with a bay window I'd like to know? - we've all been shoved into the back rooms." No one could supply the answer at the time, but we were able to counter the improvement in our living conditions with a good grumble on the first day.

A classroom had been set up in one of the houses and there we were introduced to the world of electricity and its associated equipment; to the world of high frequency sound and radio waves; to cathode ray tubes and their application and uses in measuring and displaying the behaviour of those waves. The importance of utmost secrecy was again impressed upon us when we were all required to acknowledge it on oath.

"You are about to be introduced to the latest development in detection equipment, using ultra-frequency waves which the enemy is incapable of detecting as far as we know," the instructor was an enthusiastic but rather untidy-looking officer. "You may know of existing radio detection equipment known as HF/DF, or "huff-duff", that is high-frequency direction-finding which enables us to determine the direction from which radio signals are being transmitted. This is altogether different - we transmit a very accurate directional signal which is reflected back by any solid object it encounters and from the time it takes to get back we can establish how far that object is from us. It is a range and direction finder - hence its name - RDF."

Our introduction to the actual equipment, the 'Set' (271), took place on Douglas Head where it was housed in a building with an uninterrupted view across the Irish Sea. It was not in the least bit impressive and consisted of two light grey steel boxes, one above the other and an aerial housed in a turret on the roof. In the upper box was a small cathode ray tube about six inches in diameter with a graded scale marked horizontally across the middle. The aerial was operated by a handle and the direction in which it was facing was indicated on a round plate above the handle, its rim coloured half in red (port), half in green, (starboard) with each half divided into 180 degrees.

The signal was transmitted via the aerial which also received the waves reflected back by any object which it encountered. The delay between transmission and reception was recorded by a spike or blip on the signal trace of the cathode ray tube, and the distance travelled by the signal could be determined from the horizontal scale; the bearing of the object was read from the indicator of the aerial's direction.

It was an early and primitive version of what eventually developed into the radar we now know; the operator had to work with the tube and its green tracer line facing him but the aerial handle and indicator were alongside his right ear. The ideal operator would have had eyes at right angles to each other; unfortunately no such recruit could pass the medical.

Rationing was not as severe on the Isle of Man as it was on the mainland; chocolate and eggs were freely available and we discovered it was possible to buy jars of honey which went well with the thick slices of bread issued at tea time. Discipline was more relaxed; the lessons were interesting and, although the actual operating of the set became dreary, the march to and from Douglas Head was usually enjoyable. Even the heavy mists and occasional rain failed to spoil the outings.

As the course progressed we carried out practices and tests on board a small steam yacht which had been privately owned before being taken over by the Navy. It was fitted with an RDF set and stationed at Douglas. When not operating the set we chipped and scrubbed the paintwork on the upper deck or repainted the treated areas with red lead and battleship grey. Aspiring sailors found sea-legs were not acquired overnight and the nauseous smells of fuel oil and paint compounded their distress. We calculated the whole of the upper deck of the ship must have been re-painted every six weeks.

At the end of the course we were examined on the theoretical work, which I had enjoyed and found relatively easy to absorb; even so my marks amazed me and I broke with tradition by emerging at the top of my class. With the new qualification of Ordinary Seaman RDF I was now considered suitable for active service and was sent home on seven days leave.

My return from leave was still a wrench but it was to a life to which I was more adjusted. Naval terminology came more readily to our lips and in the unusual environment that was Valkyrie we gradually absorbed many of the Navy's customs. Profanities prevailed in day-to-day language without achieving the ridiculous levels of Ganges. Some men developed their use of expletives almost into an art form; our Divisional Officer, when upset, would favour a duck with wishes calculated to delight or distress the poor creature.

To get ashore in our free time we had to catch a 'liberty boat' after being inspected by the officer of the day. In reality we simply turned left after the inspection and marched a few steps to the gate before stepping out into the town. The familiarity of civilian life was still within reach and our transformation into sailors was made easier as a result.

Jon Pertwee, who had yet to earn his later reputation in the world of entertainment, was our divisional officer. He organised a memorable ship's concert at the Villa Marina in which his outstanding contribution concerned a ships' company which had been blown into the beyond being detailed off to work 'part of ship' the next morning. The duties varied from Jacob's ladder

17

working party to polishing the Pearly Gates - apart from poor old Pertwee who was put on 'Harpin' - harpin' on a cold damp cloud.' It delighted the audience and brought the house down.

Church parade on Sunday mornings entailed a march through the town to the church; the 'other denominations' at Valkyrie did not find this much of a privilege however - they attended Loch Parade Chapel just outside the gate. What they found was a very happy minister and a congregation which enjoyed singing good rousing hymns. The happiest church parades I attended in the Navy were at Loch Parade.

Those of us who had completed the course were detailed off for general duties; after several days of scrubbing, cleaning and peeling potatoes I was told to report for duty as a cell sentry. Two lock-up garages in a cul-de-sac behind the Sefton Hotel had been converted into the naval prison and I found it consisted of three cells, a guard room, kitchen and toilet. Only one prisoner demanded our attention and he was locked in the cell immediately to the right of the outer door. Through the small, square, barred window in the cell door I could see him picking oakum as he sat on a broad wooden bench/bed, with a solid 'U' shaped block of wood at one end for a pillow. Apart from the rope and oakum on the floor along with a 'slop' bucket the cell was bare. Anyone who was unwise enough to offend the Navy could obviously say goodbye to anything that could provide a vestige of comfort.

"What's the prisoner in for?" I asked my fellow sentry at the first opportunity.

"Ginger's from the training ship; he was caught making cocoa in the middle watch whilst on duty as quartermaster. The trouble was he was caught using the officers' supplies in the wardroom pantry. He got fourteen days cells."

The sentence seemed to be very harsh but it provided me and one or two more with a job and I soon discovered it to be one of the best jobs on the island. Unfortunately it separated me from the first real friends I had made in the Navy; I was on four hours on, four hours off, twenty four hours about whereas all my room-mates were on different duties. I had every alternate day free and no friends to share it.

Supervising my duty was CPO Keohane, a quiet, self-contained reservist. On his chest a white medal ribbon held pride of place; with his ribbons from the 1914-18 War and other ribbons he had quite an array. My curiosity was aroused by the pure white ribbon and I plucked up the courage to ask the Chief what it represented.

"That was for volunteering for the Antarctic Expedition; for two years in a freezing white hell. I never volunteered for anything again once I was lucky enough to get home; nor will you, lad, if you take my advice."

Whereupon he turned back to the book he was reading, the conversation at an end. I sought more information from his opposite number on the alternate shift.

"Paddy Keohane found the diary under Scott's head when the relief party found the bodies but you won't hear him talk about it. Just let sleeping dogs lie if you want to remain on good terms with him."

Every afternoon I would sit with the Chief in the small guard room, the few chores long done; content with his book, our conversation was minimal.

Apart from the basic civilities I never heard him speak much, yet I never tired of his company and admired him tremendously.

Most of my leisure time was spent on my own; on fine days I explored the surrounding countryside and bathed in the cold sea once or twice. On one rather wet evening I was in the queue for the cinema on Strand Road when a lady touched my arm.

"My daughter tells me you buy honey from her."

She was a friendly soul accompanied by a girl of about sixteen and a boy of ten or eleven; I realised the girl had probably served me at 'Boots' when I had bought my honey.

"Don't you get enough to eat?" she asked.

I explained the position and was drawn into a conversation which continued until we were seated in the cinema. After the show came an invitation to 'have a bit of supper at home'. Ma Smethurst chattered away, her son John asked endless questions about the Navy whilst his sister Audrey said little but contributed a happy smile.

"You'll have to excuse the mess, find yourself a seat if you can - move the ironing off that chair Audrey and give the lad a seat - John, try and find somewhere else for those comics and newspapers - whatever you'll think of us I just don't know."

My hostess buzzed about a kitchen that was clean but cluttered as she kept up her chatter. Out came some potatoes.

"You'll have some of my chips won't you? Everyone says there's nobody can make chips as good as mine, don't they Audrey?"

Setting the table took no time at all; everything was already on it. We dined in comfortable chaos and the chips were out of this world. I had found my first 'up homers' as they were known in the Navy.

From then on my visits to Hawarden Avenue were regular and enjoyable. I discovered that the kitchen was filled with more than clutter; it was filled with the kindness of a lovely lady and her family; a kindness which came so simply and naturally that they were totally unaware of its existence.

Ginger turned out to be a decent lad who had been a little foolish and extremely unlucky, not only was he deprived of the physical comforts, his food was restricted to a bowl of soup with ships' biscuits and only water to drink. It was not long before we were slipping him some of our grub which we prepared and cooked in the small kitchen. Each morning we drew rations for the day from the galley at Valkyrie. They were usually generous. Ginger claimed he was a passable cook and so, when the Chief had gone off duty at the end of the afternoon watch, our prisoner was released to peel the spuds and help in the cooking of our evening meal. There was always a surplus of food and I was able to repay some of Ma Smethurst's kindness by providing something in which to fry her delicious chips.

One of the cells was used as a store for the oakum the prisoner was required to pick from the short lengths of rope supplied for the purpose. Each morning the required amount of rope was weighed out before the Chief and passed in to the prisoner who had to reduce it to the individual fibres by picking it with his bare hands. We collected some of the rope from within the cell when the Chief went for his dinner and replaced it with a like amount of oakum. The relatively small change in the respective stocks of rope and oakum never aroused any comment.

Prison life in the relative isolation of the cells behind the Sefton Hotel soon became quite civilised; with no one in authority present in the evenings we saw no reason to lock Ginger back in his cell after we had eaten. A double metal bunk with mattresses, pillows and blankets was set up in the spare cell for the use of the off-duty sentry through the night; our prisoner took advantage of this until about eleven o'clock when we all had supper and he would then stand the middle watch while his warders slept. We squared the Wrens who manned the switchboard at Valkyrie to forewarn us when the officer of the day set out on one of his 'spot checks' and Ginger was always safely locked away long before we heard the knock on the prison door. The sound of a different voice on the telephone alerted the Wrens as to what was happening and they entered into the spirit of the thing; Ginger enjoyed many long conversations with the opposite sex in the course of his solitary confinement and had two dates lined up long before he was released. A supply of paperbacks from Valkyrie's library provided cultural comfort; we had rest and good food - it was a life of plenty. All that was missing was Ginger's freedom and he was prepared to be patient under such conditions.

Ginger eventually achieved his freedom and there was no more need for cell sentries or my presence at Valkyrie. A draft chit to LDD (Liverpool Destroyer Depot) marked the end of my 'settling in' period in the Navy.

I had discovered great kindness hidden beneath a curtain of constant chatter.

And I had experienced the strength of silence, the silence of a man who had been taken to the outermost limits of endurance and had found the peace and composure of true humility.

FOUR

Liverpool was the home of football pools and Vernons Football Pools were one of the early casualties of the war. Vernons released its vast array of young ladies from their large, single story shed in Bootle and the Royal Navy replaced them with matelots. It became Liverpool Destroyer Depot - a clearing house, a warehouse stocked with naval personnel to replenish the crews of the ships using the Port.

The turnover was impressive for the ships were many and the wear and tear on their crews considerable. Liverpool had become the centre of operations for the Western Approaches to Britain and had suffered for it. Air raids had left their marks on the city and casualties had been tragically heavy but the mood of quiet determination was unmistakable and the irrepressible humour of the 'Scousers' unavoidable.

Docks along the city's waterfront hummed with activity; giant cranes stirred the skyline with their jibs as they gathered up the supplies and provisions from ships newly arrived from far-off lands. Engines trailed assorted trucks and wagons in and out of the docks with impatient bleats on their whistles to impress everyone with their industry. Trains loaded with servicemen and servicewomen chugged in and out of Lime Street station, for it was here that leaves began and ended. Faces shone with anticipation as dreams approached realisation, or lapsed into serious reflection when they had been transformed into memories. Movement was everywhere: steady, remorseless movement filled with purpose: Liverpool knew what had to be done and knew how to do it.

Home still pulled at my heartstrings but I had been able to come to terms with naval life and become more settled during my time at Valkyrie. Now I was on my own once again and for the first time since joining the Navy I had to sling my hammock. There were no beds in Vernons shed, just rows of rails about 7 feet above the floor and the hammocks were slung between them in the evening. Instead of opening my bedding out on to a wire mattress as I had done previously, I had to conquer the art of slinging a hammock so that it would hold

21

my body securely and not tip me out whenever I moved. Older experienced hands came to my assistance once I had provided them with some amusement; they taught me how to transform my hammock into the snug, comfortable cocoon that I was to value highly in days to come.

There was a marked change in the atmosphere from that of a training establishment. Allowances for inexperience were few and far between as most of the personnel were transient and preoccupied with their own immediate welfare. They presented a wide cross-section of service and experience from three-badge veterans to wet-eared 'sprogs' like myself.

It was difficult to find kindred spirits amongst such a fluid complement and most of my off-duty time was spent on my own. In such a vibrant city it was difficult to be bored. The magnificent new Cathedral with its wonderful organ enthralled me; across the river lay New Brighton and I spent a Sunday mixing with the holidaymakers in nearby Southport; an evening of variety at the Empire was balanced by a night of opera at the Royal Court. The demands on my pay were so heavy that I had no money to spare for refreshment.

During my stay a wide variety of duties started with another spell as cell sentry but this time the prisoners were really 'hard cases' who had to be handcuffed to a sentry escort during the exercise period. There were potatoes to peel, floors and messes to be scrubbed; I joined a working party that was billeted in a church hall near Orrell Hey, Captain 'D's' Headquarters; the sun shone and we became gardeners for a few days. I helped a Welshman with the installation of the new RDF set on the Cruiser 'Aurora'; he had a fine tenor voice and lived to sing - they were two very musical days. They were followed by a spell with two divers who were working on the bottom of a very murky but peaceful Albert Dock. After helping the divers into cumbersome suits and leaden boots, we screwed on the big brass helmets before they went over the side and plummeted to the bottom, trailing air and life lines behind. Divers were rewarded by extra pay but I'm sure it would be nowhere near enough for the job they were doing.

Everyone at LDD, apart from the permanent staff, checked the draft particulars on the notice board at every opportunity. One of my messmates decided to break the news to me before I discovered the fact for myself, "Your draft's up on the board," he announced importantly.

I rushed to the notice board with mixed feelings; anticipation, excitement and apprehension and the realisation that another major change was about to occur in my life. I was to join HMS Polyanthus along with two other RDF ratings, Fraser and Leach.

As everyone gathered for supper I tried to obtain some information about Polyanthus without much success.

"Probably a corvette with a name like that," was the most positive response.

No one knew where she had been or what she had been doing.

My fellow draftees were sought out, they had met with a similar response and were no wiser than I was. Both had been on later courses at Valkyrie. Ernie Leach was my age and from Runcorn; unfortunately a childhood accident had left a large scar along his jaw and the side of his neck and drew his upper lip into a permanent sneer which was most misleading for he was a very pleasant and inoffensive lad. David Fraser was in his mid to late twenties and claimed he had been a newspaper editor in Wolverhampton, a position which should have entitled him to exemption from service in the forces; he told us he was married with a baby son. There was a hint of smug superiority in his attitude towards his younger companions.

Several draftees peered out from the naval truck that drove on to Albert Dock the following morning. Alone in the dock alongside the red brick warehouses on the outer wall, and painted in pale shades of grey, blue and green, the camouflage of the North Atlantic Escorts, was a ship with K 47 in large black symbols on her bows and stern. Gladstone Dock, down river was the home of the escort ships and that was where we were expecting to be dropped. The driver appeared at the tailboard,

"Draft for Polyanthus - this is as far as you go."

Three very 'green' sailors stood beside their kitbags and hammocks as the truck drove off with the rest of the men who were destined for ships berthed down river. Together we surveyed our future home, **HMS Polyanthus**, in solemn silence.

She was about half the size of the Manx ferry and the prospect of spending our future on something so small increased our mounting apprehension.

Staggering under the weight of our awkward kit bags and hammocks we struggled across the lock gates, along the dock wall and over the gang plank.

It was June and the week before Whitsuntide; I had been in the Navy five months.

H.M.S. Polyanthus
"A ship with K47 in large black symbols on her bows and stern".

23

FIVE

"You're in Number One mess," the quartermaster informed us as he led the way through the watertight door and along a passageway on the starboard side of the ship. When we reached the broadest part of the hull where it turned inwards towards the bows and formed the base of the triangular fo'c'sle, we were left to our own devices. Along the port side were the heads and washroom. Two hatchways leading to the deck below occupied much of the central deck space and two messes with their tables and benches filled even more. Six bunks, a large refrigerator and a wire cage which contained electrical gear and a small desk, added to the general congestion and left barely enough room for gangways. Ventilation trunking and tracks packed with electric wiring claimed most of the headroom and we made our way forward with heads slightly bent.

"Not a big lot of room, is there?" observed Ernie.

No reply was expected or given.

Roughly eighteen feet nearer the bow a bulkhead divided the triangle into two parts. We dropped our hammocks and kitbags by the hammock bins that were inboard of the heads and climbed through the watertight door into the forward mess deck; Number One mess (communications) was on the port side as far forward as we could go. There was just enough space between the hawse pipe of the port anchor chain and the hull to accept a bench, a mess table and a row of lockers. The pronounced flare of the corvette's bows swept inwards from the upper deck and gave the mess a pinched look.

The area we had just left immediately assumed spacious proportions compared with the space confronting us. A large part of the washroom together with Number Two mess and our own occupied the port side of the narrowing hull; the starboard side was fully taken up with a double tier of bunks chained back at 45°. Two fat hawse pipes led the anchor chains down through the mess deck to the cable locker below and a large hatch occupied centre stage. A third mess was jammed between this hatch and the bunks whilst the fourth and largest mess, that of the stokers, ran across the base of the triangle from the watertight door to the starboard bunks. Overhead was the same proliferation of trunking and wiring but in addition, cooking utensils hung down over each mess; large 'fannies', 'billies' and kettles invited unsuspecting heads to join in combat at all times.

Through the mess deck speakers an American voice sang of the delights to be found 'Deep in the heart of Texas' followed by a calypso which extolled the virtues of 'Rum and Cocah-Colah'. It was a relaxed, if a little noisy, atmosphere; the scuttles were open and a draught of fresh air helped to dry out the newly scrubbed messes. Two men were setting cups out on the table of Number One mess and they greeted our arrival with undisguised dismay.

"Corvettes were designed for a complement of 56, we must have over 80 in this crew," one of them grumbled as he put a handful of tea into a large brown enamel tea kettle. He walked towards the bulkhead of the washroom by Number Two mess where cooks from the other messes were already lining up with their tea kettles; a water geyser on the bulkhead was coming to the boil.

Meanwhile, the other mess cook stabbed two holes in the top of a tin of condensed milk and, when his mate returned, poured the contents into the kettle of freshly infused tea. The timing was spot on, the bosun's pipe signalled 'stand easy' as the last drop of milk dripped from the can and the mess deck was invaded by the watch aboard. I realised that if half the ship's company was on leave, the task of accommodating twice the number of men who were now seated in the mess was daunting; it provided the main topic of conversation as we drank our tea.

The tea was terribly strong and its flavour was in no way enhanced by the presence of a whole tin of condensed milk; it tasted like the waste from a tannery and not even the addition of a strong helping of sugar could make it in the least bit palatable.

The assorted clothing of the mess deck was a revelation; in our regulation No 3 (everyday) uniforms we felt distinctly overdressed. The only concession to rig of the day appeared to be a cap. Rollneck sweaters out-

"In our regulation No. 3 uniforms we felt distinctly overdressed" With O/S Ernie Leach

25

numbered regulation jerseys; white short-sleeved cotton vests and open necked denim shirts worn with light blue denim trousers added colour to the general disregard of the regulation dress.

No one was very interested in putting the three of us to work on the first morning so we took the opportunity to examine the brand new set we were to operate. A steel cabin which was just big enough to house the set together with an operator and his relief, had been fitted behind the bridge and immediately in front of the funnel. The aerial was housed inside a turret with perspex windows, very much like a small lighthouse on top of the cabin. Our examination did not take long, there was no possibility of testing the set within the confines of the dock basin and as I came down to the upper deck I was stopped by a leading seaman.

"What's that all about," he asked and looked up at the turret. Remembering my oath I replied:

"Sorry, but that's top secret."

"Thought it was so we could grow tomatoes," chuckled 'Shorty' Grant - I would soon learn there were few secrets on small ships.

Our difficulty in discovering anything about Polyanthus at the Destroyer Depot was soon explained; she had spent her first year in commission with the Newfoundland Escort Force based in St. John's, and Iceland was the eastern boundary of her voyages into the Atlantic. Shortly before her return to the UK she had been in Galveston, Texas, for a refit and the records we were constantly hearing were nostalgic reminders of the Deep South.

Only the more senior ratings could lay claim to the bunks and when the watch on leave duly returned the scramble to find a vacant hammock sling became desperate. There were one or two other newcomers who had joined as replacements, and as the existing crew claimed their established slings the unlucky ones had to resort to locker tops for their beds.

With a full crew and a new Captain, the ship was ready for sea: the shrill shriek of the bosun's pipe was followed by the call that would become all too familiar in the weeks and months to come. "Hands to stations for leaving harbour - special sea duty men close up - fore part forrard - after part aft - fender party 'mid ships."

We cast off. Polyanthus was gently coaxed through the dock gates by a helpful tug and sailed out into the Mersey bound for the open sea.

Tales of Newfoundland and the North American continent had aroused the interest of most of the new members of the crew, who were already anticipating the 'big eats', the 'T' bone steaks and the large blocks of ice-cream which awaited them in St. John's.

But before we crossed the Atlantic we were required to undergo a spell of training at the Tactical School based in Tobermory and my first voyage was from Liverpool to the Isle of Mull.

As we left the swept channel of the Mersey, Polyanthus entered into an argument with the Irish sea. The argument developed, and my world diminished until it was reduced to the confines of the ship as it lurched and swayed and tossed and rolled incessantly. A general nausea overcame any enthusiasm for my first voyage; even the Isle of Man failed to arouse my interest when it passed by on the starboard side, its outline blurred by a sea fret which clung to its shores and created an ethereal image.

Following the return of the watch which had been on leave, I spent a couple of nights trying to sleep on a locker top, before finding a spot to sling my hammock in what had been originally intended as a 'recreation space' - the entrance to the fo'c'sle which had absorbed an overflow of two messes. The sling was directly over the hatchway leading to the seamen's bunk space below, and my hammock was in constant danger since it added yet another hazard for the unwary.

Despite many bumps and knocks I was grateful to be in a hammock on my first night at sea. Much of the movement which had given me a bilious headache through the day was countered by the hammock; my misery became almost bearable until a hand grabbed the side and a quiet voice informed me that it was time for the morning watch. I pulled my blanket to one side and, reaching up to grasp a convenient hand-hold on the deck-head above, quietly lowered myself out and down. Crouched beneath the gently swaying hammocks, I pulled on my pants with one hand as I held on to the rail around the hatchway with the other. The bent figure of the bosun's mate, huddled in his duffle coat, moved around the darkened messdeck, checking his list of watchkeepers with his torch, a list he would dispense with in a very short space of time, once he had become accustomed to the newcomers. One by one, other members of the watch quietly emerged from their cocoons and, bent almost double in order to avoid the other hammocks, stumbled about as they struggled with their clothes and the continual motion of the ship.

No one spoke on the dimly-lit messdeck apart from the bosun's mate, in the glum broody silence all the sounds, and the feel, and the smell of a living ship were inescapable. The pulse of its engine as it strained and throbbed; the groans and the protests of a creaking hull and the grumbles of the waves as they thudded along its sides. Fumes from the fuel-oil, the lifeblood of the ship, found their way on to the messdeck and joined the pathetic supply of air which was now exhausted by its frequent voyages through our lungs. As we stumbled out to the waiting dawn the assault on my senses by the foul air and the remorseless rolling and pitching could not be controlled. My agreement with the sentiments being expressed by others was absolute - Polyanthus was indeed a wanton hussy of questionable morals and dubious parentage.

The mess I had joined now contained four signalmen (bunting tossers), three coders, three telegraphists and three RDF ratings. There was also a rating with

27

a public school education and a family that had achieved high rank in both the Navy and the Army but with nothing to justify his inclusion in a communications mess. The leading hand was a tall and heavily-built telegraphist who was one of four regular service ratings, the other ten were H.O.'s (hostilities only).

There were two 'oppos' (friends) from the London area, both around thirty years old, in more normal times one had been a bank clerk and the other a traveller for Carr's Biscuits. The eldest member of the mess was a three-badge signalman whose participation in its affairs rarely went beyond a wry smile. The newly joined Fraser was probably the same age as the leading hand and the rest were in their early twenties. Several members of the mess had professional or banking backgrounds and most of the academic education present in the fo'c'sle was packed into Number One mess. Not that it impressed anyone.

Language on the lower deck was subject to the same rules and adjectives which applied throughout the Navy. Some words may have been pronounced with a rather better class of accent in Number One mess but there was a greater degree of versatility to be found amongst the regulars, particularly in the stokers' mess. One leading stoker considered it a matter of honour never to repeat himself when he embarked on a 'good cuss'. A minority employed a restricted vocabulary which had the advantage of a more pronounced effect when brought into use, and there was one outstanding individual who could never be provoked into using a stronger epithet than 'Christmas!'. Initial ridicule was gradually replaced by amused acceptance of a character with the strength to hold on to his convictions.

In glorious sunshine and a less argumentative sea we sailed up the Scottish coast and into the Sound of Mull. On either side, magnificent views brought me back to the beauty of the real world, a world that had seemed lost such a short time before. The opportunity to spend off-duty spells on the upper deck allowed me to escape the cramped conditions below decks and my outlook improved by the hour.

A Spanish galleon which escaped destruction at the time of the Armada was reputed to have been sunk at Tobermory; the story went round the mess deck that her treasure had never been recovered because the bay was too deep.

Shortly after we had sailed into the bay we secured to a buoy; other escorts already there had dropped anchor. It was a picturesque anchorage but it contradicted the story of the galleon somewhat.

The following day various parties were ferried ashore in one of the dinghies to attend classes in their particular activity. Others remained on board to practise their drills. It was an intensive course and renowned for the ruses and tricks thought up by a dedicated senior officer who inflicted them on unsuspecting crews from captains down to quartermasters.

It was claimed that this SO had once thrown his gold-leafed cap down in front of a startled quartermaster and shouted "That's a bomb, what are you going to do about it ?"

Without hesitation the lad kicked the cap over the side whereupon the SO yelled "Man overboard! - save him."

Not to be outdone the lad immediately piped "Away sea-boats crew, man overboard!"

In the early hours of the middle watch another quartermaster heard a dinghy approaching very furtively; realising who was probably in charge he allowed it to pull under the stern before he stood up and, whistling happily, relieved himself over a startled SO.

Warnings of such events prepared us for the unexpected and although Polyanthus was spared such experiences her crew was in a constant state of readiness throughout her stay.

Tobermory had two hostelries. The Western Isles occupied a position of importance on the headland at the entrance to the bay and was for the exclusive use of the officers. The other was a 'wet' canteen, it stood in the middle of the waterfront and was not much bigger than the front room of any of the houses at either side. For the first time 'liberty boat' and 'going ashore' had the literal meaning; dinghies filled to the gunwales with libertymen chugged ashore under the power of an inadequate outboard motor.

Once ashore they set course for the wet canteen which was swiftly packed with a mass of struggling seamen, three or four deep inside the door. For the officers who came ashore in respectable numbers the Western Isles no doubt provided reasonably spacious and comfortable accommodation. For the far more numerous ratings the odds on getting a drink were no more than even. Ernie raised his arm to ease himself through the doorway only to find it was impossible to lower it in the throng and our attempts to get a drink proved to be too frustrating. We opted for a walk around the rocky headland before catching an early liberty boat back to the ship.

Exercises at sea brought all departments of the ship into play from guns to depth charges. Asdic and RDF played hide and seek with an evasive submarine, and several new members of the crew, including myself, wondered if a corvette could ever remain steady at sea.

Simulated attacks of all kinds were made on us both day and night in an intensive programme designed to bring escort vessels up to a high standard of competence and efficiency. It tested their response to emergencies of all descriptions and at the same time it tested my will to survive.

There was no doubt that in her on-going argument with the sea Polyanthus was coming off second best. Her behaviour became more and more boisterous to the point of eccentricity. Men assumed ridiculous angles as they tried to counter the heavy roll of the ship only to find a greater challenge facing them as the bows reared up and hung for an eternity before crashing down with a thud which jarred every bone in the body and every rivet in the hull.

What had been a bad bilious headache descended into abject misery and my stomach surrendered. I carried out my duties without interest or enthusiasm and the pathetic state of Ernie, who was even worse than myself, gave me no comfort. I followed him on watch and the atmosphere in the RDF cabin reeked of his misfortune.

Along with the rest of the ratings who were not on watch, I lined up each morning along the port well-deck where the Buffer detailed us off to work 'part of ship'. At the height of my misery I was made 'Captain of the Heads' and I became responsible for the cleanliness of the toilets. I could not have cared less if the heads stayed dirty for all time as I gathered the cleaning gear together.

"Oh no!" I groaned to the leading seaman who was supervising.

"Look at this toilet bowl, it's blocked solid, how do I clear that lot?"

L/Seaman Pearson broke into a wide grin and made an observation to the effect that my luck was being subjected to rape.

"You roll up your sleeve and stick your 'effing' arm down, mate" he said. "No one else is going to do it for you. It's up to you to do the job you've been given and to do it right. If you don't the lot of us suffer."

My stomach exploded and I had even more of a mess to clean up.

When stand easy was piped I could not face the thought of the terrible tea nor the fug of the mess deck; instead I made my way out to the well deck through the port waist and gave my stomach free rein. As it had not been receiving any donations for some time my retching was unproductive. Life on these terms no longer held any attraction. I managed to drag myself back from the side just in time to avoid a 'green one'; tons of water crashed down to fill the well deck then rushed and tumbled along the scuppers in its race to escape. My eyes floated in and out of focus as the waves of nausea took their toll.

A tap on my shoulder brought me back from the depths of despair. It was Alec Massie.

"If you see a brown ring come up mate, swallow it quick, 'cos it'll be your arsehole." He stood behind me and grinned as I turned for yet another retch. "Come and get something down, then you'll have something to bring up. Tie a lump of fat pork on a piece of string and grease your

Port Well Deck.
"Water .. rushed and tumbled along the scuppers in its race to escape."

throat with it."

"Go away" I groaned and wondered if I would ever recover.

After five days my seasickness more or less disappeared and my interest in the future was re-awakened: Alec resumed his more detached attitude to life.

By the time we had anchored on our return from the exercises it was too late for shore leave, but it was a balmy evening and we were given permission to bathe. The peaceful bay quickly became the scene of noisy enjoyment as men leapt over the side, some wearing swimming trunks, many wearing nothing at all. We splashed around until someone shouted for a race to a buoy about 200 yards away; whereupon the water erupted under a flurry of arms and legs. It was only when we neared the buoy that a small skiff was seen heading into the middle of the swimmers. A hefty female pulled steadily on the oars until she reached our midst where she stopped and stoically surveyed our antics and our torsos. There was not a lot of entertainment in Tobermory but Polyanthus did her best to provide some light relief that evening.

After a week at Tobermory we sailed for Lough Foyle in Northern Ireland.

The ship maintained its mad motion day and night without respite until hopes of stability faded into impossibility: poor Ernie, along with several others of the crew, had no alternative but to suffer his seasickness stoically.

Meal-times were a test of tenacity and endurance for them, nowhere more so than in Number One mess up in the point of the bow where every movement of the ship was most exaggerated. Five men packed the tops of the four lockers outboard of the narrow mess table, and were faced by four more jammed together on the form opposite. With a greatly reduced air circulation, the atmosphere was oppressive, and all too often the sight of the unattractive food was the last straw. Although Ernie and his fellow sufferers tried to position themselves on the fringes of the mess, escape, when it was called for, was hampered by the presence of so many of their mates and the behaviour of the ship. Bitter experience taught me to keep a constant watch on Ernie, who usually sat near me; if his eyes widened and took on a despairing look, his mouth would be sure to bulge and it was time to shield my food and give him space. With a similar reaction from others and the cooperation of the ship, he could escape from the tightly packed mess before he was overcome - but not always. It was no comfort for Ernie to know he was not alone - every mess seemed to have at least one member who was similarly afflicted at the time.

Dining difficulties were but a small part of the unending discomfort endured by everyone who served on a corvette. Personal space on the lower deck was limited to a bunk or a hammock and even that was vulnerable to anyone thrown off-balance by one of the ship's more violent tricks. Quite apart from the difficulty of avoiding each other, daily life developed into a running battle with normally inert objects, suspended mess kettles and dixies displayed an amazing ability to hit and hurt passers by. Anything vaguely resembling a normal walk

31

was impossible; progress became a sudden spurt forward followed by a sideways stutter and a desperate effort to cling to the ground gained until the next spurt could be achieved.

Sleep was at a premium. The nausea arising from the motion of the ship was replaced by a general tiredness that was not helped by standing four hour watches. Even the luxury of an 'all night in' every third night failed to overcome my body's yearning for uninterrupted rest.

SIX

Tucked away in Lough Foyle in Northern Ireland was a tanker. Her part of the war effort was to refuel the escort vessels prior to their departure into the North Atlantic and she was anchored directly opposite the small village of Moville in the Irish Republic, where every evening twinkling lights reminded us of pre-blackout nights at home.

Small boats headed out from the village in our direction and clustered around the hull as we slowly circled the tanker. Butter and cheese, stockings and underwear, trinkets and cheap souvenirs were offered up by the Irishmen in the boats. They quickly realised from our lack of interest that we were outward bound; our mothers, sisters, sweethearts and wives were not likely to see us laden with gifts for some time.

"They'll be telling Jerry to expect us as soon as they get back" was the bitter observation as the boats headed back to land.

When our fuel tanks had been topped up we sailed out to join the Escort Group C2 and its convoy destined for North America.

In the first few days the North Atlantic demonstrated its superiority of wave strength over the shorter waves we had experienced off Scotland. The dull grey sea and sky became steadily darker and cheerless: the waves were longer and higher and hid their fearsome power beneath a deceptive lethargy. For long periods the ships of the convoy filled the horizon before they disappeared beyond the wavecrests, leaving us very much alone and hidden in a long deep trough of sea. Every movement of the ship, every sound of the fearsome struggle I had previously experienced was now greater and more violent as we tossed and bounced about at the whim of the elements.

Meals at sea became far more difficult to master. As the bows reared up in one of their spiralling ascents our plates would slither along the mess table sharing their contents as they went; the bow's sudden descent then left the unsuspecting plates trailing behind in mid air and confused their contents even more. The skilled diner caught his plate and lifted it clear of the table immediately any of these acrobatics were about to take place, but such skill

33

could only be acquired gradually and the combined efforts of the ship and a capricious sea frequently conspired to defeat even the experts.

Enormous 'seventh' or 'rogue' waves crashed down on the bows, often at an angle, to shiver the hull and the teeth of everyone aboard.

"Milestones, mate," said Alec.

"Turn right at the 396th for Iceland - that was the 98th in case you haven't been counting."

We struggled to recover our plates and what we could recognise as our own food. Meal times attracted such waves; there was no question about that.

A voice from the next mess confirmed Alec's observations.

"It's that Southampton tram driver who's on the wheel again, Lobby .... Ludd, he could find a 'milestone' in a puddle."

"Why does he have to be on at every ..... mealtime I want to know?"

Another lurch threw the mess deck into even more turmoil. Those trying to hang on to their plates pressed against others who were already seeking support. A short-lived sullen silence gave tempers an opportunity to cool before we resumed the normal meal-time topic - sex.

Our food was now showing signs of distress at the hands of the uncompromising sea. Even the bread taken aboard just before we left Ireland was turning green; the loaves were torn from a large block and the only crusts were at the top and bottom; we cut off all the crusts and edges but the sour soggy taste overwhelmed whatever we ate along with it. Our 'Chef', the cook, showed no inclination to try his hand at baking bread so it was down to 'hard tack', biscuit blocks constructed from an identical recipe to the one used for dog biscuits with an added whisper of sand and cement.

Fresh vegetables, offended by their storage in a well ventilated bin on the upper deck, simply dissolved into a dank evil-smelling mush. Their replacements were the ubiquitous 'Pusser's Peas', dried marrowfat peas, a commodity no self-respecting ship would be without. They were in the same category as 'kye', that drink peculiar to the Navy, made from shavings taken from a block of hard cocoa/chocolate and scalded with water before sugar and condensed milk were added; it was an open question whether it was to be drunk or chewed.

The adjustments to my life since joining the navy had been constant and very demanding but none had been as drastic and shattering as those I faced on my first venture into the North Atlantic.

All our exercises off Tobermory were soon put to the test; at the first action stations our previous times to reach the fully 'closed-up' state were beaten. We charged round the ship, bumping into stanchions, bulkheads, doorcasings and each other, setting up a tremendous clatter on the steel decks. Watertight doors clanged shut amidst loud shouts from the various action stations reporting that they were 'closed up'. Now it was for real and I found my pulse racing with the excitement and the fear of what fate might have in store for us. As it happened

Polyanthus was not closely involved in the activity which was ahead of the convoy but the experience proved to be a powerful purgative.

The leading telegraphist claimed to have a special cork for use at critical times during action stations.

Away from land, we were denied any opportunity to keep up to-date with the news and the time honoured method of broadcasting was brought into play - the 'Buzz'. By tradition it was always attributed to that seat of learning, the heads. Any rumour with a hope of acceptance earned the ultimate accolade of a 'Shithouse Buzz'.

For the sixty-odd men jammed into her fo'c'sle, Polyanthus provided two urinals and three stalls with lavatory pans fixed on platforms about six inches clear of the deck. The stalls were open at the front and the space available as a passage was narrow enough for an occupant of a stall to brace himself against the bulkhead at the other side of the passage with his extended arm. This was a considerable advantage in heavy weather since it provided a certain feeling of security and helped to maintain contact with the pan at all critical times.

Shortly after being stood down from action stations the news of a U-Boat kill reached me. The 'house' was in session. Three members were 'sitting', their belts draped around their necks like chains of office; heads down and with one arm outstretched they made their individual contributions to the proceedings. There were two members ahead of me in the queue.

St. Croix, a Canadian destroyer had sunk a U-Boat ahead of the convoy and had picked up some gruesome proof.

It was heartening news but it was not long before we were very much occupied with other U-Boats which were keen to avenge the loss of one of their number. In the early hours of the following morning they torpedoed three ships but only sank one. Polyanthus was ordered to remain with the two survivors as the convoy continued on its way.

When dawn broke we were circling round the two completely disabled ships. One was a new British ship festooned with torpedo nets; the torpedo had apparently found one of her two unprotected areas, her stern, and left her immobile. Some of her crew had remained with her but the other vessel, an American, had been hurriedly abandoned by her crew immediately after being struck. The torpedo had left a great hole in her bows but to all outward appearances she seemed to be salvageable.

As the morning watch passed into the forenoon watch all who could find an excuse to be up on deck spent as much time as possible surveying our charges. Word went round that our remaining supply of fuel was causing concern and for that reason our speed was being reduced; until we were relieved we could only maintain steerage way. Communications were set up with those members of the crew who had remained aboard the British ship; her ample fuel supplies had survived the torpedoing and the obvious thing to do was to attempt a transfer.

35

Fanciful hopes of taking the abandoned American in tow, with ideas of shared salvage money and personal fortunes, added a touch of much needed zest to our outlook.

Despite valiant efforts of improvisation the enterprise was doomed to failure by a restless and uncooperative sea. The helpless ship had a displacement of around ten times that of Polyanthus and with our single screw it was an unequal and hopeless struggle to maintain a reasonably steady distance between the two ships. Lines parted as the sea flexed itself and the ruptured hose spilled the precious oil into the hungry sea.

Where there had been optimism there was concern; our fuel was limited, there was no way of knowing how and when we would be relieved - and where were the U-boats that had created the situation?

Suddenly the vibrations of the propeller stopped; we lost way and began to drift. It was all we needed.

Morose groups gathered on the upper deck as we drifted along with the two merchant ships. For two days we wallowed with only a few turns of the screw at rare intervals to help us maintain contact with our charges; hour after hour of aimless drifting spent in near silence when nerves became more and more taut, a silence that developed into sullen resignation in some and nervous tension in others. Two wooden minesweepers eventually appeared on the horizon and took over guard duty. We were finally relieved in more ways than one.

Every ruse to save valuable fuel was brought into use as we slowly and carefully completed our voyage through the fog on the Grand Banks. At this point the value of RDF made its impression and the first indication of a landfall was a 'blip' on its screen.

Suddenly the sheer cliffs of Newfoundland emerged from the fog. We clung to them until the entrance to the vast inland harbour of St. John's appeared and the dull dual tones of a dismal fog horn welcomed us to Newfoundland. The Chief Engine Room Artificer maintained Polyanthus was running on vaporised fuel oil as she entered the Narrows. We were only too thankful that she had made it safely.

Small timber shacks clung to the steep barren hillsides at the harbour entrance, each with a rickety platform on which quantities of

Harbour Entrance St. John's.
"Small timber shacks clung to the steep barren hillsides."

36

cod were laid out to dry. The weathered, unpainted timber testified to years of exposure to the harsh elements, to the endurance of the structures and of the folk who lived in them.

I was totally unprepared for 'Newfy'; everything I saw as we eased our way into the harbour at St. John's suggested an unending struggle for survival. The 'land of plenty' looked distinctly depressing and down at heel to a lad accustomed to the solid stone buildings of Yorkshire.

Several escort vessels were already in residence at St. John's, including all those of our Group. They had beaten us in by three days and were tied up alongside the wooden jetties which stretched along the 'South Side', a long barren hillside that protected the harbour from the wild sea beyond. All the available space was taken. Polyanthus was obliged to sidle up and slip into a berth alongside a Canadian corvette that, so far as we could see, appeared to be in the sole charge of a quartermaster and a very disinterested rating. No one else could be raised to take our lines and it was left to a couple of our own lads to scramble across her upper deck to the jetty before we were secured.

Adjustment to a strangely stationary ship took a little time as legs continued to anticipate movements which had been discarded when she passed through the Narrows. The washroom was under constant siege from men who were desperate to remove the stubble from their faces. Throughout the voyage, in deference to superstition, they refused to 'shave off' because it would cause the weather to 'blow up rough' - my experience so far suggested it was a misplaced belief that the inevitable could be avoided.

There was only one opportunity to get ashore before we were on our way out through the Narrows to join an eastbound convoy. On that first short sharp visit we were hard-pressed to make up for the time lost in playing nursemaid. Fresh provisions were taken on board to give a pronounced lift to the meals. Fresh bread for the first time in ten days had the added advantage of being made with white flour instead of the less refined flour of the U.K. No one could ever explain why each white loaf we obtained in St. John's had a sultana in it.

The short time we had spent lying alongside the Canadian corvettes provided an opportunity to compare the standards of discipline observed by some of our fellow escorts. They varied considerably. It came as quite a shock to realise that the man in shirt sleeves, sitting on a depth charge and smoking a cigar, whilst reading the 'funnies' in the Sunday newspaper, was in fact the Captain.

Canada's Corvette Navy was being cobbled together at a great speed; with insufficient resources of experienced manpower it had yet to establish and enforce the standards which were essential in any Navy.

There was no question about the knowledge and experience of the men who had spent their working lives at sea in the Merchant Navy; the ships fortunate enough to be commanded by such men could be readily distinguished, but few men in their crews shared their background. A few had been fishermen: tough,

37

hardy men who retained a determined individuality and resented the disciplines they were now expected to observe. Equally independent lumberjacks and farm hands, more accustomed to the vast prairies than the open sea, made up great parts of the crews.

Evidence of the individuality was displayed on the shields of the four-inch guns of the Canadian ships; colourful emblems, caricatures, and interpretations of tribal art enlivened the bland grey, green and blue camouflage. HMCS Wetaskiwin was outstanding in depicting an attractive, crowned lady, sitting in a puddle with her legs in the air. Faced with such frivolity, we of the Royal Navy, maintained a stiff upper-lip and admired their initiative.

Nowhere was there a straight ringed sleeve of an R.N. or R.C.N officer to be seen amongst the escorts gathered in St. John's and it took many months before I came to appreciate the tremendous advantage enjoyed by the British ships in having a hard core of regular ratings to establish and maintain the discipline and stability essential to an efficient ship.

Polyanthus had sailed with the Canadian corvettes from the outset and was one of the family, sharing the same objective and all the dangers and the hardships entailed in fighting the war against the U-boats; the Canadians surprised us constantly in so many ways, but their courage was never in doubt.

Across the harbour the city of St. John's gazed at our assembly of escorts and switched on its lights in the evening to remind us again of the pleasures denied our families back in England. The fog horn maintained a steady warning for much of our short stay. Its deep intonation of two notes was echoed by the radio commercial for toilet soap which asked "What is the most dismal sound in the World? - B-O - use Lifebuoy!".

During our spell in St. John's the sea beyond had quietened down; we emerged to find the ship behaving with much less violence towards its crew. In place of the rough weather we were faced by a very aggressive enemy who kept us closed up at Action stations for the better part of three days.

My action station was on the bridge where I acted as Captain's messenger and relayed his orders by means of the various voice pipes. In the middle of the bridge the Asdic operator, Pearson, sat on a high stool carefully turning the control wheel. It was Sunday morning and there was a lull in the proceedings. Suddenly he pulled the headphones back from his ears and shouted to me.

"Jump up on the back of my chair, quick!"

His outstretched arm pointed to a merchant ship about a mile away on the starboard bow. A wall of water had risen up around her and was cascading back into the ocean. Pearson slid the earphones back over his ears and continued with his Asdic search as we watched the stricken ship's death throes. For a while nothing seemed to change until, slowly and deliberately, her bows began to dip lower into the sea and sliding gently forwards, she lifted her stern until it was almost vertical. Her final plunge had a strange dignity and grace. As she disappeared another vessel was hit and sank quickly and quietly shortly after her crew had taken to the boats.

All the previous action had been in the dark hours and I was astounded at my reactions to the tragedies I witnessed on that clear sunny Sunday morning. I might just as well have been seated in a cinema watching a news reel, isolated from the terrible reality.

On the other hand, Pearson began to chatter excitedly and he embarked on a graphic and detailed description of the various delights he had experienced in a pre-war Alexandria with its incredible 'exhibitions'.

Our adversaries remained undetected despite our searches and we took advantage of the lull to devour a thick corned beef sandwich and a hot drink each as we maintained our uneasy vigil.

The Captain remained on the bridge for three days and nights and I had to remain with him.

"Get your head down in that corner, lad, I'll give you a kick when you're needed" he told me towards the end of the second day.

I curled up for almost two hours before he called me. On the third day I had a longer spell and when the Captain eventually decided he could leave the bridge I went below to seek oblivion in my hammock. I had been allowed just a few hours' sleep and I was absolutely whacked, The Captain had borne all the responsibility with no sleep or respite of any kind.

In mid-Atlantic the convoy was handed over to an Escort Group based in the U.K. and our Group took over responsibility for a Westbound convoy. Our return to St. John's was not without incident but much less dramatic than when we had been outward bound.

Life on board continued to be extremely hard and demanding: everything had to be battened down tightly in order to keep out the sea. The atmosphere in the confined space of a small mess deck, which housed more bodies than it could accommodate, quickly became foul and unhealthy. With all the outlets tightly closed, the incoming air from the ventilation trunking was reduced to a feeble trickle, unlike the water from the untiring sea: that always succeeded in gaining entry to enclosed spaces which in turn, were equally successful in preventing its escape.

The foul tasting fug created condensation on the cold steel hull, it dripped and dribbled down and on to the deck where it joined the water that had already accumulated there: with each roll of the ship it rushed out from under the hammock bins, across the deck and disappeared under the lockers on the opposite side. Each swish collected whatever was on the deck until the liquid thickened into a cold murky soup of filth and scum that defied all the efforts of the mess cooks; every morning they struggled to transfer it into dixies with floor cloths which quickly became slimy and lost their absorbency.

Our brief respite in St. John's became a dream; a deliverance from a nightmare of wet mess decks, clattering alarm bells, foul air, poor food and lack of sleep. Cleanliness was vitally important but impossible to achieve completely. With everyone wearing several days' growth of stubble and scruffy clothes we were more like a bunch of cut-throats than representatives of the Royal Navy.

Despite all the difficulties discipline remained sound and tight. The Captain had set his standards in all the important areas and led by example. Captain's Rounds were made meticulously and all nooks and crannies revealed their secrets to the beam of his torch. Perfection was impossible but the knowledge that a diligent Captain would be round ensured much more effort was applied to its pursuit.

Once again the dismal tones of St. John's' fog horn proclaimed its warning and its welcome; and once again we sailed through the Narrows and secured alongside our fellow escorts.

Polyanthus was ready for a rest and so were we.

SEVEN

With more opportunities to become acquainted with the city I found my first impressions had been misleading. St. John's was the first place outside of the United Kingdom that I had seen and could not be judged by my standards and limited experience. On board there were no opportunities to spend money apart from cigarettes and as these were duty-free they were hardly a drain on pay. The attraction of all the good things which were no longer obtainable at home was overwhelming and groups of matelots became tongue-tied as they bought silk stockings and underwear in Bowrings, along Water Street, from salesgirls who found their embarrassment amusing.

Corvettes were on 'canteen messing' which meant every mess was self-sufficient as far as catering was concerned. Each man had a daily entitlement of about 10d to cover the cost of his food and provisions and this was credited to his mess. At the end of the month the mess was charged for all the food and provisions supplied and the total was set against the accumulated entitlements.

Someone had to be appointed as mess caterer in order to provide a scapegoat for the inevitable problems and shortages which could accumulate during the accounting period of a month. Number One mess had a marked advantage in having one or two more numerate members, yet even they were pleased when their term of monthly duty had passed. Mess caterer could be a thankless appointment.

Probably because of my previous occupation I was detailed off as mess caterer at the start of my second month aboard and, thanks to the basic sense of responsibility of the mess in general, it was possible to create a reasonable menu that did not break our budget.

Every morning two men were detailed off to be mess cooks for the first part of the forenoon watch and it was their duty to prepare the food for dinner and take it up to the galley. There the food from all the messes was cooked on a large iron stove by the ship's cook, the 'Chef'; a man who went through life acquiring countless burns on his arms and constantly changing his socks; his feet were unbelievable.

The mess cooks then scrubbed out the mess as thoroughly as possible and made the tea ready for stand-easy. After that they worked 'part of ship' along with everyone else who was not on watch.

My first month as mess caterer started well: I nipped along the jetty to a fishing boat freshly in from the Grand Banks and with hardly any bargaining purchased a large cod for five packets of 20 cigarettes - a cost to the mess of 1/8d. Whenever we were in St. John's I followed the movements of the fishing boats very closely and if one came in from sea, the mess ate fish.

For the first few days of any voyage the standard dinner was a roast, irrespective of the joint of meat available. The mess cooks simply stuck it in a flat square cooking tray and surrounded it with potatoes before taking it to the galley where it was surrendered to the whims of the 'Chef'. Whatever fresh vegetables remained would be boiled on the top of the range but for the greater part of the voyage the 'veg' was invariably 'pusser's peas'. As the quality of the meat deteriorated, 'pot mess' became the main course; scrag ends of beef, potatoes, pusser's peas and any remaining vegetables that appeared edible, cooked in a billie together with a large tin of 'red lead' - canned tomatoes. Given good weather and an enterprising mess cook there were days when 'doughboys' or dumplings might be added to a pot mess, but the combination of good weather and an enterprising cook was rare, and the cooks who could make successful doughboys were even rarer still.

'Home on the Range' - bacon, bangers and beans - was popular but relatively expensive and only eaten when funds permitted. Although the beans were reasonably cheap the other ingredients could seriously damage a day's catering budget.

For 'afters' we again had to rely on the initiative of the mess cooks: there were a few who were prepared to attempt a 'duff' with dried fruit or jam, or a Manchester tart - a pastry base spread with jam after it had been cooked and covered with a thick custard topping made with lashings of custard powder, sugar and boiling water. Again, a combination of favourable factors was required if results were to be acceptable: the humour of our constant foe, the weather, the cleanliness of the mess cook and his ability in pastry making, the space available in the oven and the unpredictable mood of the Chef. Manchester tarts always shared the same ingredients but no two were ever alike; given the absence of measures and scales a great deal depended upon the size of the cook's hands and what he considered to be a handful.

The most frequent 'afters' was cake - Chinese wedding cake - or rice pudding to the uninitiated. Yet even something as simple as a boiling of rice with the addition of sugar and a tin of condensed milk could produce some strange results.

Mishaps in the galley in heavy weather were inevitable and could only be guessed at. Mess tins often contained unidentifiable cremations when collected and any show of reluctance on the part of a mess cook to accept a particular item was an almost certain sign that it had been rescued from the deck during its journey from the galley, usually at the foot of the companionway between the galley and the port passage.

Stokers suffered most from the inadequacies of their caterers; they loved 'afters' and large tins of fruit - pears, apricots, plums - would appear at their table whenever a new month started. As every month-end approached the same table would be lucky if it saw 'Chinese Wedding Cake' every other day.

Harbour-time always represented rest from the demands of the sea, a good night's rest and better food, yet work still has to be done when a ship is secured against the wall; the ravages of the sea have to be remedied and painting ship's side was inevitable - it was also unfriendly to clothing. Catamarans consisting of two large baulks of timber, inevitably covered with the efforts of countless painters and with the discharges of assorted ships, were dragged alongside to provide a working platform. 'Skimming dishes' (small one or two-man motor boats) scuttled around the harbour and set up waves. Catamarans rocked in their wake, paint was spilt and paint brushes touched up parts they were not intended to reach. Poor Ernie was known to have felt sick even on a catamaran.

In the middle of the harbour was the American ship which had been in our charge during the previous convoy. Someone had managed to take her in tow and had no doubt claimed the salvage money we had dreamed of. The great gaping hole in her bow was a tremendous temptation for the 'skimming dishes'; they found it a lot of fun to scoot in and out of her bows.

During our stay in St. John's the buzz went round the ship that convoys would be escorted to and from the UK by the same escort group instead of the groups changing over at WOMP (Western Ocean Meeting Point). We set out again with the attraction of a UK port at the end of the voyage and the possibility of a short leave.

The acquisition of an RDF set must have transformed the life of the ship's officers when keeping station on the convoy. "Bridge - RDF! - Range and bearing of the nearest ship?" was the constant demand throughout the dark night watches. Anything other than a prompt response was unacceptable regardless of the effect on the sweep being carried out by the operator. No officer assumed responsibility for the RDF department nor did any of them fully understand the limitations of the set as a means of detecting a U-Boat. The radar screen which presented its echoes in the form of a plot was still a long way off, what we had was very basic.

Our training as RDF operators had been minimal and because the equipment was only just out of the experimental stage, no firm rules or procedures had been established, we simply made our own and learnt from our own experience.

The aerial could be swept through 180 degrees either side of dead ahead but not through a continuous arc of 360 degrees, and due to its position immediately in front of the funnel there was a 'blind spot' astern of the ship. Signal quality became a problem out in the Atlantic where the sea rarely cooperated with any of our activities; the firm green trace on the tube became fuzzy, we called the result 'grass', and a small signal, such as the one produced by a U-boat's conning tower, could be obscured and easily missed. A slower and more careful sweep was called for in such conditions and demanded more concentration, it became almost impossible to retain the positions of the convoy's ships in the head. If a request for a station bearing was received when the aerial was pointing to the opposite quarter a furious winding was required to turn the aerial through anything up to 300 degrees, the sweep sequence was destroyed and it was always the area away from the convoy which suffered from reduced coverage.

Each RDF operator had a non-specialist seaman with him on watch to act as a relief; training and instruction was left entirely to the individual who alternated with the relief throughout the watch, each one doing half-hour spells, the one off-duty curled up in the cramped space between the set and the corner of the cabin by the door.

My efforts to discuss the operational aspects of RDF with any of the officers met with little interest or response; this was hardly surprising since my observations involved restrictions on their newly acquired solution to station keeping. The claim that exposure to the UHF transmissions could make a man impotent may have had a bearing on their reluctance to become too deeply involved with the equipment.

It was at about 2300 hrs on a cold black night when a small 'blip' appeared on the screen at the outward limits of the extended scale. Such a possibility had not even been considered in our course because the chance of detecting anything at maximum range was out of the question. To the request for the range and bearing of the nearest ship by the officer of the watch I replied:

"Sorry sir, but I've just picked up something and it must be really big."

The Captain was summoned. To the question "What do you think it is?" I could only repeat that it was something much bigger than anything I had experienced before.

Speculation by the officers as to the whereabouts of the enemy's battlewagons was very unsettling as we turned away from the convoy to investigate. I would much rather have been setting out on the bus for Ilkley.

The 'blip' grew bigger and bigger as we closed the gap, so did my apprehension.

It was the biggest iceberg imaginable.

We returned to take up our station on the convoy and resume the dull, dreary routine which was the fate of a convoy escort. An endless round of watch keeping, eating inferior food and trying in vain to get more sleep. And over all else was the strain which no one was prepared to acknowledge openly.

We had left our Jack Dusty (supply assistant) in St. John's. He had been picked up by the shore patrol leading a pack of dogs along Water Street, each one secured by a length of spun yarn. His mission was to round up all the dogs he considered to be strays in order to save them, and it did not take the doctors long to decide that he was the one who needed saving. It transpired that he had survived the sinking of his previous ship but hardly anyone knew of it until he finally cracked.

He was not to sail into Liverpool again for a very long time. His war was with his personal hell and we could only speculate on what it involved.

When we left 'Newfy' the Captain decided to dispense with the doubtful help of a messenger at action stations. From my position of privilege on the bridge I was relegated to the crew of a depth charge thrower down aft in the starboard well deck.

From now on, action stations usually meant a very wet and strenuous spell of duty on a deck which was not much above the water-line. We huddled inside our oilskins and duffle coats hoping the cold, grey sea would spare us a drenching but it rarely did. Immediately after a depth charge had been fired, it had to be replaced by another from the cradles along the deck and they were heavy - extremely heavy.

Before a depth charge could be loaded a 'stalk' had to be lifted high in the air and dropped into the barrel of the thrower; the stalks were heavy and awkward too, and they were covered in a thick coating of grease. The charges had a will of their own, and resisted all our combined efforts to coax them on to the cradle atop the loaded stalk. On a cold dark night their savage attacks on limbs and fingers numbed by an ice-cold sea brought forth an unbelievable concerto of curses, blasphemy and obscenity.

Re-loading usually coincided with the ship heeling over as she turned to come back along the line of attack. A depth charge suspended on the end of a block and tackle, and poised to drop into position, quickly becomes a pendulum under such circumstances and defies restraint.

It was then that the sea, which had been gathering itself for just such a moment, hurled a great wall of water at us. There was no escape. Secured to a demoniac depth charge we spluttered helplessly at our most formidable foe - the sea.

Thoughts of U-Boats disappeared and with them any remaining standards of normality. This was naked aggression. A fight for dominance between a steel barrel of high explosive and the individual. Each one of the struggling crew was convinced that those who were supposed to be helping were dim-witted, useless idiots and said so.

Intervention on the part of a raw, remorseless sea simply added to our torment. Blood covered our hands and we wondered as we struggled if it was our own for no pain could be felt beneath the bitter numbing cold. Seaboots filled with water, pockets on soaked duffle coats and oilskins filled with water;

cold, cold water. It tortured our very souls.

And when our struggles were over, we, who had not to resume an interrupted watch, made our unsteady way back to the shelter of the fo'c'sle: decency gradually regained control of our behaviour: snarls were replaced by sullen acceptance of a common misery as we emerged from our sodden clothing.

A railed catwalk crossed above the boiler room to provide a gangway between the port and starboard passages of the ship. It was here that the hot air, laden with oil fumes, rose up to meet the cold air which we brought with us from the raw world outside. The two formed an unholy alliance, consummated their union and produced high humidity and condensation.

And it was here that we draped our soggy bundles in the forlorn hope that they would dry out. Before long it resembled a Turkish bath - an Anglo-Saxon Turkish bath according to many dripping patrons.

Those who were to stand the next watch out on deck made the most of the dry respite; steaming clothing freezes more quickly than dry. Theirs was a chilling prospect.

"I reckon I'd have been a lot better off if I'd been sent down the pits, I'd be a damned sight drier and able to stand."

The voice came from within a scrum of half-naked and demoralised men, most of whom were struggling to towel themselves down and stay on the same bit of deck.

"And a bloody sight better paid" added another of the unsteady throng.

"If you were a miner you could go on strike and nobody could touch you, not like the 'Andrew' - they'd charge you with mutiny and throw the book at you. They can 'top' you for it, you know."

"No they couldn't; not now. They stopped that years ago. Anyhow, nobody can go on strike while there's a war on."

"'Course they can, that's what I'm on about. Didn't you hear about the miners in Kent, they were on strike the last time I was 'up the line'."

"What was it about?"

"I dunno, more money I expect; they've probably heard about our extra 3d a day 'hard-lying' money for being on this tub - want a share of it."

"What a shower, as bad as dockyard mateys; it makes us look a right lot of stupid bastards. I know what I would share with 'em if I had a chance."

Polyanthus heeled over and caught a heavy cross-wave; the mess utensils clattered each other as they swung on their hooks overhead, filthy black scum shot out across the deck from under the lockers and the 'discussion' group became an untidy heap of bodies yet again.

"Oh! my effin' back" yelled the one underneath as he was trapped against the edge of the mess-table. At least he now had something to take his mind off tormenting seas and striking miners.

46

EIGHT

"Wakey! Wakey! Rise and shine!. C'mon, mi lucky lads, all the hands - off cocks, on socks; Heave ho! Heave ho! Heave ho!, lash up and stow ! - Maggie May's gone away but Lime Street's where it always was before - Wakey! Wakey!. Show a leg there."

It was an unusually steady ship and an unusually chirpy bosun's mate who bounced through the fo'c'sle repeating his call. On this morning there were few groans from the bunks and hammocks.

"How near are we, mate?"

"Formby light's coming up any time now."

There was a civilised note in the conversation which had been lacking for some time.

Polyanthus lost way and we sat out in the channel awaiting instructions. All eyes searched a sleepy shoreline for the flashes that would reveal what Liverpool held in store for us. Decks were washed down and paintwork was cleaned but our minds were elsewhere as we waited. On the skyline ahead the towers of the Liver Building were outlined by hazy sun as it climbed steadily into clearer blue sky above. On top of the towers the Liver Birds maintained their impassive surveillance of the Port of Liverpool. It was so near and yet so far; we waited, and waited, and still we waited.

Suddenly there was a clatter from the 10-inch signal projector on the bridge. Over the water a light was blinking furiously in our direction. An off-duty signalman became momentarily popular.

"What's the 'gen', Bunts?."

"They're berthing instructions, Gladstone."

"What about leave?"

"All shore leave cancelled," announced our interpreter, who quickly put on a glum face and disappeared, leaving us open-mouthed and unconvinced.

'Boiler-clean and three days' leave.' The word spread throughout the ship in a flash and no one cared about the false message put out by the bunting tosser.

47

We went below to prepare for leave, to check our 'rabbits' and make sure everything would be ready for the 'off'.

Presents for the folks at home were always referred to as rabbits, a name which covered anything acquired legitimately or otherwise. Payment of duty on rabbits was something to be avoided at all times, since they frequently included items such as duty-free cigarettes and tobacco, and very often a small bottle of rum.

Not surprisingly, a great deal of care and ingenuity was exercised in the packing and concealing of particular rabbits.

The lock of Gladstone Dock engulfed Polyanthus. Sheer walls towered above us and demanded superhuman efforts to hurl the heaving lines up to the dockers who were gazing down from above. Wearmouth was pretty good with a heaving line and gloried in the opportunity to demonstrate his prowess.

With joy and relief we secured alongside the outer wall within Gladstone Dock and put the gangplank down. A bunch of dockers who had been watching our arrival and avoiding any involvement in the proceedings immediately clambered aboard.

"Boiler cleaning party," they proclaimed and disappeared down the starboard passage.

"Hope you've got your rabbits stowed away safely," warned 'Shorty' Grant, the leading hand of Number Two mess. "Nothing's safe from those shitehawks."

Shorty had joined as a boy seaman and came from a naval family; he rarely gave bad advice.

"You can't move in the starboard passage, those greedy bastards have found the canteen and are waiting for it to open,"

The good-natured mood in the fo'c'sle changed when the 'dockyard mateys' refused to budge and demanded that they be served with some 'duty-frees'. Fortunately a bowler-hatted figure appeared and they quickly dispersed to escape their foreman.

A customs officer was one of our visitors: he came on board to check the ship and deal with our 'declarations'.

"Always declare something, mate," advised Alec with the wisdom of long experience. "It gets you a pink chit to show the blokes on the gate and they're less likely to bother you."

I stood in line and declared four pairs of silk stockings, paid the duty of about 1/8d, received a pink chit as a receipt and returned to complete my packing. It filled a case and a large cardboard box. There were all the ingredients for a Christmas cake, all my allocation of cigarettes, two pricks of tobacco, tins of fruit, cigarette lighters; there were even some silk stockings.

Now that the ship was secured alongside the dock, most of the crew had only one thing in mind - to get ashore, and the washroom became the centre of activity. Behind each one of the men at the three wash bowls another two were jammed impatiently awaiting their turn. More men stood outside and the rich odours of after-shave filled the space that was more accustomed to the foul fug of BO. Clean underclothes appeared, 'Number One' uniforms were being brushed vigorously, blue collars, neatly folded and stretched tight, were pulled around stanchions to give them a 'cold iron', Burberry raincoats were brought out.

The routine for the first run ashore was as standardised as the routine for the ship entering harbour and it was being strictly adhered to.

General good humour was as much in evidence as the after-shave and above the constant back-chat someone was singing an unexpurgated version of a popular song. It brought forth the traditional response.

"Don't sing that song, Jack."

"Why, does it make you feel homesick?"

"No, it gives me the screaming hab-dabs," we replied in unified derision.

An infectious excitement built up as extra-long ribbons were tied and re-tied around the black silk worn under the sailor's collar. Eventually a satisfactory 'tiddley' bow was achieved to produce evenly draped tails on the ribbon. Shoes were given an extra polish and Burberries were re-folded to give a smarter drape over the arm

"Oh boy, just let me get through those gates. I'll take the first bit of skirt that comes along between eight and eighty."

"You mean they'll be either eight or eighty. The ones in between won't let a lecherous sod like you near them."

"A fat lot you know about it. With my technique it's a cinch. A crafty nibble at their ear so that they get a whiff of my after-shave and it's away sea-boats crew. Never fails."

"I could go a bit of rape myself tonight, nothing like a good struggle to get me really roused."

"You're a randy lot of bastards. Thank Christ you're all talk."

"Listen mate, after being cooped up with a bunch of ugly matelots like you lot I could shag a little pig."

"After you with that pig."

"A pig's about all he'll get, if he can catch one."

"Dry up, will you. You'll all end up swilling so much ale you won't be able to stand, much less raise one."

"You can say that again."

The watch for leave waited impatiently for their leave passes and railway warrants and repeatedly checked their cases and their rabbits. I had hidden a prick of tobacco inside each leg of my pants and they were most uncomfortable - they also restricted movement and prevented me from sitting down. Then our mail arrived and our frustration was pushed to one side by the thrill of receiving the eagerly-awaited letters.

49

Half of the other watch waited with equal impatience for the liberty boat which would release them to the temptations and pleasures of Liverpool and our impatience was approaching annoyance as we watched them disappear ashore. When our passes and warrants were eventually handed to us we turned our backs on Polyanthus and rushed towards the dockyard gates without so much as a backward glance. I would have been first to the gates had it not been for the weight of my case and box but I still managed to catch the first bus to Lime Street station.

NINE

At sea on Polyanthus, with nothing to differentiate one day from another, the Sabbath could quite easily pass un-noticed. In the activity and excitement of our arrival in Liverpool, few gave any thought as to the day of the week until they were faced with the restricted train services available at Lime Street station on Sunday evenings. I boarded the only train bound for Yorkshire, it took me to Dewsbury and it was packed.

Four ATS girls occupied the seats around a corner table at the end of the carriage, they took a marked interest in the sailor who struggled through the door with a large suitcase and an even larger box. One of them spoke.

"You can sit on the table if you like, sailor."

The opportunity to share female company could not be denied, but the two, fourteen inch long pricks of tobacco I had hidden down my trouser legs had, by this time, become embarrassingly uncomfortable. I unbuttoned the top of my pants, and after fumbling around inside one leg, extracted a prick of tobacco. My totally unexpected behaviour proved too much for the curiosity of the girls and their animated chatter faded into silence as they watched, wide-eyed and open-mouthed. When I extracted the second prick, one of them could no longer contain herself,

"What are those?" she exclaimed.

" Rabbits," I answered.

They turned out to be a most effective conversation piece and by the time the train moved off I was sharing a double seat with two happy, friendly girls. One of them had a bag of freshly picked plums which, after the food on board the ship, were irresistible: I gave her a packet of cigarettes and gorged myself on juicy, fresh plums.

The journey was slow and the train was late: when it arrived in Dewsbury there was no further transport available and I was faced with a long lonely walk of more than four miles. Fortunately I had used ample cord to bind the box containing many of my rabbits and I tied one end to the handle of my suitcase to form a sling across my shoulders: it provided sufficient assistance to my

51

aching arms as I struggled homewards with a suitcase in one hand and a large cardboard box in the other.

Shortly after two o'clock in the morning I threw a handful of gravel at the window of my parent's bedroom.

Mary had started her nursing training at St. Luke's Hospital in Bradford the previous week, but there were no concessions for nurses whose boyfriends had come home on leave and our few hours together were all too short.

On Wednesday afternoon I returned to Liverpool and the prospect of at least two round trips to 'Newfy' before I had any hope of seeing home again. I had been at home for two days.

That evening I climbed into my hammock quite early and wrapped myself, along with my memories, in my blanket. For a fleeting moment I had glimpsed another world and now it was gone; it was just as if I had never been on leave.

Five days after we had entered Gladstone Dock we sailed out into the Mersey. The ship's argument with the open sea appeared to be on a far more friendly basis than it had been three months before.

Unless we were diverted to another sphere, Russia or Gib', our future could only be an unending round of convoys backwards and forwards across the inhospitable North Atlantic. A bare, raw existence stripped of all but the most basic necessities of life. Next time round it would be the turn of the other watch to enjoy leave.

Resentment filled our minds as we thought of all those 'barrack stanchions' with their office hours or alternate days off, who always managed to avoid a sea-going draft; the 'squaddies' and the 'brylcreem boys' who enjoyed the same

Off Duty
"Behind the funnel casing around the grating over the boiler space."

52

privileges - all became the object of our envy. Then, as we left the Irish Sea, such useless thoughts quickly disappeared and were replaced by the thoughts of St. John's with its promise of a brief respite.

The North Atlantic was less antagonistic in the autumn. During afternoons, when the sun shone, there were opportunities to spend off-duty hours up on deck and we gathered behind the funnel casing around the grating over the boiler space. The starboard boat deck was the Captain's domain and no one dallied on it until he had taken his solitary exercise - ten paces forrard and ten paces aft, backwards and forwards with his eyes fixed straight ahead, yet missing nothing.

It was a time when yarns were spun and jokes told, when amusing and often embarrassing incidents were recalled from our days ashore; when the well loved hymn tunes we had learned in an innocent childhood, provided the melodies for irreverent verses; when popular songs were sung with alternative words. Rude, crude and bawdy sessions relieved our tension and broke the monotony.

Certain characters demonstrated a wide and varied knowledge of unscripted ditties and given suitable encouragement, entertained the rest who joined in any chorus they knew. The sessions were not allowed to end until everyone had joined in the chorus of what was probably one of the best known ditties,

"Roll on the Nelson, the Rodney, Renown,
This one funnelled bastard is getting me down."

Clear afternoons provided opportunities to observe the behaviour of our fellow escorts when they came within a reasonable range. Much as we were pitching and rolling around ourselves, we felt sure the other corvette must be having a far worse time as it reared up and flaunted the red underside of its hull to expose the asdic dome which was directly below the bridge - a third of the way along the keel. Unable to accept that our own behaviour

"Pitching and rolling around."

was no different, we expressed our sympathy in the customary way.

"Now she's payin', just look at her go - poor bastards, you shouldn't have joined."

There were days when meals were undisturbed by milestones, when Polyanthus

53

restrained her violent behaviour to the point where it was little more than boisterous and we moved about using a steady rolling gait; sudden changes in pace were no longer required to counter violent antics on the part of a tormented ship.

Days when action stations no longer held the threat of a thorough soaking to the depth charge crews. The sea merely tossed occasional contributions our way, to let us know we were not forgotten down in the open well deck. Watertight doors could be left open, clean fresh air circulated through the fo'c'sle; our congested and stark, comfortless conditions would have been almost bearable had it not been for the endless dreary routine, the debilitating loss of sleep.

After supper, when everything had been washed up in a mess fanny filled with scalding hot water and lathered with the frequent dunkings of a perforated can containing scraps of soap, we peeled the spuds in readiness for the next day's dinner. Then, on a relatively clear table, we would write our letters or play solo, or patience, or cribbage. Number One mess had an on-going game of cribbage that dated back to the commissioning of the ship.

It was at this time during the calmer spells that the mess deck enjoyed a quiet hour. Those due to stand the middle watch climbed into their bunks or hammocks hoping for sleep and everyone spoke in quiet tones.

And on the occasional clear night, when the stars shone brightly in the sky, I would stand on deck and gaze at the Plough and wonder if Mary could be looking at it too. We liked to think of it as our permanent link, that no matter how many miles might come between us, the Plough would always be there, visible to us both.

Polyanthus carried no torpedoes but she had a torpedoman. His job was to look after the depth charges and electrical equipment, and the wire cage in the recreation space was his private domain. His name was Barton and he came from Liverpool. The Navy had never fully curbed his natural behaviour and, despite a length of service that qualified for two good conduct stripes, he had never worn more than one and that was for a very brief period. 'Barts' was an irrepressible 'Scouser' and an opportunist.

On one of the occasions when the ship was on her best behaviour he set up a crown and anchor board on the end of the table in the stokers' mess, alongside the door. Gambling was regarded as a serious offence in the Navy but it was obvious from his patter that Barts had never been deterred by such considerations.

Punters were not long in seeking the fortune which Barts assured them was there for the taking.

"Would you like to buy your bird a fur coat? - you can ride around in a limousine - c'mon m' lucky lads, now's the time to double your money!"

The danger signs were soon in evidence as the most unlucky became reckless. Freddie Faulkner was unlucky but convinced it could not last, and from time to time an odd win bolstered his hopes. The eventual outcome was sad and certain, in one last despairing gesture he had bet, and lost, his partly used packet of soap powder!

News of the new activity reached the PO's mess and in a sudden foray the Coxswain confiscated the the board and its proceeds. Bart's appearance at Defaulters was assured, a further set-back for his good conduct stripes unavoidable.

Too much money had found a new owner by this time, petty theft broke out on the mess deck and possessions disappeared. The case for the ban on gambling was proven beyond doubt.

Ken Holland, a coder, was the ship's messenger and 'postie'. It was a prized job that gave the holder more time ashore and a reasonable degree of freedom with which to enjoy it. Sadly for Ken the amendments and updates to the code books were like Topsy - they just growed and growed - until the point was reached where his fellow coders felt his trips ashore added far too much to their work load; someone else would have to take on the duties of postie.

I was only too pleased to take over the duties of postie and ship's messenger when Polyanthus came back to Liverpool. This time she had a longer stay.

The dockyard mateys made a take-over bid for the mess deck shortly after we had secured alongside. They were not subject to our discipline and restraints, and were seated in our messes banging our mugs on the tables and demanding tea when stand easy was piped. The mess cooks were complaining and arguing with the intruders, but they were considerably outnumbered. We added our protests as we tried to reclaim our messes, only to be told: "We were here first." Within an hour of our arrival we were confronted by scroungers who enjoyed far more pay, had ample freedom in which to spend it, and a home and bed waiting for them every night. Tension built up rapidly as arguments and tempers became more and more heated. Above the din, Wearmouth could be heard announcing there would be no tea poured until the intruders cleared off, and simultaneously, the melody of 'Just like the Ivy, on the old garden wall' came from the stokers' mess. We all knew the naval version and joined in.

"Dockyard mateys' children, sitting on the dockyard wall,
Watching their fathers, doing 'eff' all;
When they grow older, they'll be dockyard mateys too,
And just like their fathers, they'll do 'eff' all too."

Amidst a stream of curses, threats and obscenities, they eventually departed and we made the best of what was left of the stand easy. Several rabbits were found to have disappeared along with them.

Now I was postie I could walk through the dockyard gates virtually unchallenged with my orange postbag over my shoulder. It contained the post, hand signals for Captain 'D's' office and a little something extra which I posted independently to my father. I saw no reason why my folks should be denied the rabbits I had for them simply because I was unable to get home.

One of the Union Castle boats was in Gladstone Dock. She had arrived from South Africa and was secured along the west wall. When I returned from the Fleet Mail Office I could see from the dockyard gates there was a lot of bustle and activity around her; yet when I eventually reached the dock alongside it was deserted. A sudden shout summoned me into the large open doorway of a shed filled with a crowd of dockers. Their eyes were fixed on a crane from which a sling was swinging quite violently back and forth along the line of the dock. It was immediately above the place I had just left. The sling was filled with crates containing oranges and a couple of crates were balanced most precariously at its edge. They eventually fell to the dock and burst their sides.

It was the signal which released a horde of dockers from the shed and I joined them as they cleared up the mess. The exodus left behind the solitary figure of a customs officer who stood just inside the doorway of the shed, gazing up into the roof and apparently unaware of the excitement. A docker dashed back with several oranges for him to hold.

My postbag contained oranges when I returned on board Polyanthus and they were delicious.

From time to time, some of the artists who appeared at the theatres in Liverpool, would come along to the wet canteen on the outer wall of Gladstone Dock to entertain those men who were unable to leave the dock. I was about to turn in when the quartermaster told us the Western Brothers were expected in the wet canteen and, along with most of the watch aboard, I dashed off the ship. Using the well-worn piano and a makeshift stage, they entertained us with what was probably their full act and spent quite a long time chatting to the lads before they left. It was in the canteen that we picked up a buzz from the crew of another ship - the routine was to be changed - in future, Londonderry was to be the U.K. base for most of the North Atlantic escort vessels. It might shorten the voyage and save fuel, but it would also shorten our leave and no one relished the prospect of the long, dreary journey back and forth to Ireland. We soon found it was one of those uncannily prophetic buzzes with untraceable origins that often appeared in the fo'c'sle before it reached the wardroom.

TEN

When Polyanthus left Liverpool she left Barton behind.

Using his local knowledge and experience he decided not to leave by the main gate of Gladstone Dock and made his way through Huskisson and adjoining docks until he reached the gate which he believed to be 'safe'.

It wasn't.

"What have you got in your case, lad?" asked a voice from the hut by the gate.

"Just my dhobying," replied Barts without breaking step.

A policeman came out of the hut. "Don't be in such a hurry; I like to see what you lads carry around with you."

Barton failed to get home that night. He failed to get home for a great many nights. About two thousand cigarettes were removed from his case for use as evidence at the subsequent trial. The Crown became the main beneficiary of his enterprise with his crown and anchor board and he spent the next 28 days picking oakum in a cell.

His temporary replacement kept a very low profile and spent most of his time in the small cage filled with the electrical stores inboard of the forrard end of the starboard passage.

A small cabin on the opposite side of the passage had been cleared in readiness for a further addition to the ship - a sick bay complete with a sick berth attendant. An initial stock of medical supplies and equipment was provided and in accordance with time- honoured procedures it appeared to be made up of items that were the least likely to be of use on board a corvette.

Everything was to hand in our new sick bay - it had to be - there was just enough room for the sick berth 'tiffy' to close the door when he stood inside. Treatment was provided through the door; the 'tiffy' stood inside the sick bay; the patient stood outside in the passage.

Fortunately my only call on the tiffy's services at sea arose when the ship had difficulty in recovering from a heavy lurch and hung for a heart-stopping age before slowly rolling back. At that moment the mess cook who was making a jug of custard had just filled the jug with boiling water; I had the misfortune to

57

be alongside as he and the jug came my way.

Amongst the supplies that we had believed to be inappropriate the sick berth tiffy had some gel which did a great job once I had rid my neck, shoulders and chest of the scalding sticky custard. As a result my 'war wound' left me unmarked.

Apart from minor incidents of a similar nature our 'Doc' had few calls on his 12 weeks or so of medical training. On one occasion he stitched up a cut on someone's head. The patient was laid on the table of the stokers' mess before an unusually quiet and unhelpful audience and the sick berth tiffy's needlework underwent a critical examination.

Our new 'Jack Dusty', wasted little time in enrolling the sick berth tiffy into the responsibility for the canteen which was also situated in the starboard passage. It was another job that was far from onerous; the stock consisted of a variety of brands of cigarettes, some soap and razor blades. It was open for half an hour each day and could not be regarded as serious competition for Harrods.

Between the sick bay and the canteen was the ship's office, all three were narrow and cramped but the office was favoured with more length. A flap about seven or eight inches wide could be lowered to form a narrow desk across the doorway and it was here that we drew our pay, made our requests or received our punishment.

Whatever the purpose of our presence at the office it was impossible to retain any sense of propriety in the passage. Two persons could barely pass without turning sideways and Requestmen and Defaulters could become a farcical performance. With the Coxswain in mid-salute a mischievous sea had suddenly thrown him off-balance and on to Barton, who was making one of his appearances as a defaulter. Before the bodies had been sorted out and returned to their original positions for another try the irrepressible Barts was trying to register a complaint of assault.

The ship's 'scratch' or secretary was Sub/Lt. Whitehead and the office was his domain apart from those occasions when it was required for Requestmen and Defaulters. He was friendly without being familiar as I quickly discovered after taking over the duties of postie and ship's messenger.

As the ship approached the berth at the end of a voyage I would join the midships fender party already dressed in my No. 3 (working) uniform. Once she was secure I would report to the office to collect the mail and hand signals.

I was usually first ashore and last aboard and Sub/Lt. Whitehead was the officer to whom I reported.

The starboard passage was where the ship's unofficial barber, Percy Tidy, a stoker petty officer, carried on his trade and lived up to his name, usually towards the end of a voyage and when the ship was in harbour. Whenever the weather was fine and mild enough he preferred to work out on deck; the pleasure of fresh clean air was more precious to the stokers than to anyone else. Outdoors the barber's chair was a depth charge.

It was in the starboard passage that I learnt how to roll a prick of tobacco and it was Percy Tidy who taught me.

Each month we were allowed to buy our ration of naval tobacco; it could be taken in the form of cigarette tobacco (Tickler's), for those who 'rolled their own', in the form of pipe tobacco, or as leaf tobacco. Although a non-smoker I was most interested in the preparation and production of the true navy tobacco and accordingly bought my ration of leaf.

For the top quality product it was necessary to remove the stalks from the leaves by careful separation; it also resulted in the loss of half the weight. The leaf was then placed on a clean piece of cloth and dampened with plain water or rum and water and allowed to stand for a day in order to absorb the liquid. It was then dampened again and wrapped tightly in the cloth which was tied with light twine. It was at this point that the need of a length of uninterrupted deck space was required.

Under the supervision of one of the regular ratings I carried out these preparations prior to making my approach to P.O. Tidy who asked for my 'tot' as payment for rolling the prick of tobacco. Corvettes unofficially issued their rum neat instead of in the form of 'grog', the watered down version that was generally issued throughout the Navy.

He offered to do all the preparation in addition if I would give him another tot to put in with the leaf. It was widely believed that the tot fortified Percy rather than the tobacco and I was told by the pipe-smokers who smoked my tobacco that the rum did not make any appreciable difference to the flavour or enjoyment.

PO Tidy threaded a long length of spun yarn through a suitable steel eye on the deck head, walked down the passage, tied one end to another eye on the deckhead and the other end round the middle of the parcel of tobacco. He then sat astride the yarn suspended from the deck head and looped it around the parcel. The weight of his body tensioned the yarn and as he slowly rolled the parcel round and round all the moisture was squeezed from the contents. At the same time the yarn was being bound tightly around the parcel. When the finished product was finally tied up it resembled a large cigar.

My father and Mary's grandfather were most appreciative of my efforts. I could only accept their word for its quality.

Life followed the routine we had come to accept as our lot; our natural resistance to its unreasonable demands and to the harsh conditions was being steadily eroded. No one could escape the constant tension that tested our nerves and bodies to the limit, yet at the same time a general mood of resignation became increasingly evident.

Despite our disreputable appearance cleanliness was our constant concern. Given the intense overcrowding on the lower deck disease of any form would run riot if it had half a chance and anyone who displayed any tendency to slip from the accepted standard was shown no mercy.

One character who fell by the wayside was stripped, scrubbed and then treated with 'Blanco' which he then had no alternative but to scrub off himself. There was no doubt that his fall from grace resulted from an accumulation of nervous tension and overall tiredness; his strength of will had almost disappeared.

Winter was gradually gathering us into its grasp when the convoy we were escorting was instructed to follow a more northerly route. Ice floes like giant water lilies packed tightly together and covered the surface of the sea. As we forced our way through they crunched and bumped along the hull; the sea was much calmer for their presence but it was at the price of their constant din.

The harbour at St. John's was partly frozen when we arrived but we still had to paint 'side of ship'. Trying to drag the heavy timber catamarans around the hull was difficult because of the large blocks of ice, and one or two adventurous individuals actually painted whilst standing on the ice. The fact that we were attempting to apply paint on to ice which covered parts of the hull was of no importance - it was the routine to be followed and follow it we did.

When in due course the ice melted it took the paint with it. Poor 'Poly' looked as if she had a notifiable disease.

"Ice floes like giant Water Lilies"
Clunny Blandford on the bow.

ELEVEN

The news that the Captain had been promoted and awarded his 'half-ring' aroused very little interest on the mess deck. When it was subsequently realised that he was now the most senior officer in our Escort Group and that Polyanthus would become the Group leader our attitudes changed.

With his new half-ring the Captain also acquired a replacement navigation officer, Sub.Lt. Bradshaw RNR, and with his help it was decided that Polyanthus should set an example to the other ships in the Group.

On the first Sunday after reaching St. John's, Polyanthus held 'Divisions' on the wharf; a far from enthusiastic ship's company mustered in No. 1 uniforms and formed up under the direction of the Coxswain.

Groups of bemused spectators gathered on the adjoining ships to witness this betrayal of the accepted nonconformity of escort vessels in general and corvettes in particular. Canadian skippers put aside their Sunday newspapers to stand and stare, some even put down their cigars.

At the appropriate moment the officers made their way down the gang plank followed by Sub.Lt. Bradshaw, resplendent in shiny black gaiters and the Captain who proceeded to inspect every man on parade.

Despite all the muttered comments and grumbles my pride was given a boost and before the parade ended most backs were just a little straighter and heads a little higher than they had been.

Our new 'Sub.' was viewed with deep suspicion by the other ranks. Divisions was bad enough but anyone who turned out in gaiters could pose a threat to our whole way of life.

Before the day was out I had been issued with a pair of khaki gaiters for wear whenever I went ashore on duty as Ship's postie and messenger. I soon discovered that they gave me an extra bit of pride in the job I was doing, in my appearance and in my ship.

It was essential for a senior officer of an escort group to have an experienced and reliable navigating officer which was no doubt the reason for the appearance of Sub.Lt. Bradshaw. It was also essential for him to have an experienced and reliable yeoman of signals. In Alec Massie the skipper had everything other than the rank. The acting yeoman of signals for the Group was not even a leading hand, he was Signalman First Class Alexander Massie and no senior officer ever had a better yeoman.

From time to time signalmen indulged in games of 'one-up-manship', usually a matter of speed on the signal lamp. A meeting with an American destroyer created difficulties for the duty signalman and a message was sent below to Alec. The 'Yank' who had ignored earlier requests to drop his sending speed suddenly found the tables turned as Alec unloaded all his years of experience and ability on him.

Life became more demanding for the signals staff but most of us hardly noticed any change in the daily routine. The Atlantic continued to be cold, grey and wet, the ship continued to be cold, cramped and uncomfortable, the bulkheads continued to dribble condensation on to decks that defied all our efforts to mop up. Above all there was always insufficient sleep.

Oiling at sea became the normal mid-ocean exercise which made wire ropes sing as they stretched and sometimes broke under the strain; then the hose would part and spill precious gallons of fuel oil into the ocean before the supply-cock on the tanker could be turned off.

As I came off duty at the end of the first dog-watch one evening I crashed into 'Flash' Braithwaite. A heavy sea was running, the ship was changing course and great 'green ones' were cascading over the bows; we dived for cover behind the wheelhouse simultaneously.

Polyanthus rolled as only corvettes can and we clung to the same stanchion, unable to avoid the spray which managed to search out victims no matter how well they were protected.

"Just heard an idiot on the radio," spluttered Flash, "Spent 10 days in an open boat after being torpedoed. Says he can't wait to get back to sea again."

The ship reached an angle approaching 40 degrees and showed no sign of returning to the vertical; we grasped the stanchion harder than ever, "Come on you lazy old cow" we urged, "for Christ's sake get up."

Slowly she began to return only for the roll to gain momentum until it swung straight through the vertical and over to the other side. We found ourselves fighting to retain our hold once again and our feet slithered on the steel deck as the angle changed.

"If ever I get off this bloody tub no one will get me back on the 'hoggin' (sea) again." Flash continued to speak but his voice was lost in the din of yet another wall of water hitting the ship.

"I reckon these blokes they put on the wireless are about as authentic as Lord Haw-Haw," concluded the disillusioned and by now drenched Braithwaite.

I agreed with him entirely. Only I was too miserable to even grumble at our lot.

My mood was shared by the occupants of the mess deck in general who had their own problems in trying to dry themselves out and eat their evening meal.

I was in the midst of my meal when I was summoned to the bridge to report to the Captain. Struggling back into my wet coat I made my way back along the same hazardous route, at a loss to understand the reason for the summons. If the Captain was on the bridge during a dog-watch there was every likelihood that someone would be in trouble, and all the signs pointed to that someone being me.

The Captain stood on the open bridge with his back to the wind and spray that howled and lashed into my face as I stood before him; he was clearly annoyed.

"We have just narrowly avoided a collision with the escort which was ahead of us. Why did you fail to report that she was not on her station before you came off watch?" the Captain demanded.

Completely nonplussed I could only tell him I was not aware of her being off station and plead the reduced efficiency of RDF in heavy weather.

I was given jankers - 7 days 'Number Elevens' - for negligence and dismissed.

Back in the mess I began to do a few sums as I smarted under the accusation and judgement of an event in which I found it difficult to understand my involvement. With time to collect my thoughts and calculate the distances between the ships and lapse of time from handing over the watch to the 'near miss', it was clear that the other ship, a Canadian corvette, was more than likely to have been on station as I believed her to be when I handed over the watch. Taking into account the interlude I had shared with Flash Braithwaite there had been time for my relief to have carried out further 'sweeps' before he reported the danger, a great deal depended on the time he had taken over those sweeps before he became aware of the maverick behaviour of the other escort.

Having satisfied myself on the facts I sought the advice of the most senior member of the mess, Alec, when he came below at the end of the second dog watch.

"How do I get a chance to clear myself?"

"You don't, you put it down to experience and forget it" was his answer.

Realising I was far from happy at his advice he pointed out that the 'old man' would not take kindly to a request for him to reverse his decision. "Those who were on duty were so busy covering their own yard-arm, mate, that they didn't care who they shit on and you caught the lot; even if you manage to throw most of it back, some will still stick on you and no one's going to thank you for stirring up an even bigger stink."

There was an awful lot of common sense in what Alec had to say but I was in no mood to accept it. Fortunately for me it prompted one of Alec's rare disclosures about his past and it put my own problems into perspective.

At the time of Dunkirk Alec was in Pompey Barracks. Along with some other

63

long-service ratings he was issued with a rifle and two clips of ammunition, some emergency rations and a steel helmet; then told to collect his gas mask and oilskins and report to the dockyard. There he was given a whaler which, along with others, was towed along the South Coast and across to Dunkirk.

For three days and nights Alec and the others like him ferried troops from the shore to the larger ships before they were eventually taken in tow once again and brought to Dover.

Alec was a signalman not a seaman, he had never handled a whaler before; nor had he ever fired more than 10 rounds with a rifle and that was in his initial training. He arrived in London en route for Portsmouth bedraggled, unshaven, and minus his ammunition and gas mask. With his steel helmet stuck on his head he stumbled bleary-eyed through the barrier to be faced by an immaculately turned out officer who considered him to be a disgrace to the Service and told him so.

Two military policemen marched a dishevelled and disinterested sailor to the RTO's office to be put on a charge. It seemed the RTO was one of the few people to show any sense because he dismissed Alec without any ado and told him to get back to Portsmouth as quickly as he could.

His troubles were far from over.

The returning hero reported to the 'Jaunty's' office at Pompey and was immediately put on report for losing two clips of ammunition; in addition he had to replace his gas mask at his own expense.

Commanding Officers lost whole battalions of tanks and guns, whole fleets of transport vehicles were abandoned and destroyed. Many of those accountable for them were decorated for arranging their destruction.

Thanks to the diligence of a regulating petty officer aboard the stone frigate, HMS Victory, however, Signalman Massie. A. was duly brought to task and made to realise the significance of his negligence. There can be no excuse for losing two clips of .303 rifle ammunition.

"Don't ever expect any recommends in the Andrew (Navy); never volunteer for anything; keep your nose clean and always watch your back," was Alec's rueful conclusion.

I never found out why the Canadian corvette had turned on to a reciprocal course and had charged towards Polyanthus without warning; nor did I discover if the officer responsible received any reprimand.

I did my number elevens and resented it.

When we approached home waters once again the convoy split into small groups; we escorted some of the ships part of the way to their destination in Loch Broom and then turned towards Lough Foyle with its captive tanker and its supply of fuel.

The bum-boats came out from Moville to greet us. Fresh butter and eggs and a variety of tinned goods were roughly set out along with silk stockings and clothing of doubtful quality in an effort to coax any spare cash from our pockets. When cash was not forthcoming offers to barter for duty-free cigarettes and tobacco brought an increase in trading.

On their return to Moville some unfortunate Irishmen found their one-pound tins of 'Pusser's' tobacco contained dried tea leaves and newspaper beneath a top layer of tobacco.

The Navy had its share of rogues and 'spivs' and the men of Moville discovered that Polyanthus carried her full quota.

We took a pilot aboard and sailed up the River Foyle for the first time. Through lush green Irish fields, trees and meadows, we slid quietly and gently between the river banks up to the city of Londonderry. On we sailed until we passed the Guildhall and tied up almost under the parapet of the bridge. We had left the unrelieved cold grey monotony of the Atlantic behind and taken a journey through some delightful country before arriving in the centre of a city.

The transition was difficult to assimilate; it was also difficult to appreciate, for our thoughts were concentrated on the protracted and time-consuming journey which faced those who were entitled to leave.

The city of 'Derry' did not hold many attractions to lads who had recently experienced three visits to the flesh-pots of Liverpool.

Libertymen from the watch aboard went ashore in search of whatever delights Derry could offer. Some of us found a dance hall which gradually assumed a dual role as the evening progressed. Brawls broke out from time to time and then it became a battlefield; some of them spilled out into the forecourt.

A diminutive and extremely drunk Irishman loudly denounced the Royal Navy and everything British. His avowed intent was clearly to destroy them all single-handed, starting there and then; with arms swinging wildly in all directions he was bound to make contact sooner or later with anyone who stood before him.

When four matelots retired hurt in the face of his unrelenting aggression we decided there were better places to spend our evening despite the loss of our admission fee to the dance.

'Was he by any chance from Moville?' We asked ourselves. 'Did he own a bum-boat perhaps?'

No one was prepared to stop and enquire.

Our opinion of Londonderry and its welcome was not enhanced by the experience, yet on our return to the ship we discovered there were some who had apparently fared rather better than we had done. They did not return until morning.

One of them brought a varied assortment of dresses and ladies' underwear which he had removed from the wardrobe of the 'lady' with whom he had spent the better part of the night. At the first opportunity he declared he would 'pop' them at the nearest pawnbrokers in order to recover some of the money his lady had stolen out of his pockets.

Others became withdrawn and said little about their escapades. We were left to draw our own conclusions when they put in a request for the Roman Catholic priest to be called. It was a request which was granted automatically and the Captain had to make his cabin available as a confessional when the priest arrived on board.

Abject and troubled creatures suddenly became carefree and happy within the space of a few short minutes as their sins and misdemeanours were absolved.

Our Canadian friends, tied up alongside and outboard of Polyanthus, had arranged things differently. One or two selected ladies of the town had been smuggled aboard for the night. Their departure on the following morning was witnessed by our quartermaster, 'Darby' Allen.

"Could I help you ladies?" he enquired solicitously, "You look absolutely worn out."

"Some other time, Jack, m'darlin'," they replied as they stumbled across our deck in order to get ashore.

Derry's image was receiving some very rough treatment.

With nothing better to do on my next run ashore I found myself eating beans on toast at the Salvation Army canteen. A large hearty man was busy by the cash till counting the money; he looked up and caught my eye. A short time later he walked over and we exchanged the usual type of pleasantries; cashing-up at some of the canteens I learned was one of his contributions towards the charities concerned.

He asked me if I would like to visit his home.

"It's nothing grand but there'll be a warm welcome from my wife and a warm fire to sit beside."

We walked up to Pump Street, in the shadow of the Cathedral, and I found a second home.

Fortune smiled on me that evening; he was right about the warmth, I could never visit Derry again without visiting Pump Street and the Bell family. They were my first contacts with all those people of Londonderry whose warm hearts and unfailing kindness came to mean so much to me.

TWELVE

The bread supplied to us in Londonderry was dreadful.
The ship's cook was prevailed upon to make a really determined attempt at baking a batch of bread but what he produced was indescribable and he was never prevailed upon again.
On the slow convoys where the voyage extended to twelve or more days we had a problem with the freshwater supplies. The dwindling remains in the tanks became brackish and unpleasant to drink and had to be rationed. Even the basic necessities of life began to taunt us. Our thoughts turned to the plentiful food of St. John's and as our appetites grew they added to the torment of drawn-out voyages which dragged on until they seemed everlasting.
Given the appalling conditions and the inadequate food available during the winter of 1942/43 it was not surprising that the strain became increasingly difficult to bear.
I was asleep in my hammock in St. John's when I suddenly awoke to find myself being sick. There was no warning. I had felt perfectly well when I turned in, and felt almost no after-effects.
The following morning I reported sick and was sent along to the Depot Ship at the end of the wharf to see the Doctor. His examination was perfunctory and his remedy drastic; I had to swallow 2 ounces of castor oil there and then.
Back on board Polyanthus, the Buffer's forehead creased into a scowl as he listened to my report and left no doubt in my mind that he did not believe a word.
"Do I look as if I'm wearing a green coat?" He asked, "Try that again, my lad, and I'll have you up the stick, painting the crow's nest."
With my recent intake of castor oil that was the last place I wanted to be.
My sudden attack remained a mystery and I continued to follow the normal routine, enjoying a bowl of cornflakes and a cup of coffee at the Caribou Hut each morning as I returned from the Captain 'D's' Office with the signals. For someone who has endured a slow convoy aboard a corvette, cornflakes in a bowl filled with cold fresh milk are like ambrosia and nectar.

The Caribou Hut boasted an excellent canteen and the ships' messengers provided it with a steady mid-morning custom as they dallied on their return journey with their signal bags.

One of the civilian clerks in the Signals Office was awaiting the opportunity to return home to Yorkshire and for the last few trips I had been acting as her personal messenger by bringing funds from her family.

Kathleen Rhodes had gone out to Labrador as a Moravian missionary just before the outbreak of war and when her tour of duty came to an end she managed to reach St. John's where she became stranded. With few funds to speak of she was largely dependent upon the goodwill and generosity of others.

Each time we arrived in St. John's we were allowed to exchange a maximum amount of £10 to enhance our spending power, and with the co-operation of Sub.Lt. Whitehead I was able to change a further £10 in addition to my own, which I then passed on to Miss Rhodes. Until she was able to find employment I believe these few gifts from her family were all she had to spend on herself and they had to be wangled through illegally.

Visiting her in St. John's was always an enjoyable experience; despite the difference in our ages and only the most slender links in Yorkshire we got on well together. For many months in the year she had been isolated and responsible for the care and welfare of a group of Eskimo children whilst their parents were away hunting. Her nearest neighbour was the Mountie who called on her and her brood from time to time. The highlight of her year was a trip by dog sled to the trading post accompanied by the Mountie.

Her reward for her years of isolation, endurance and dedication had to be found in the minds and memories of the children she had cared for. There was little to be found during her enforced stay in Newfoundland.

A fine and lovely lady, she eventually reached her home in mid 1943.

Each visit to St. John's provided an opportunity for our former Jack Dusty to keep in touch with his old ship and his former shipmates. Accompanied by a sickberth attendant he was allowed to leave the Naval Hospital for a couple of hours, and once aboard he sat at the corner of the stokers' mess at the entrance to the messdeck. There he could see and be seen and there he would chat and talk quite normally, telling of his life of ease, secure on dry land with a comfortable bed and good food.

"You're all mugs," he insisted. "I've got it made. I'll have worked my ticket by this time next year, just you see."

"But what do you do with yourself all day ?" asked Raggie.

"Oh, I read a lot and I play with my cars," Jack replied happily, then added in a more excited voice "and if I behave myself I've been promised a new Dinky toy next week - its a lorry."

His audience exchanged glances with each other; there was an awkward silence until someone ventured,

"I guess you really do have it made, Jack."

It was difficult to find a great deal to talk about from then on.

Our brief spell of glory as senior ship came to an end when the Captain was given command of a larger and better class of ship. Although Polyanthus never had any spectacular or dramatic action she had acquitted herself well and there was a strong 'buzz' of impending medals and awards.

In recognition of what he considered to be outstanding service the Captain proposed to recommend Alec for immediate promotion and was surprised when Alec was not interested. For a man who was proud to have earned his promotion through hard work and efficiency it was very difficult to understand the philosophy of someone who was equally efficient in his job without being dedicated to it.

Whatever his recommendations no awards ever came the way of anyone aboard Polyanthus in the ensuing months. Sub/Lt. Whitehead was awarded his second ring but that was for time served. No one really expected any recognition: ours was a thankless existence.

Freddie Cox was one member of the crew who certainly had no expectations of medals or glory; very few of us looked our best at sea but Freddie looked scruffier than most. Even after a few days in harbour and several good washes he fell short of the Navy's idea of a well-turned-out able seaman.

Fate had it in for him. No matter how much he tried to remain inconspicuous he found himself very much involved in memorable events.

Three survivors who had been rescued from the Mediterranean by an American ship had been landed in New York and sent to St. John's. Despite the acute shortage of accommodation, we were ordered to take one of them back to the UK with us. He did not attract much attention and kept himself in the background until the day of departure, but as the time for sailing drew near he suddenly went berserk and stormed on to the mess deck, challenging anyone brave enough to face him to a fight.

"I could whip Joe Louis" he yelled, as he glared at the rest of us.

Just at that moment Freddie Cox came through the watertight door dressed in singlet and pants, having just left the washroom; puzzled, he gazed around at his startled shipmates and sat down on the form alongside the water geyser at the end of Number Two mess. The 'bird of passage' dropped on to the other end of the form and slowly slid towards Freddie; he leaned out, took hold of Freddie's bare arm and caressed it gently.

"That's a lovely arm," he said. " I could eat that arm; I once ate a man's arm in the 'Med'."

"Well you're not eating this one," gulped a captive and badly shaken Freddie who realised he was very much on his own.

After another caress, the madman dropped Freddie's arm and jumped back on to his feet, repeating his challenge to fight anyone and everyone. At the same time he grabbed the mess fanny above Number Two mess and brought it down on his forehead with a sickening thud; dropping the fanny, which now displayed a pronounced bulge, he resumed his seat for a brief moment before getting back on his feet and heading unsteadily across the deck.

There was a noticeable exodus from the stokers' mess when he sat down and slumped over the table.

A marine, who was a fellow survivor, was summoned from the ship on which he was taking passage, in the hope that he could pacify his former shipmate; but he met with little success.

Any normal person would have been knocked out by the force of the blow our passenger had inflicted upon himself with the fanny, and although it had obviously restricted his energy, it was not long before he got back on his feet again and staggered out of the fo'c'sle shouting,

"This ship isn't going to sail because I won't let her."

Following at a safe distance several lads kept us informed of his progress.

"He's gone down to the wardroom flat and grabbed the fire-axe off the wall - - he's battering at the Skipper's cabin and yelling that he won't let us sail."

"He's been drinking 'Bluebell'. There's a couple of empty tins in the heads."

"What the hell's he been drinking metal polish for?"

"Because there's supposed to be some alcohol in it."

"Poor sod, he must be bad."

The marine confirmed that the claim to have resorted to cannibalism was correct. It was not at all comforting to know and we wondered how long it would be before he grabbed the Skipper.

By this time the whole ship's company was alerted. The Buffer had mustered a few of the larger members of the crew and was hiding behind the largest, 'Lofty' Pratt.

"Go down and grab him," ordered the Buffer.

"No bloody fear," answered Lofty, "I've just remembered I'm a coward."

Without any warning the man charged up from the wardroom flat and back to a mess deck which had never had so much open space to move about in.

The impasse ended when a naval patrol made up of half a dozen enormous Canadians came aboard along with a diminutive Surgeon Lieutenant.

Putting us all to shame, the little 'Doc' walked straight up to the wild-eyed one. "Come along with me," he said quietly.

His new patient smiled and began to cry as he walked meekly off the ship.

He was no longer concerned about the ship sailing because he would not be on it.

Following his incarceration, Barton had rejoined the ship. He came from the same part of Liverpool as Freddie; they were both 'Scousers' who shared the same background, were both regulars serving on the same ship and were about the same age.

They hated each other's guts.

I never discovered what brought their hatred to a head, but the point was reached where they were at each other's throats and bloodshed was inevitable.

Barton was reputed to have been cruiser-weight champion of the Navy in the 'Med' before the war, a title which had so many claimants that it was meaningless. He looked as if he would be handy with his fists, however, and was the obvious favourite in any battle between the two.

He also had considerable experience in battles with authority and had no wish to invoke its wrath when there were regulations available to protect him.

He put in a request for a grievance fight as provided for under Kings Regulations and Admiralty Instructions; and both protagonists refused to be dissuaded from such a fight despite the strong arguments of their superiors.

The fight took place on the wharf alongside Polyanthus when she arrived in St. John's and most of the crew poured off the ship and on to the wharf, to witness an event that was rarely seen.

The duty officer stood to one side with a stop-watch and signalled the start and the end of each round; there was no ring other than the one formed by the spectators and the fight continued until one of the contestants was unable to fight any more.

It was a brutal, debasing spectacle. Cheers of encouragement quickly died away as round after round reduced both men into bruised and bloody hulks. With no clinches to give relief from the constant bombardment, the unrelieved aggression was total, it became a matter of endurance and pointless pride.

The fact that Barton was the one finally to concede defeat was no longer important, Cox was in as bad a state and in need of help to get back aboard. We were only too anxious to get them below decks and out of sight of all the spectators who had witnessed the fight.

The two men had put their own pride and courage on public display but there was no winner, just a loser and that was their ship - Polyanthus.

For some days neither man could take advantage of the spell in harbour. Others took every advantage available to them.

With the greater part of the crew ashore the ship was quiet and relatively peaceful when 'Raggie' Coulin burst on to the mess deck. It was around nine o'clock in the evening.

"Lend me your duffle coats and oilskins, lads", he cried as he gathered up his own oilskin. "I've got a bird waiting for me up on the hill."

With hardly a pause for breath he was away again and panting up the hillside beyond the wharf, watched by an intrigued bunch of his shipmates who had come out on to the upper deck. A gallery of spectators gathered on the bridge and all available binoculars and telescopes were directed towards the hopeful Casanova. Skirmishes broke out as we jostled for position or fought for a chance to use the glasses; everyone was anxious to view the progress of such an unusual tryst.

It was not long before the four-inch gun began to move; slowly and steadily it turned and the muzzle began to lift until it was trained on to the target. Shorty Grant and his opposite number on the gun's crew, Davey, had no intention of struggling for a glimpse through binoculars when there were perfectly good telescopic sights on the gun. Shorty was no mean gun-layer and between them they provided an accurate direction and elevation for all and sundry to follow.

The activity did not go unnoticed. It aroused the curiosity of our counterparts on other ships who, with the assistance of our four-inch gun's crew, became voyeurs too. Men making their way along the wharf slowed and hesitated, their progress handicapped by their anxiety to know what was behind our activity. Denied our knowledge of the motivation, the spectacle of a couple struggling up the barren hillside with a bundle of clothing must have presented them with quite a puzzle to solve.

Freddie never got over his dispute with Barton. On the voyage out from 'Newfy' he rarely came below deck and could be found curled up amongst the hawsers and ropes on the funnel casing, wrapped in his greatcoat with a duffle coat over his shoulders. He emerged to stand his watch and immediately retreated into his own lonely and silent world when it ended.

All efforts to persuade him to come below for food were ignored and eventually someone would take a plateful up to him regardless of the general view that starvation would eventually force him below.

It was an accidental movement of the engine-room telegraph which brought Freddie's plight to the notice of the officers. It made a short, sharp ring and it startled Freddie who mistook it for the alarm bell.

He shot up to his action station on the port side of the bridge and whipped the cover off the oerlikon. A startled officer of the watch demanded an explanation and Freddie was put on Defaulters.

It was then that Freddie's service history came to light.

He too was a survivor. His previous ship had been sunk in the North Atlantic and he had been in the water for some time, smothered in fuel oil which half choked him. As it was February it was a miracle he had survived in the cold. For months he had sailed with us unable or unwilling to confide in anyone and enduring his private hell until he could carry on no longer.

He left us on reaching the UK and was sent home on six months' compassionate leave.

THIRTEEN

The afternoon train for Larne represented the way out of Londonderry for those going on leave. The journey around the Antrim coast seemed endless and we were far too frustrated by the slow pace and the number of stops to enjoy the scenery. Every station appeared to be Bally something or other; we fully expected to end up at one called Ballylost.

Eventually we climbed aboard the ferry crowded with men and women from all three services. The small saloon was jammed with a struggling mass of humanity and we had no wish to join it; huddled in our coats we gathered on the upper deck where the air was fresh and clean, unable to break the habit of constantly scouring the sea and the skyline with our eyes.

At Stranraer we disembarked on to the train, the 'Paddy', and began our journey through the night. The more fortunate ones who were able to find a seat snatched some sleep between stops.

"We'll get a cup of tea at Preston," observed someone "and it's free."

Preston lived up to his expectations. At 3 a.m. the train was met by some cheerful ladies with a trolley complete with a tea urn, cups, buns and cakes which they quickly handed out to servicemen and servicewomen, without question.

The train stopped at Wigan shortly before 4 a.m. and the solitary porter on an otherwise deserted platform informed me that, not only had I to change trains, I had to change stations. The certainty of rest and sleep in my own bed within a few hours boosted my spirits as I struggled across a cold and deserted town with my rabbits.

I didn't have to knock anyone up, my parents were already up and about by the time I got home. The journey lasted 20 hours and I had 5 days leave.

It was too much to hope for Mary to have any days off during such a short leave. We snatched a few hours together on her time off duty before I embarked on the return journey to Derry via Manchester and Preston.

The Paddy drew into Preston and the window of a first class carriage dropped down. A bleary-eyed staff-officer stuck his head out and was somewhat taken aback to be confronted by a lady on the platform who asked "Would you like a cup of tea?"

"I would indeed," he replied, "how much will that be?"

The realisation that it was free appeared to overwhelm him. Taking a ten shilling note from his wallet he pressed it into the lady's hand.

"God bless you, my dear" he managed to whisper as he choked on the hot tea.

A soldier who was standing at the trolley turned to me.

"Did you see that? He must be bloody thirsty, he's just given her a week's pay for a cup o' char."

In the middle of the night I suffered another sudden attack of sickness and as the night wore on I became colder and colder. It was a miserable journey.

The following morning I reported to the sick bay, where my temperature was taken repeatedly during the next two hours with various thermometers. No matter what was done it refused to rise to normal and I was put ashore.

For some reason unknown to me I was billeted in the Sailors' Rest in Gt. James Street; it was in the town and handy for the sick bay, and from my point of view it was a most satisfactory arrangement. There were only four or five merchant seamen staying there at the time, the food was quite good, and it had a piano.

For the first time since joining the Navy I had the chance to make my own music, my temperature returned to normal within twenty four hours, no one at the sick-bay seemed to know what to do with me and I was quite happy for things to continue as they were.

The Sailors' Rest had a big, heavy door which remained wide open from morning until night. There were times when it was not fully open however and when I tried to push it back one evening I found an attractive 'colleen' hiding behind it.

"Do you know a sailor called Jack who might be staying here?" she asked. "He arranged to meet me tonight."

I passed on her enquiry to the other occupants of the dormitory upstairs although none of them answered to the name of Jack.

"She's there most nights between six and seven," I was told, "she's met a lot of blokes called Jack since she first stood behind that door."

In complete contrast were the carefully chosen local girl volunteers who served and helped out in the canteen at the Sailors' Rest. One of them showed some interest in my efforts on the piano and chatted to me. I told her that I had met the Bell family and she asked if I knew Marie.

"She's a music teacher and I'm sure you'll be more than welcome to practise on her piano and use her music at any time. Come along to the service at the Seamen's Mission tonight and I'll introduce you."

Vickie duly introduced me to Marie and so I met the Longwell family: to my 'up-homers' at Pump Street I added others on Nicholson Terrace where I was assured of an equally warm reception. The wonderful folk of Derry welcomed me into their homes and treated me as one of their own; their daughters and their friends welcomed me into a happy group in which sailors could forget their harsh existence for a brief spell and I became one of the fortunate lads who discovered, and enjoyed, the dances at Richmond Hall.

It was only when I had been given sufficient time to recover from whatever my problem had been that it was decided to send me to the US Navy Hospital at Creevagh for X-rays and further tests.

I was the only Englishman in a ward containing seven survivors from an American merchant ship who were suffering from frost-bite.

"Have you still got your tonsils, Limey?"

"Yes."

"Not for long you haven't."

"Why?"

"Because there's a pharmacists mate first class who was a butcher back home and he's just qualified to remove tonsils. He does the job in the small ward at the end of the hut down there. The only ones in this ward who had tonsils when they came in don't have them no more. He just snips 'em off with his fancy wire noose whilst you're standing there. Don't even let you lie down on a trolley. Just like shelling peas, I'd say."

I avoided the removal of my perfectly good and healthy tonsils and was able to enjoy an unbelievable variety of food; an everyday meal of pumpkin pie and turkey with vegetables and ice cream was a luxury beyond my wildest dreams. It was served, all at the same time, on a stainless steel tray, each item in its own section, a marked change from the conglomeration of food I often faced on board when the weather blew up rough. I began to feel disgustingly healthy very quickly.

Following numerous tests, barium meals and X-rays, the doctors decided that I had a scar on my duodenum which was probably the remains of a former ulcer and I was put on a light diet. My good health ceased to be quite as enjoyable.

Since my only previous problem of a similar nature had occurred only a few weeks previously, my 'ulcer' must have come and gone with unusual speed..

One survivor was considerably older than the others; he was a Texan and occupied the bed at the opposite corner of the ward to mine. Most of his mates found difficulty in being quiet but he said very little and was something of an enigma. From time to time I found him studying me and after a few days he suddenly called across to me.

"You know something, boy? You remind me of a guy back home. This guy looks like he's forty and yet he's only twenty-nine."

It hardly seemed appropriate to tell him I was only nineteen.

When I was discharged from Creevagh someone had an incredible flash of common sense and realised it would be much cheaper to send me home on leave than to keep me at the Sailors' Rest in Londonderry. I was delighted to have the chance to endure the long journey home.

A fellow traveller who had worked on the railways proved to be a tremendous help.

"We're due in Carlisle at ten past one in the morning," he told me. "The Leeds train is due out ten minutes before we get in but it usually hangs on for the Paddy; have your gear ready by the door as we pull in to Carlisle; if they've held the Leeds train it will be across the platform ready to pull out."

From then on I always made the unscheduled change at Carlisle and saved the long and uncomfortable 'Cooks Tour' round Lancashire although it meant my homecomings were again in the middle of the night.

During the time I was at home Mary celebrated her 19th birthday and we became engaged.

I returned to Londonderry to find Polyanthus had been routed to Liverpool. She was due to arrive at the oiler in Lough Foyle the following day so I caught the duty 'drifter' as it made its daily journey down river but arrived too late. She had sailed without me.

H.M.S. Sherwood was a 'four stacker', one of the First World War destroyers which the Royal Navy acquired as part of the Lend-Lease deal with the United States, a long and very slender ship with an entirely different character and nature to that of a corvette.

I took passage in her to St. John's.

From October 1942 the weather in the North Atlantic had deteriorated steadily with winds rarely falling below gale force 7 for days on end. In January, 1943, the escort groups experienced some of the worst weather ever faced throughout the whole Battle of the Atlantic; Sherwood and Polyanthus were in the group that was caught in a hurricane.

Mountainous waves whipped into a fury by unbelievable winds hurled the ships around in a frenzied

H.M.S. Sherwood after the hurricane. "Threatening walls of water which bore down on us from all sides".

76

cauldron of sea. The horizon became but a memory and the convoy was scattered with all hope of cohesion lost. Completely separated from one another it became a case of every man for himself: a fight for survival amidst the terrifying forces of nature. There were times when it was impossible to make any headway at all through the threatening walls of water which bore down on us from all sides. Suddenly the ship would be carried up high on to the crests where she would shake and shudder from the vibration of her propellers as they thrashed the air before she embarked on the plunge back into a fearsome, deep yawning trough. For three days no one was allowed on the upper deck unless he was secured by a life-line. I realised how accustomed I had become to the behaviour of Polyanthus - she was like a cork on the sea - Sherwood was like a stick.

Polyanthus had not fared very well. Her visit to Liverpool had arisen from her need for a major re-fit and overhaul. When I re-joined her I found her need was even greater; one boiler room fan had collapsed beyond repair and the other had shaken most of its securing rivets loose. For the last stages of her struggle to reach St. John's it had relied to a large extent on lashings of spun yarn for security.

Of the ships caught in the hurricane, not one had escaped unscathed. Escorts had lost sea boats and funnels, and hardly any of those which were in St. John's at that time could be considered operational. The fate of the merchant ships was difficult to ascertain; the Commodore had been lost along with his ship and only seven of the merchant ships which had set out were said to have completed the crossing.

Beneath the veneer of normal composure it was possible to detect an apprehension which was unlike any I had known before. We had experienced the full and frightening forces of a merciless nature and had been to the brink of oblivion. By comparison the war against the U-boats counted for little; that was a war in which we could fight back, take the initiative even. Against nature we were helpless and defenceless.

At such times even the noisiest of men often take refuge in silence as they search for peace of mind. My conception of fear was changed beyond recognition.

The gales were waiting for us when we emerged from 'Newfy'. They stayed with us for most of the voyage home and it was a slow convoy.

Since Polyanthus could not manage more than 7 knots it was just as well. The chief ERA wore a frown as part of his everyday uniform; now it was overlaid with an expectation of imminent doom as pipes began to show signs of fracturing and new groans and creaks could be heard from the bowels of the ship.

The Canadian corvettes were keeping fairly close to us and indulging in the customary indecent behaviour adopted by corvettes in heavy seas. They tossed around, flaunting their red bottoms, and increasing our own discomfort; we knew that Polyanthus was behaving in the same way and her creaks and groans sounded even louder in our ears.

The shelter of Lough Foyle was never more welcome. It was down to Derry for the briefest of stops before we were out again and on our way around the North of Scotland bound for the Tyne and the desperately needed refit.

The huge towering waves, up and down which we sailed as if they were hillsides, were replaced by the shorter chop of the coastal waters. Taken by surprise the greater part of the crew fell victim to seasickness and those who avoided that misfortune benefited from huge helpings of dinner.

De-ammunitioning ship at North Shields was completed by willing hands in record time and we sailed across the river to South Shields where the refit was to take place.

Anxious enquiries were made as to the presence, strength and attitudes of the customs officers at the dock, for this was unknown territory and a refit leave of 14 days was much too valuable to risk. The problem was that everything was being stripped out of the ship and we had to get our rabbits off with us somehow.

Following my usual procedure I declared my quota of silk stockings and breathed a huge sigh of relief when I cleared the dock gates. Before I could go too far I had to remove several cigarette lighters from my socks and redistribute many other items about my person.

Shortly before midnight I arrived in Bradford station. The ticket collector sympathised with me and a packet of duty free cigarettes put me on the footplate of a light engine which took me to Low Moor. I felt unable to face the long walk home and spent what was left of the night with my godparents who happened to live there.

My godfather was a policeman and he took as many of the lighters as I could spare to Bradford Police Station when he went on duty that morning. He sold the lot within minutes.

Instead of two or three days at home I now had two whole weeks; it was marvellous. A telegram arrived during the second week granting an extension of a further seven days. That was unbelievable.

I returned to South Shields to find a bare ship, littered with wires and pipes, welding torches and assorted equipment; it was early evening and the workers had gone home. Ernie emerged from the shelter of the doorway to the starboard passage carrying a rifle.

"Bloody awful welcome isn't it?" he said as we surveyed the utter shambles around us. "There's no heat of any kind and only emergency lighting and with my usual luck I've dropped for sentry duty."

"Any idea of the reason for the extra leave."

Ernie chuckled at my question. "Well, the buzz is that it's down to Barton: when the dockyard foreman came aboard with his gang, Barts saw him marking off parts of the bulkheads with a lump of chalk and writing 'off' on them. Blokes with acetylene torches began cutting the bulkheads, so old Barts found himself a piece of identical chalk and did a bit of marking off himself. Nobody has any idea who did it, of course."

Most of my watch were already back and I found most of the 'digs' on the list provided aboard the ship were full. My hopes of finding a bed for the night had almost gone when I found a house with a spare bed. No sooner had I been shown the bed than the air-raid sirens sounded and I spent my first night in South Shields in an Anderson shelter. My luck changed on the following morning when I was given the name of family who had not taken boarders before; they were typical 'Geordies' and Mrs. King knew how to spoil a lad.

Throughout my service in the Navy I had never received any dental treatment and it was decided that this was the time to do something about it. I was told to report to the Naval Dental Centre at North Shields where a very enthusiastic young dental officer had a great time sorting out my teeth.

Each morning for a fortnight I took the ferry across the river and he put in a lot of practice with his drills and forceps. I lost my fear of dentists in North Shields.

Responsibility for the alleged sabotage was never established, nor was the true reason for the extension to our leave, but there was certainly no doubt about the gratitude of the crew and of the mothers, sisters, sweethearts and wives who enjoyed all the precious extra days with their loved ones.

FOURTEEN

Polyanthus sailed out of Dawson's Yard at South Shields wearing a fresh coat of paint and looking good.

Her mast had been moved; it was now behind the bridge, which had been completely re-designed with the Asdic cabin stuck on the front. She also had a new weapon, a 'Hedgehog' which could fire a pattern of bombs ahead of the ship and hopefully add to the discomfort of any U-boat which happened to be in the vicinity.

We rounded the North of Scotland and faced the Atlantic once more with little enthusiasm.

With our limited capability, our role in the Battle of the Atlantic was very much a supportive one. Corvettes were not the most glamorous of ships, they were uncomfortable and unattractive, not in the least like the flowers whose names they bore. We were stuck with a job which had to be done and it was not one we enjoyed.

Our leave and spell in South Shields had created a break in our routine as a convoy escort and an opportunity to adjust to a more civilised lifestyle. The return to sea was accepted with a degree of resignation bolstered by a stubborn determination to cope with whatever fate might throw at us.

There were some who indulged themselves in the pubs ashore by telling tall yarns of their individual contributions to the Battle of the Atlantic, men who 'just couldn't wait to get back to sea'. They had very little to say when they found themselves back at sea. The Navy has a description of them, "bloody good kids in harbour but oh! my Christ at sea." Fortunately they were few in number but they added to the frustration felt by the rest.

Our attitude was not unlike that of Barton and Freddie Cox when they embarked on their grievance fight; we knew it was going to be painful and not particularly enjoyable but our stubborn pride would not let us turn our backs on it and walk away.

The news we had received of Freddie brought us some cheer.

During their leave a couple of the lads had met up in Liverpool one evening and decided to find out how Freddie Cox was getting along. They eventually knocked at his door which was opened by a smart young fellow holding a baby.

They failed to recognise Freddie at first, so great was the change from the scruffy and nervous individual they had known. Before them stood a proud and very presentable parent.

It was great to hear their tale of a domesticated Freddie bathing the baby in front of the fire as he apologised for the absence of his wife.

"She didn't have much chance to have a night out before I was sent home," Freddie explained. "She can get out a lot more now and I enjoy being with the baby."

The ship's notice-board always displayed the latest available copy of the C in C Western Approaches Daily State. The one which was pinned up when we set out for 'Newfy' after our refit carried an item which was of no interest to anyone aboard other than myself.

It announced that applications would be considered for training as air crew in the Fleet Air Arm from personnel at present serving in other departments of the Navy and Marines.

I put in my request for transfer immediately.

The rest of the crew thought I was out of my mind.

The refit brought other changes; several members of the crew were replaced and there were additions to aggravate the overcrowding. I acquired a bunk in the seamen's bunk space below the 'recreational area' and was moved into a new mess along with Ernie Leach.

Several eighteen year olds, straight from training, had now joined the crew; it was remarkable how great a gap was created by a year's experience afloat. They seemed so green and innocent that I could not believe I had been just like them less than a year before.

Three of the youngsters were Scots lads. Two of them were fine but the third, from Glasgow, was a shocker; a typical 'Jaimie' who considered himself to be a hard man. He had not been aboard very long before he threatened one of his fellow Scots with a razor and let it be known that he was not one to be trifled with. Few of us were impressed by his bravado and it came as no surprise to find him wanting once Polyanthus got under way.

'Raggie' Coulin thoroughly enjoyed himself with the young lads. After a prolonged bout of seasickness the victim was often left with a great desire for sweet food and this was very pronounced with the younger lads. Choosing his moment carefully, Raggie would sidle over from the stokers' mess with his plate of afters. Placing it temptingly in front of one of the newcomers he would then assume a disgusting leer and in a husky voice whisper "Duff for chuff, mate? Come along with me and I'll show you the golden rivet while you're eating your duff. Every ship has a golden rivet, you know."

Most of the lads were aware of the proverbial golden rivet and were under no illusions as to what they thought Raggie wanted as they agonised over the tempting duff.

They were the only ones on the mess deck who felt uncomfortable about Raggie and he took full advantage of their fears; they would discover his good nature soon enough.

My action station was changed. I realised that if I got a soaking from then on I really would be in trouble - it was in the ammunition locker down below the bunk space on the keel of the ship.

There were two of us down there, charged with the task of passing ammunition, by way of canvas bucket on the end of a simple rope hoist, to the four-inch gun crew on the fo'c'sle. My companion, one of the several Jones's in the crew, found relief in talking constantly about his amorous exploits, real and imaginary. His achievements were quite remarkable and varied if I were to believe all I was told.

When he tired of his favourite topic, which was not often, he would speculate on our fate should the ship be hit.

"I reckon we'll be nothing more than two red splashes on some crumpled grey metal."

It was not a pleasant prospect, since we were confined in a space little more than a yard square, our only escape a steel ladder fixed on the bulkhead.

My thoughts dwelt on the conditions aboard the U-boats. If I was unhappy with this lot, theirs was no better. They had my sympathy, even though they were the enemy.

Jones kept up a constant monologue during our confinement. I have no doubt it helped him; my reaction was just the opposite, the last thing I wanted to do was to talk.

We did a quick turn around at St. John's and as we sailed it seemed as if all the Group were trying to get through the Narrows together. I was with the party which was hoisting the dinghy off its chocks preparatory to swinging it outboard, when there was a sickening shudder and Polyanthus ground to a stop.

She had been forced to the wrong side of the channel and had struck a submerged rock. We returned to the berth we had vacated such a short time before to assess the damage, which proved to be quite serious.

It was necessary to have temporary repairs carried out in the dry-dock before we could proceed to a better equipped base for a full repair. We shared the dry-dock with the 'Oribi', a tribal class destroyer which had just rammed a U-boat. Where her damage was honourable, ours was rather ignominious.

Our stay in St. John's was unexpected and longer than any before, and it provided an opportunity to hold a ship's dance, the first and only one as far as I know. It was fitting for the Newfoundlanders in our crew and our attachment to the Newfoundland Groups that our dance was held in St. John's. It gave Cluny Blandford a chance to show off his new wife and the officers a chance to lavish their hospitality on the staff officers of the base in surroundings which were more spacious than our wardroom.

Every morning I enjoyed my cornflakes, or occasionally some toast, at the Caribou Hut and became known to some of the volunteers. The wife of the manager for Marconi was one of them and it transpired that she had a friend who knew my mother. This apparently established my credentials and she volunteered her daughter as my partner for the ship's dance.

On the evening of the dance, I called at her home and met my 'date' for the first time; she was a very nice girl but we had difficulty in finding any common ground. We arrived at the hall to find there was a marked shortage of girls and, of the ones present, there were several who preferred the bar to the dance floor. For a time we sat at the side of the hall and sipped coke: I instinctively knew not to mention beer, and in due course we made a valiant attempt to dance. Our incompatibility was even more pronounced on the half empty dance floor where I stumbled and floundered around and prayed for the music to stop. I was a very disappointing beau, I regret to say, and the evening was not a success from our point of view.

Polyanthus was ordered to proceed to Baltimore for the repairs to her hull and we sailed down the Gulf Stream in weather which became warmer and sunnier with each day that passed.

More of our time off watch was spent out on deck and the unaccustomed

The Gulf Stream.
"Our time off watch was spent out on deck".

83

warmth and sunshine tempted many into long spells of sunbathing. Inevitably there were some who overdid it. 'Lofty' Pratt became ill and unable to go on watch; he felt even more sick when he was put on a charge for what was considered to be a self-inflicted injury.

Small airships or 'Blimps' hovered above us on anti-submarine patrol along the eastern seaboard of America and in a strange way added to our sense of well-being, despite their obvious limitations. Eventually we turned into Chesapeake Bay where a pilot came aboard accompanied by a doctor and a customs officer.

"What's your cargo - sugar?" Was our first greeting.

We were told that we were the first British warship to venture as far as Baltimore and no one was quite sure what to make of us.

The doctor insisted that every single man aboard should be examined for transmittable diseases from the Captain down. Feeling very insulted, we assembled on the mess deck and dropped our pants, determined not to make his job any easier than was necessary. He seemed pleased when he could leave.

We were given a clean bill of health but it all seemed to be so unnecessary and offensive.

On a sunny Sunday afternoon we sailed into the Coastguard Yard at Baltimore and as no one had any American money we were unable to go ashore. In the warm sunshine the water in the dock looked very tempting. Permission to bathe was sought and given and with a dinghy to act as a safety boat we were soon splashing around like kids just out from school.

Swimming in the dock - Baltimore.
"We were soon splashing around like kids".

Our bold young Glaswegian, now that he was back in harbour, was 'skylarking' and making lots of noise, ridiculing some of the bathers. He was not making any attempt to jump into the water however, a fact that was not lost on Buck Ryan who climbed back on board. He called to Cluny Blandford and the two 'Newfies' hoisted the noisy Scot up from the deck and hurled him over the side into the dock.

The lad could not swim. Amidst a great frenzy of spray and thrashing limbs he was clearly reduced to a state of abject terror; he squealed like a stuck pig, watched by a highly amused but unsympathetic Ryan.

"The poor bastard can't swim, Buck," someone called.

"Then now's the time for him to learn," guffawed Ryan.

The dinghy was quickly brought over. Jock was well and truly waterlogged and helpless when Ryan dived in and helped to get him out.

He was half drowned.

"Roll him on a depth charge and get some of that dock water off his stomach," Cluny ordered.

Buck rolled him back and forth none too gently until 'Jock' was able to drag himself away.

Our hard man from Glasgow learnt that Newfies can be hard men too. He became far less noticeable from then on.

85

FIFTEEN

The C.O. of the Coastguard Yard at Baltimore proved to be very helpful. He sympathised with our currency problems and loaned our skipper the greater part of the spare cash which was available on the base on the Sunday of our arrival.

It meant that one watch could go ashore that evening with an advance of two dollars for each man.

It was quite a thrill for many of us to go ashore in the U.S. for the first time even if we were virtually penniless. Our two dollars was unlikely to cover much more than the fare to and from the town plus a beer but we set out determined to make the most of what could only be a very quiet run ashore.

We were in trouble as soon as we climbed on the street car; there were empty seats at the back of the car and some of the lads headed for them. It was difficult to know who was the most upset, the indignant white folk at the front or the astonished black folk at the rear. The remonstrations were loud and clear and the driver refused to move until we were standing in our rightful place at the front of the car despite the empty seats at the back. Colours were not to be mixed.

For the second time that day we were offended by the customs of our hosts.

Older members of the crew who had visited Galveston and Charleston with Polyanthus in 1941 had previous experience of the U.S. and had adjusted to many of the cultural differences. Unfortunately they never thought to warn the rest of us.

We walked the streets and the parks in preparation for the big event of the evening - a drink of beer. No matter how much we tried to prolong its enjoyment we were soon back on the street again and counting the remaining few cents in our pockets.

Setting aside the fare for the ride back to the yard we found we still had enough to buy a hamburger each with a few cents left over, just enough to buy one cup of coffee between three of us. This gave rise to some argument as we awaited our turn for service in a busy hamburger joint; our voices and uniforms attracted quite a lot of attention.

Three girls were nearby.

"Are you boys English?" one asked.

"Sure they are, that's HMS right there on their caps see, I bet they're Royal Navy."

"Gee, you talk just like the folks up in New England. I know that 'cos I have an aunt who lives there. Will you talk to us some?"

Ernie looked at me, his eyes were full of disbelief and despair.

"I don't believe it," he whispered through clenched teeth. "A chance like this and we have to be skint."

There was nothing for it but to tell the girls that much as we would like to share their company we had nothing in the kitty.

"That's no problem boys, please talk to us; we just love listening to your English accents; what do you say we go and have a beer when you've finished your hamburgers. You just leave the paying to us. We're earning real good money building 'planes right now."

As we turned to leave I felt a tap on my shoulder and a voice with a strong Yorkshire accent observed, "I'll bet tha knows where Smiddles Lane is."

Smiddles Lane in Bradford formed part of the route from the Nurses' Home at St.Luke's to my home. To be able to identify my accent with such accuracy was no mean feat.

"You're five miles out," I laughed, "I'm from Cleckheaton."

He was a merchant seaman who had come to Baltimore as part of the crew which was to pick up a new Liberty ship from the shipyards of Fairfield Bethlehem in Baltimore.

My party was not particularly interested in my chat with a fellow 'Yorky' and the conversation was curtailed as a result.

We thoroughly enjoyed our free beer and the girls seemed to enjoy our 'talking to them'.

We returned to the ship with the feeling that Baltimore might turn out quite well, providing we could afford it. After a week a special allowance of a dollar a day was added to our pay for the duration of our stay - it brought us up to about half of the pay of our opposite numbers in the U.S.Forces.

With Washington D.C. and New York comparatively near at hand the possibility of visiting one or both was very much on my mind. The repairs could not be completed in less than two to three weeks and at the first opportunity I asked Lt. Whitehead if there was any chance of being granted a weekend leave pass.

New York was my first choice and I calculated that I could just about manage the train fare and the cost of bed and food at a hostel on about three weeks pay. Lt. Whitehead agreed to my suggestion of an advance of a fortnight's pay on the following pay day which would provide me with a whole month's pay in my hand.

The opportunity to visit New York may never come again I told my mates.

None of them showed much enthusiasm and so I went alone.

The United States looked after its servicemen and women extremely well during the war and nowhere better than in New York. It also looked after me extremely well.

As a stranger to the city I had no difficulty in finding my way around. Organisations like the YMCA always had hostels for servicemen and all the various centres which set out to help us were well publicised on posters around the station.

I went to the Soldiers and Sailors Club on Lexington Avenue where, not surprisingly, I was the only British serviceman. I was treated like royalty.

"Would you like to eat on Times Square? - Schrafts donate a table every lunchtime; you can have a ticket if you think you might enjoy that. Oh! - Say! - here's a pass for the Rockefeller Centre and Radio City. You can see all around; watch them making programmes an' all; go to the very top of the building too. Now wouldn't that be nice? You could go there in the morning and then go to Times Square from there - and don't forget to come back here in the afternoon whenever you're through eating, we never know what else that's interesting might come in."

Glen Miller was broadcasting with his orchestra when I got to Radio City but we were only allowed to look through the soundproof glass windows of the studio and listen to the relayed music before being whisked off by the guide to the top of the building in one of the express lifts. Everything had to be done at speed.

My companions at lunch were men and women from the American Services and I was a novelty to them. Early on in the meal I became aware of their attention: they had stopped eating and were watching me use my knife and fork.

"Gee, that's really something boy, both hands together, where d'you learn to do that?"

Each of the men sported a medal ribbon and I could not resist the temptation to ask, with assumed innocence, "Where have you boys been serving?"

As I suspected, none of them had been outside the United States. The ribbons had been awarded for proficiency and similar attainments. They found it difficult to believe that their allies had no equivalent awards.

"Have you got a pass for the show at Radio City Music Hall?" I was asked, when I told my companions of my morning's activities. I was quickly told how to get one.

It was a good lunch and following their advice I found the centre where they were handing out the tickets for the show. "You're in luck, boy, we just have this one ticket left." New York was simply great.

A white grand piano held pride of place in the foyer of Radio City and it was being played by a pianist of some ability when I entered. My seat was way up in the 'gods' and a long way from the stage and screen but I was not grumbling in the least, it was, after all, completely free.

The show was lavish: the inevitable theatre organ was followed by a symphony orchestra, a corps de ballet, a dance troupe and a couple of solo turns. The full-length feature film was overshadowed, as far as I was concerned, by the spectacular stage show.

An English sailor could not help becoming a figure of curiosity in America at the time and I soon realised that there was a big advantage in making the visit alone. The young couple who were sitting next to me were soon plying me with questions. It was a rare celebration for them; because of their young children they rarely got out together.

"Will you join us for a drink after the show, just a quick one before we head off home?"

I agreed quite happily.

"Let's go to Leon and Eddy's, have you heard of it? It's a really famous night spot."

We stood by the bar in the long narrow entrance and my host disappeared into a larger room inside. I saw no reason to ask why. The band was showing signs of life as he returned and the leader took hold of the microphone to announce the next number.

"Before our next number ladies and gentlemen, I would like you to give a big hand to these boys of the US Army Air Force, the brave boys who are sitting at that table right there."

Everyone clapped and so did I, although I was not sure why.

"And tonight we have a special guest; one who is fighting that great battle out there on the wide Atlantic Ocean; one of our brave Allies from England. He's sitting at the bar there. Stand up sailor and let us all see you."

I had no option but to obey.

The barman put another drink in front of me.

"I didn't order that," I protested.

"The guy over there." He pointed and as I acknowledged a waving arm I heard another voice calling, "What's the Limey drinking, Bud, set him one up on me."

A further four drinks followed and although I understand the song for which Leon and Eddy's was renowned was sung later on, I cannot remember hearing 'Virgin Sturgin' needs no urgin'.

The only disappointment was the Stage Door Canteen, another facility which had free entry; it was reputed to have a constant stream of celebrities of stage and screen calling in. There were no celebrities to be seen on the two occasions when I looked in. It was about the only part of the whole weekend which failed to come up to expectations; everything else exceeded them.

It was entirely due to the unstinting generosity of the American people that I returned from New York with money still in my pocket and a head filled with great memories.

Because I was not penniless when I got back to the ship I was able to have a day in the Capital and see the White House together with all the other sights of Washington: only this time I had company. Jack Hirst realised he had missed something by not making the trip to New York and the two of us hitch-hiked. It was another memorable experience but something of an anti-climax for me after New York.

Once the citizens of Baltimore became aware of their British visitors a number of invitations came our way. I went to a graduation party at one of the churches along with 'Taffy', one of the young ratings who had joined us recently.

The graduates were a bunch of young people who were decked out in their caps and gowns and after the ceremony several of the girls headed straight for us, each clutching a be-ribboned diploma in one hand and a cap in the other.

It was difficult to know which question to answer first as Taffy and I were put to the test. All was going well until one of the girls asked Taffy where he was from.

"Wales," said Taffy proudly.

"Now tell me," continued his inquisitor seriously, "Is that a large or a small town?"

It was not the sort of question to put to a proud young Welshman and our image was a little tarnished before I was able to get him away.

I concluded that geography was not one of the strengths of their High School but for those who were paying attention there was a unique opportunity to learn some colloquial Welsh that evening.

Confusion with our mail was inevitable following our mishap and we had been in Baltimore for some time before the first mail-bag reached us. Jack Hirst received a letter which had been written five weeks previously and it upset him.

We were good friends and without telling me anything beyond the fact that he had received some bad news he suggested we should go ashore to help put it out of his mind. It was not a good time for a 'special' run ashore in view of the kitty so we each took our savings from our rum ration - a small bottle of 'neaters'.

Two bottles of beer at the Oasis night club in down town Baltimore took the greater part of what money we had but with the help of the rum which we surreptitiously added to the glass of beer from time to time, we soon took a more philosophical view of life and Jack was able to pass on his distressing news. His wife Eleanor was serving in the ATS with an anti-aircraft battery and had been hurt by a shell; all he knew was that she was seriously ill in hospital and had suffered a miscarriage. As he fought back the tears we realised the stripper, a lady well past the bloom of youth, was on the stage. She finished her act, slipped her dressing gown on her shoulders and walked up to the table next to ours. As she flopped down on a chair she pulled a cigarette from a pocket on the gown. A brave attempt at a smile wormed its way out of her worn face and she leaned over, obviously seeking a light for the cigarette. As she did so her dressing gown fell open and we were confronted by her sagging breasts and belly.

The sight was too much for Jack, he could not get out fast enough. With only half the night gone, we were back on the street with hardly any money and even less sense.

We decided to ask at the next bar if they would accept English money in payment for a drink.

The next bar happened to be in a hotel which was the venue for a doctors' conference; the bar was full of doctors and some of them showed an interest in English money.

"Now what's that coin there and how much is it worth? - give the boys a drink barman - tell me, would you by any chance be prepared to sell me one of these coins?"

Things were looking really good until we were invited to join them up in their room where we would 'be able to get to know each other rather better'.

Jack and I turned to each other and made determined efforts to pass warning looks. Drunk as we were, both of us recognised that it was time to leave.

Our story of how to get drunk in Baltimore for sevenpence ha'penny just had to be told on the mess deck. We thought it was rather good, especially when we had rumbled the further plan of our new doctor friends.

Two nights later three of our shipmates, all regulars, went ashore. They returned the following morning with a doctor's bag full of equipment and some fine underwear.

"Those guys had it coming to them," they observed and promptly requested a visit from the priest.

Overall, our relations with the local population of Baltimore were very good, but encounters with US Servicemen were not always friendly. Groups of soldiers who were out on the town and looking for some action would shout across the street "What about Dunkirk, Limey? What's the matter, couldn't face the Kraut?"

It so happened that as part of their recruitment campaign the US Government had a strong poster presence on the hoardings imploring its citizens to 'Remember Pearl Harbour'. We quickly cottoned on to the value of these posters when faced with the taunts and there was usually one within sight when the need arose. With a wave towards it, we would repeat the message - "Remember Pearl Harbour," and fortunately, the exchanges invariably ended on that note.

Following his encounter with the graduate section of Baltimore society, Taffy decided to seek his pleasure elsewhere. The accounts of the tremendous opportunities, not to mention favours, that were available to British sailors --- d his curiosity. For a young lad on his first voyage out of the UK he was anxious to savour all that life had to offer. He set out to establish his virility and manhood.

He returned on board with a burning desire to impress everyone with an account of his prowess and achievements. Fortified by his intake of beer, both his imagination and his voice were somewhat exaggerated.

Alec had come on board not long before. He had followed his normal procedure and had got quietly drunk before making his way somewhat unsteadily back to the ship. Alec believed very strongly that once aboard, silence was golden.

Taffy was completely taken aback by the intensity of the verbal onslaught that Alec hurled at him in a subdued voice. In this mood Alec commanded respect and attention, drunk or sober.

"Pipe down, you little runt," he hissed. "When you get back aboard you shut that big hole in your face and let everyone get their sleep. I'm pissed, I usually am when I've been ashore but you never hear me making a din. A young kid like you should look at a stupid old fart like me and see what a mess I've made of my life. All I'm good for is going ashore and coming back pissed out of my mind."

Alec appeared to be sobering up by the minute.

"Take a good look, son" he went on. "Do you want to end up with nothing to look back on, nothing but runs ashore, drinking God knows how much beer and being all the worse for it?"

Taffy swayed as he tried to keep Alec's face in focus and opened his mouth as if to speak, only to find his balance required all his concentration. With a look of confused irritation he managed to put his backside on the form and steady himself against the mess table.

His performance was viewed by Alec with undisguised disdain.

"As for getting yourself a woman, a chance to play with her suspenders will give a kid like you all the excitement you can handle for one night. Anything else is a waste of money, believe me."

Alec stared at the deck, his face thoughtful:

"There was a time when I fancied myself as a bit of a lad; when I picked up a woman and got something I have been ashamed of ever since. There are no medals or battle honours awarded for that kind of service; just remember that."

As the end of our stay in Baltimore drew near there were one or two members of the crew who were displaying signs of unease. Their furtive visits to the sickbay fooled none of their shipmates, who quickly diagnosed that the cause of their worries did not arise through a casual contact with a lavatory seat.

The people of Baltimore had been friendly towards us, and the lads had not been slow to capitalise on their curiosity value. Many of the numerous and often lurid tales of sexual conquests and extraordinary activities obviously had a basis of truth in them. Now the day of reckoning had arrived and with it the realisation that the 'conquests' had been somewhat careless with their virtue in the past.

When we sailed out into Chesapeake Bay there was no sign of the officious customs and medical men we had encountered on arrival; a fact that gave rise to some sarcastic comment.

"They were keen enough to make sure we brought nothing in but no one wants to know what they've given us to take away."

The dockyard workers at the Coastguard Yard in Baltimore did a first class job on Polyanthus. She emerged looking brighter, with a new coat of paint in slightly lighter shades of grey, green and blue than she had been wearing when she arrived.

Our voyage northwards along the eastern seaboard of the United States was interrupted by an overnight visit to the US Naval Base at Norfolk, Virginia where we were berthed immediately astern of the aircraft carrier 'Bunkers Hill'. As we sheltered under the overhang of her flight deck she towered above us, perfectly still and apparently immovable. The prospect of landing a plane on such a large expanse of deck did not appear to be an insurmountable problem and my determination to become a pilot became even stronger.

I kept my thoughts to myself. Practically everyone on the mess deck thought I was completely mad for even thinking about flying.

The purpose of our call at Norfolk was obscure and unexpected. Even more unexpected was our call at Staten Island, New York. The purpose or justification for this was just as obscure but no one questioned an opportunity to visit New York; we simply made the most of it.

Each watch had the chance to enjoy a half-day leave and we poured on to the Staten Island Ferry to savour the sights and sounds of the city. Where I had been a lone English sailor on my earlier visit, I was now accompanied by the rest of my watch ashore and New York was not quite as big an adventure.

When I had set out on my solo weekend visit I believed it would probably be my only opportunity to visit one of the great cities of the world and within a couple of weeks I was back again. I had no regrets. The sacrifice involved in the earlier visit had been relatively small and it had been rewarded by a really great experience.

Two days later we were on our way back to St. John's and the familiar routine of a convoy escort; our American interlude, like our Tyneside refit, drifted into memory. A few more members of the crew found they too had become casualties as a result of their amorous adventures in Baltimore. They had tangible reminders of the interlude which detracted from the pleasure of their memories.

When we finally returned to our escort duties it was felt that Polyanthus had probably suffered more casualties during its brief visit to Baltimore than at any other time since she was commissioned.

SIXTEEN

The summer of 1943 brought a pronounced lull in the activity of our U-boat adversaries and we enjoyed the luxury of working three watches for a complete voyage across the Atlantic.

My request for a transfer for pilot training had been approved by the Captain and I became increasingly impatient as I awaited the overall approval from the powers on high in the form of a draft chit.

Release from the convoy and the sight of land triggered off a sequence of events which had become all too familiar.

Neutral Donegal was indifferent to our steady progress along its coastline until we rounded the headland into Lough Foyle. Our appearance in the lough awakened the villagers of Moville who were far from indifferent to the prospect of some trade. The bumboats emerged to move around Polyanthus and the other ships from the group as we idly awaited the arrival of the boat which would bring our pilot.

When he arrived the bumboats sheared off and we were under way again down the lough and headed for the mouth of the river.

Once again green fields with trees and hedgerows replaced the cheerless expanse of grey sea we had left such a short time before, it was almost as if they embraced us. Cattle and sheep grazed contentedly, undisturbed by our appearance. Occasionally a small farmhouse came into view and small children shouted and waved. Above a larger house a Union Jack fluttered, displaying the allegiance and support of the owner, who was rumoured to be Montgomery's mother.

At the after end of the upper deck our own Ensign fluttered bravely in reply, its outward edge weathered and tattered by the constant attention of the elements. It was little more than half the length it had been when we left 'Newfy'.

Grass and foliage assumed an added lushness with the progress up river; the fields and hedgerows closed in even more and then opened out again to be replaced by the buildings of Londonderry.

It was a vastly different scene from the one which greeted Polyanthus on her first visit. The American base was down river from the Guildhall and housed a wide variety of warships. A couple of American destroyers, a sloop of the Royal Indian Navy and corvettes of the Norwegian, Netherlands and Free French Navies were in residence. Our own familiar ships which were on the 'Newfy run' had first tied up beyond the Guildhall in the shadow of Craigavon Bridge. Now they were lost in the crowd. It was difficult to pick out our family and friends in the crush.

The engine room telegraph 'tringed' and the throbbing propeller came to rest. Polyanthus glided gently towards the wooden jetty with an apparent innocence. Her ropes were soon ashore and she slid alongside with remarkably good manners.

The telegraph 'tringed' again and the ship shuddered as the river foamed and boiled when the propeller went full astern. It was then that she produced her gesture of independence and swung her stern at the jetty in a playful, crunching nudge. The jetty creaked and groaned loudly as it buckled in pain,

I dashed ashore with the mail and the hand signals the moment we had secured alongside the wharf. I could hardly wait for the gang-plank to go down.

"Hello Polyanthus, long time no see," greeted me as I entered the Fleet Mail Office on Strand Road.

"Iris, here's Polyanthus to see you," brought the younger of the Bell sisters to the counter. She had joined the Wrens shortly after I had been befriended by the family.

All the latest news concerning my friends in Derry was passed on under the ever watchful eye of the Petty Officer Wren, known to all as 'Chiefie'. Eager to discover what the signal bag at Captain 'D's' Office might contain in regard to my future I was on my way long before Chiefie's patience gave out.

All the ship's messengers and posties tended to be known by the name of their ship in the offices ashore; fortunately for those from the Flower Class corvettes the incongruous use of names like 'Poppy' and 'Dianthus' went unnoticed for most of the time.

To the Wrens in the signals office the messengers were their only personal contact with the ships and a special type of friendship developed as a result. I wasted no time in telling them about the signal which was of paramount importance to me - the one which would confirm my draft. No one could recall any such signal being issued.

Somewhat disappointed, I set out on my return journey to the ship taking a less direct route. It just so happened that this took me past Nicholson Terrace and since Mrs Longwell had a pot of tea 'almost made' I felt duty bound to help her drink some of it.

Back on board the customary preparations for shore leave were well under way; the washroom was under siege and the usual good-natured insults were

95

being exchanged, couched in the crude language peculiar to the lower deck.

Only the eagerly awaited pipe of 'Libertymen fall in' could silence them. The band of scruffy, unshaven ruffians that had entered Lough Foyle was transformed into the smartly turned-out group that now lined up along the port welldeck: the inspection by the duty officer was but a momentary pause in a headlong rush ashore. The clatter of feet on the steel deck ceased and a hush came over the ship.

Of those who remained on board the majority were preparing to go on leave the following day and I was one of them. We settled down to read and re-read our mail in peace. It was a forlorn hope.

"After you with the sports page Shorty."

"Get lost."

"How come so many people write to you when you can't read?"

"They draw pictures for him, stupid."

"Looks like the 'Jamaica's' out East; my 'oppo' mentions his shorts so they must be wearing tropical gear."

"I'm glad I'm not on a big ship, too bloody 'pusser' for my liking."

"He thinks he's the one who's better off. Says I can have my hard-lying money; reckons I'll never catch him on one of the 'boats'."

"Takes all kinds. You've been on the battlewagons, what do you reckon's the best bet, Shorty?"

"It doesn't pay to think one way or the other, you get your draft and you have to make the best of it. The best ships are always your last ships, or so they reckon."

Gradually the chatter died away and hammocks were slung and made ready for an early turn-in. At eight o'clock 'rounds' were piped hurriedly before the duty officer burst on to the mess deck, having left his thoughts in the wardroom alongside a large pink gin. As he ducked under a hammock in his headlong rush to get back to his drink he bumped into Ken Holland who had taken a late washdown. Ken instinctively came to attention but lost his grip on his only bit of cover, the towel around his waist. Ken had made quite a good job of his ablutions, the water had reached a good temperature and he was not only very naked, he was also rather pink and anxious to reach his bunk.

He stood his ground and the officer came to an abrupt halt; they stood eyeball to eyeball until the slight smirk on Ken's face was almost out of control.

The washroom door marked the limit of 'rounds' that night; "Carry on," ordered the officer as he turned on his heel and left us to discuss his discomfiture.

The quartermaster returned later to share in the giggle and to impart some news he had picked up from one of our family of Canadian corvettes.

"The Canadians and Yanks are having a battle royal at the Corinthian Hall. A lot of the Canadians are going ashore to help out but none of our lads are involved, as far as I know."

Resentment had been building up ever since the Americans had moved into Londonderry. They had constructed the naval base off Strand Road and their hospital at Creevagh. Compared with the Canadians and ourselves they had more of everything, food, facilities, mouths and money, particularly money, and the money pulled the girls.

We went up on deck to see groups of lads from the Canadian ships heading out of the base without a thought for liberty boats or other restrictions. Their shipmates who remained aboard passed on varied and probably exaggerated reports of ambulances collecting the injured and blood flowing in the streets. Like the flames of a forest fire the news spread throughout the ships and kindled our curiosity. We awaited the return of our libertymen and hoped they would provide a more reliable account of the situation.

As we watched the departing Canadians a lone figure appeared heading steadily towards us. It was Alec and he was displaying a pronounced tendency to yaw to starboard as he struggled to maintain a steady course. Employing amazing variations in pace he arrived at the foot of the gang-plank where he stopped, took a deep breath, and with his eyes fixed straight ahead came aboard without missing a step. He went straight into the heads.

He emerged to find many of the early birds had taken to the hammocks which festooned the mess deck like large bulging cocoons. Bending double to avoid them made Alec's progress even more difficult but with a foolish grin on his face he finally sat down in triumph.

After some fumbling he produced a tin of baked beans from the pocket of his weatherworn Burberry and placed it on the table. He then removed the coat, his blue collar, black silk and jumper. Only when they each had been carefully folded and stowed away did he return his attention to the beans.

"Nothing like a tin of beans to finish off a run ashore" he said quietly to no one in particular and threaded his way once more beneath the hammocks and up to the galley.

Alec's routine for coming aboard after a run ashore on the beer was faultless and a role model for young sailors - apart from one unfortunate detail - the explosive combination of baked beans and beer.

Later arrivals were not always as quiet as Alec had been, nor were they as careful in avoiding the hammocks. Small groups gathered around the mess tables, unwilling to turn in. The whispered exchanges of their experiences ashore gave rise to short bursts of laughter amongst themselves and outbursts of temper from those who had turned in.

It was almost midnight when Barton returned, accompanied by Pearson and another of his cronies who was wearing a round white Yankee cap at a jaunty angle. They gathered round the mess table as Barton triumphantly laid out a U.S.Navy pea-jacket for inspection.

"Where the hell did you get that, Barts? - were you at the Corinthian?"

"Couldn't get near the place; there were too many bloody Yanks fighting with the Canadians to get in."

"Fighting to get out more like," Pearson corrected him.

"Who cares which way they were going," continued Barton. "They needed thinning out a bit - especially that Yank with a half-full bottle of whisky. The way he was swinging it around someone was liable to get hurt so I persuaded him to sit down and be quiet."

"He has a very persuasive right hand has old 'Barts'."

Barton acknowledged the compliment with a grin.

"Some of his mates got their shit in a right uproar; came on a bit stroppy and tried to hit us, they did. Didn't give me chance to fold up the lad's jacket to make a pillow for his poor head."

" Shame," observed one of the growing audience insincerely.

"Then the patrols appeared and they were even more stroppy so we scarpered, smartish like. Must have dropped the poor bloke's wallet when we were running because when we stopped all I had was his jacket, his bottle and a couple of ten dollar bills."

"What happened to the bottle of whisky?"

"What do you think?" Barton breathed heavily in the direction of the questioner. "Taste that."

Eventually the foc'sle settled down. On the first night in from sea, however, the normal snores and sounds of sleeping men were interrupted by cruder muffled noises that threatened unpleasant consequences.

Where Alec was concerned the consequences were diabolical.

SEVENTEEN

When those of us who were due for leave eventually reached Larne the day after arriving in Londonderry, our mood was a mixture of excitement and impatience.

There was the usual scramble to grab a seat on the train as soon as we could get ashore from the ferry at Stranraer: the boat had been packed and it followed that the train would be no different. A deceptive swell on the crossing had caused havoc amongst many of our fellow passengers and left us with an advantage. We grabbed a compartment for ourselves and pulled down the blinds. When anyone attempted to slide the door open we slammed it shut with shouts of "Full up in here". Few people escaped long journeys standing in the corridors but tonight it was to be some other poor blighters; we had grabbed a small measure of comfort and we did not intend to give it up.

Calls of nature involved a struggle down a corridor packed with kit-bags and cases and strange beings who appeared to have more than their fair share of immovable arms and legs which they would carefully position so as to restrict progress.

Jones was the first of our number to tackle the obstacle course to the toilet as we trundled along the South West of Scotland towards Carlisle. On his return he ushered three ATS girls into the compartment. They were shivering and dishevelled and their attempts to remove the evidence of an unhappy sea-crossing from their uniforms had not been entirely successful.

"Thin out a bit lads, give these lasses a seat, they're not feeling too good."

His hospitality was not altogether welcomed by the rest of us because it disturbed our comfort; nor was it in keeping with his lecherous image. Jones was not the sort of bloke to be left alone with your sister, yet here he was behaving like a mother hen.

Everyone squeezed together and we shared each other's warmth - and discomfort.

One of the girls told us she was from Hull. In her weakened condition the prospect of the long drag through Lancashire and Yorkshire with all the changes of trains and stations filled her with dread. The two of us who were planning to make the change to the Leeds train at Carlisle promised to look after her and introduce her to the more direct route.

Across the platform at Carlisle the Leeds train was ready to leave as we pulled in with the door open and our cases in our hands. We were out before the train stopped, dragging an uncertain member of the ATS together with her kit along with us.

With a headlong charge towards the train on the opposite side of the platform, the three of us just managed to jam into the end of a coach which was already packed with a mass of travellers. The protests and insults were many and loud but the train was moving by then and we were on it.... just.

By moving and re-arranging the assorted luggage a little extra space was found and we were able to make our ATS girl fairly comfortable on a couple of kitbags. What we could not do was keep her warm as the train climbed up into the Pennines. It can be bitterly cold in the corridor of a train crossing the Ribblehead Viaduct at half-past two in the morning.

The poor lass became more and more miserable as she shivered; her teeth chattered and she began to weep. There was no chance of a hot drink on this line, no Preston Station with its 'Angels of Mercy' and their trolleys; we felt awkward and embarrassed by our helplessness.

"Have you a bottle?" Hardware asked, "I haven't bottled any rum this trip".

Neat rum as issued to us on corvettes would warm anyone or anything. For the uninitiated it could induce anything from a state of acute apoplexy through to insensibility, usually in that order.

"Do you like rum?" we enquired of the girl as I struggled to open my case and find my bottle.

"I don't know, I've never tried it," she answered through chattering teeth.

I took the cap from the bottle and held it to her lips.

"Try some of this," I said. " Don't drink it, just take a sip."

I was too late, she took quite a swig.

The apoplexy did not last long, she was too weak. Her half-closed eyes suddenly opened wide, their misery transformed into a horrified squint: her mouth opened and closed without any apparent purpose, there was no intake of breath, no sound. Her eyes began to bulge ominously before they straightened out and glared accusingly at me when she found she was unable to speak. There was a pathetic croaking noise in her throat followed by an uncontrollable bout of coughing and spluttering, and a startled expression appeared in her eyes as they filled with tears and slowly closed. The noise from her throat stopped abruptly and she fell back on to the kitbags and began to snore.

Her snores could be heard above the noise of the train.

Hardware, who had assumed a detached and impassive role throughout, finally spoke.

"She's not shivering now," he observed laconically.

We managed to awaken her sufficiently to get her off the train at Leeds. Hardware was bound for Sheffield and stayed on; he left me to cope with the problem on my own.

Fortunately there was an all-night Forces canteen at Leeds station. I put my bag, the girl and her kit on a station cart and pulled it along to the canteen.

When she was eventually seated safely in the warm canteen with a mug of hot tea I set about finding the time of a train for Hull. It was not the easiest of tasks at 4.30 in the morning.

Her train was due to leave after mine and she assured me that she was perfectly capable of making her own way home despite being a little tipsy. I suggested that another mug of tea would do no harm and walked over to the counter to buy her one.

"You should be ashamed of yourself, some of you sailors are worse than animals."

The tirade was totally unexpected and set me back on my heels. One of the lady volunteers was addressing me with her eyes ablaze.

"Getting that poor girl drunk and then taking advantage of her. I suppose you think you can just dump her here at this time of the morning. Just look at the state she's in. Whatever are you thinking about?"

The ATS girl was looking at me and shaking her head as if to say "Ignore her." I took the mug of tea across to her.

"She was at me whilst you were finding the time of my train," she told me not too distinctly, "asking where I had been drinking at this time of the morning. I told her I hadn't been well and I thought you had given me some rum but I couldn't remember much about it."

"Didn't you tell her where we've come from?" I asked.

"We're not allowed to say where we're stationed." She tried to give me a reproving look but one of her eyes went 'walk-about' and ruined the effect.

There was clearly no point in my staying, so I left. I hope she got to Hull safely.

The leave flew by as always and as I waited, late at night, on Preston Station for the Paddy I thought of what I should say to Jones when I met up with him again. As luck would have it some of the lads were waiting by the door of a carriage as the train drew in; they were looking for a free cup of tea. Jones was one of them.

"You landed me right in it," I told him when he got back on the train. He was not in the mood to be ribbed; his journey home had been far worse than mine.

The compartment had been invaded by three soldiers after we left it at Carlisle and Jones, along with the rest of our lads, had fallen asleep. When they awoke the train was standing in Preston station, the soldiers were missing and so were three cases. Three of our lads, including Jones, had arrived home empty-

101

handed. All their rabbits had been lifted.

A couple of aircraftsmen who were heading for Drummore were in the compartment; they were most interested in hearing of Jones's misfortune and joined in our commiserations. Everyone agreed that it was a despicable thing to do.

Our eyes eventually became too heavy to hold open and we slid into a fitful sleep.

During my sojourn in Creevagh I had started to smoke cigarettes and had acquired an unusual ostrich-skin cigarette case in Baltimore which, like most sailors, I carried in my jumper. I was rather proud of it.

Sailors' jumpers tended to bulge open. By the time we reached Stranraer the cigarette case had gone. So had the aircraftsmen.

Our journeys to and from Londonderry were uncomfortable, long-drawn-out and tiring; they also had more than their fair share of misfortune.

EIGHTEEN

Sub Lt. Bradshaw was not long in being accepted as a decent officer despite his 'pusser' inclinations. He was competent and he was fair; we could not expect, or ask, for more than that.

"I understand you have ambitions to leave us," he remarked in passing. "Since we're enjoying a quiet spell at present I've been thinking of providing some navigation lessons for anyone who may be interested in promotion examinations; they could be useful to you if your request is granted."

My grounding in navigation began during the dog-watches under Harry Bradshaw's guidance. At the outset there were three others who crammed into the small chart room; two of them quickly dropped out to leave Les Hardware, a regular AB who was aiming for his 'hook' (Leading Seaman), and myself.

I could not have asked for a better set-up, one instructor to two pupils. For the first time since joining the ship I had an accurate idea of her position on the broad Atlantic, a better idea than some of the officers in fact, and despite my tutor's formal approach I appreciated his willingness to devote some of his spare time to Les and myself.

Alec said little about my intentions of becoming a pilot, he didn't have to. His views on volunteering for anything at all were quite firm. Nevertheless it was to Alec I turned for help with the basics of signalling and the morse code in particular.

"Could you teach me some morse Alec?" I asked. "I'll give you 'sippers'."

He studied my face before replying. "You must be out of your tiny mind; isn't it bad enough having to sail on the hoggin without trying to land a bloody aeroplane on it? - I'll teach you for 'gulpers'."

Alec decided that I should position myself down the starboard passage to receive the exercises in morse which he sent on a hand lamp from the mess deck. My apprehensions about the size of his 'gulpers' proved to be unfounded: he was, after all, a seasoned rum drinker of many years' standing. The amount he consumed from my 'tot' was hardly noticeable.

Our relief at the lull in U-boat activity and our enjoyment of the extra rest gradually gave rise to a feeling of uncertainty and unease. The few alarms we had came to nothing and we became edgy as a result of the lack of action. Of the plans and strategies of our leaders we knew nothing, all we could do was to speculate on what might be building up ready to burst on to us when we least expected it.

The sense of unease affected me as much as anyone; I found no comfort in my fate being decided by anyone other than myself, and the prospect of flying my own 'plane, of being master of my own fate, became more and more appealing with each day.

'Woolworth' carriers carrying Swordfish aircraft were now sailing within the convoys but we were never near when there was any flying. I remained in blissful ignorance of what I would have to face if my hopes were realised.

Our quiet time was being shared by the other escort groups as we soon discovered on our arrival in St. John's. The newspaper and radio reports of losses sustained by the U-boats appeared to have an element of truth in them but we knew from past experience how unreliable and wide of the mark they often were. We preferred the news that we exchanged within our own 'family' - and nothing was happening. The knowledge only increased the fear of a storm waiting to break.

We were south of Greenland on our return from Newfoundland when the first and only rat ever seen on board Polyanthus appeared. It was the week of Cleckheaton Feast.

There had been a pleasantly warm sun for most of the afternoon and it had encouraged several of us to take advantage of the early evening air. As usual we were gathered behind the funnel casing and around the open hatch over the boiler space.

George Holland spotted the rat as he climbed the ladder at the after end of the upper deck. His was a detached existence; as petty officers' flat sweeper he lived in their quarters down aft, neither one of them nor one of us. Life had not dealt George a good hand at all. Amongst other deficiencies he was not very articulate and he had a slight speech impediment; his eyesight was deteriorating and as far as we knew he had no relatives. The petty officers' mess on Polyanthus was the nearest thing he had to home. He was anxious to conceal his growing blindness because he knew it would put him ashore. The petty officers did a 'Nelson'; they too developed a blind eye where George was concerned.

Despite his failing sight George had seen the rat but no one realised what was making him shout and splutter incoherently. Following the direction in which he was pointing they spotted the quick movements as the rat darted from beneath one locker to take refuge under another.

Our first reaction was one of disbelief and amazement. It was only momentary. Deck locker lids were thrown back and we grabbed brooms and squeegees, anything which could be used as a weapon or cudgel and began banging them on the deck in an effort to drive the rat into the open. When it did appear it displayed reactions which were far superior to ours; no one managed to hit it.

The din brought the Coxswain and the Buffer up on deck where, instead of putting a stop to it, they joined the chase.

It was not long before the rat went over the side of the upper deck as it scurried ahead of the battery of brooms. It landed in the starboard well deck and shot under a depth charge thrower. The Buffer was one of the most enthusiastic by this time and was the first down to the well deck. His furious poking forced the terrified rat out just as the sea came through the scuppers. It hesitated and was finally struck by first one and then another of the pursuers. Pearson grabbed the rat's tail and hurled it over the side and into the sea.

The makeshift weapons were returned to their appointed places and stowed away amidst considerable speculation and discussion.

"Where the hell has the rat been hiding until now and where had it come from?"

"How can anyone tell where it came from? I can tell you one thing, mate, it didn't bloody well swim aboard."

"How long has it been aboard? I'd like to know."

"It can't be the only one; there's bound to be others."

"There's nowhere for them to hide on this ship, her keel's filled with concrete: everyone knows that."

"Oh yes, and when did you see all this concrete you're on about; has some hairy-arsed stoker had you down there, showing you the golden rivet then?"

"Just get some sea-time in before you start getting stroppy with me, clever dick; I've been on her since she commissioned, don't forget."

Rats had never featured in our thoughts on Polyanthus until this one had appeared and suddenly they became uppermost in our minds. They added another dimension to our apprehensions - superstitions. Countless tales of rats and ships began to circulate on the mess deck where superstition found many disciples. Those who dismissed it with derision were in the minority; an uncomfortable atmosphere built up which was inescapable.

Polyanthus had revealed her first rat and we had thrown it overboard. It became the thought for the day in the heads; there had not been a decent 'buzz' for days.

"The only time to worry is when the rats leave a ship of their own accord, not when you chuck 'em overboard; we're not expected to provide 'em with bed and board."

"I don't care what you say, it's still bad luck. We shouldn't have got rid of it."

"Shave off," Pearson chimed in. "What a shower of old women; we saw the lousy rat and we got rid of it - now we're going to pull the bung out - I don't think."

105

The lull in the conversation was of necessity and not in deference to Pearson's derisive opinions.

"What's known as a strained silence" volunteered a voice from the end stall. "Can't say that I go for all this superstition lark but I'm not very happy about the way the subs have been leaving us alone. Something's brewing somewhere."

"I reckon they're licking their wounds after the mauling they had - what's left of them."

"More like gathering for a bigger show than ever if you ask me. The Indian summer we're having isn't just with the weather, it's the lull before the storm with the subs."

As the 'roosts' were vacated new delegates claimed the warm seats. "What's the buzz then?" one asked.

"Rats" was the blunt reply.

No other topic could displace the subject of the rat; its body might be quite away back in the ocean but its spirit remained on board. It began to haunt some of us.

Much as I wished to put the episode out of my mind I was affected by the strong waves of superstition and it increased my growing sense of unease. That night I had a vivid dream in which the ship was sunk and there were only three survivors who managed to cling to a Carley float. Two of them lost their grip and were gone before I could recognise them: the third I could clearly recognise as Davey, a regular AB.

'Brum' shared my watch in the RDF cabin and acted as second operator. He was not the most talkative of companions and spent most of his time when he was on stand-by curled up in the corner on the floor. From the occasional confidences he had shared with me I gathered his peace-time occupation was as a long-distance lorry driver travelling between Birmingham and Glasgow. He was not married but had 'shacked up' with a woman of whom he was very fond. He had found her alone with her case at the side of the road one night and had given her a lift. They had been together ever since and the arrangement obviously suited him.

A picture of the film star Carole Landis had been stuck on the bulkhead; it comforted Brum and provided him with the stuff dreams are made of.

"She's the only one of them stars as isn't married," he would remark with irritating regularity. I wondered if he considered it to be a guarantee of virginity.

Brum was not the most imaginative member of the crew and I was taken aback when he suddenly announced during the forenoon watch "I had a bloody bad dream last night."

"Aye."

"We was sunk. Only one of us survived."

I continued to turn the aerial and stare at the tube, not sure if it would be wise to say any more. My curiosity was too much.

"Who was it?"

Brum's answer simply confirmed my fears.

"It was Davey."

"You must have eaten something that was off last night to make you dream something as daft as that."

I tried to sound as normal as possible despite the pain in my bowels.

Was it a form of mass-hysteria or hallucination? These were things of which I knew nothing and there was no one who was likely to be able to explain such matters on board. I was too afraid of being ridiculed to say anything to anyone about my own dream. My thoughts became more and more concentrated on my draft to the Fleet Air Arm, for that would remove all the worries and doubts that were plaguing my mind.

Brum spoke openly of his dream to others after he had been fortified by his tot and caused an amazed 'Lofty' Pratt to reveal that he too had been dreaming about our fate; in his dream there were three survivors but he had no idea who they were.

Davey was not at all flattered by the news that he was going to be the only survivor. The discussions now commanded a wider audience than could be accommodated in the heads and we gathered outside the washroom door alongside the hammock bins.

"Its just a lot of balls," shouted Davey. "This is a lucky ship, she'll still be on the Newfy run when this stinking war's over, buzzing round the last convoy like a fly round a cow's arse."

"If she's a lucky bastard she's anything but a happy one. Two dreams following a bad omen doesn't sound like good luck to me."

"Can't you silly buggers understand what I'm trying to tell you? She's a lucky ship. What about the time we was hove to for two days playing nursemaid to those two cripples?. There'd been more torpedoes tear-arsing round the hoggin than I've had hot dinners but we came through OK; even the fuel held out until we got to Newfy."

"Next time she sails I won't be on her, mark my words; I'd rather be a live coward than a dead bloody hero. What's a bit of cell time anyway? - it can't be any worse than this."

"If you're so sure it's all decided how do you know she's going to finish this trip, how do you know there isn't a Jerry out there right now with his finger on the tit - ready to split us from arse-hole to breakfast time?"

Alec had heard enough and left no room for doubt over his views.

"If this is what one stinking little rat can do I think the whole flaming lot of you should be re-mustered into the Wrens, then you really will be able to wet your knickers."

After a couple of days the subject of the rat was hardly referred to again. Those who were disturbed and those who scoffed at them kept their own counsel and I was thankful that I had done the same from the outset. Yet no matter how I tried to convince myself of the futility of superstition the fears refused to go away.

Thoughts of shore leave, or even better, leave 'down the line', gradually regained their pride of place as we drew nearer to Ireland. Three Swordfish flew off the carrier and circled the convoy before flying alongside us on their way to Maydown, the aerodrome not far from Derry. The air-gunners waved as they passed.

"Lucky devils, they'll be there in two or three hours, we've got the best part of two days ahead of us."

Although my thoughts were echoed by the group around me on the upper deck no one, apart from me, would have joined them, given the chance.

The sight of the Irish coast was as welcome as ever but this time there was an inescapable feeling of relief at having arrived safely.

NINETEEN

My eagerness to get to the Signals Office in Londonderry quickly turned into disappointment.

The Wrens welcomed me in their customary cheerful manner before they saw the hope which must have been written all over my face.

"Sorry, Polyanthus." The Wren to the left of the door gave me a sad smile. "There's nothing come through yet on your transfer."

The Wren petty officer opposite quickly changed the subject by enquiring about our trip.

"It's the same story all round, must be as good as being on a cruise at the moment."

My response was what she expected.

Much as I appreciated the short visits to the Caribou Hut in St. John's, they could not compare with the reassuring comfort of the homes that were open to me in Londonderry. I stopped off at Nicholson Terrace on my way back to the ship and enjoyed a cup of tea beside the fire with Mrs Longwell. The simple pleasure of what had become my daily ritual, during our spells in Londonderry, was a tremendous comfort.

It provided a certain amount of diversion from the unfailing shake of the head which greeted me every day on my visit to the Signals Office.

By the time Sunday arrived I had resigned myself to another trip to Newfy. The watch on leave were due back on the following day and I had to accept that time had run out on me yet again. Lt. Whitehead called for me to do a run ashore that afternoon and immediately after dinner I departed.

The Wrens smiled when I entered the office: one of them held up her thumb.

"My draft?" I asked incredulously.

They nodded and laughed. I had not realised how great was the personal interest these girls took in our welfare. As they handed me the bag they pointed at it and gave the thumbs up again.

" There's one or two drafts for your ship, there's a Leading Seaman Grant being made up to petty officer and another draft too, they're not giving you much time; it's rather late in the day."

Not a word had actually been said regarding my own draft but it was all systems go on our communications link; the message had come through loud and clear.

"What are you hanging about here for? Your place is back on your ship; for all you know she may have to sail tomorrow."

The Wren petty officer put on a stern imitation of authority and I wasted no time in obeying.

Lt. Whitehead was still in the ship's office when I got back. The speed of my return bewildered him, it was quite out of keeping with established practice. I handed him the signal bag and remained at the door.

"There's something not quite right here, you make the fastest shore run on record and now you're hanging around, just what is going on?"

"I thought I had better wait in case you might need me again, Sir."

"And why should I need you again, could it be anything concerning your transfer."

"Could well be, Sir, but I think there's a draft chit for Leading Seaman Grant, he's been made up to petty officer."

"Anything else you can tell me before I open the bag, our sailing orders perhaps ?"

"Could be tomorrow, Sir. I was hoping the Captain might request reliefs for Shorty and me. I'm quite prepared to make another run ashore with the signal."

"The Captain's got his head down, probably snoring his head off. It is Sunday afternoon after all, man. If you think I'm going to risk giving him a shake you've got another think coming. There's very little chance of him letting you go at this late stage if we are sailing tomorrow as you claim. Now clear off. I'll send for you if I need you."

Remaining still was beyond me from then on. I was up and down from the bunk space, stalking round the mess decks and being a downright nuisance to myself and everyone around.

'Darby' Allen told me I had to report to the office just before he finished his afternoon watch.

I made my second visit of the day to the Signals Office.

The thumb of my free hand was held high as I handed the signal bag over. My lovely Wren friend put her thumb up in reply; there was a big grin on her face.

That night I packed all my kit. When my relief came aboard on the following morning I was all ready to go.

The other watch returned from leave just before I was about to depart and Ernie Leach was adrift. I was really sorry that I would be unable to say my farewells to him.

Shorty Grant was in no hurry, in fact he wanted to make another trip to Newfy

110

because there were some rabbits he had been unable to buy on his last visit.

He was still aboard Polyanthus when I left to catch the afternoon train with a couple of other men whose drafts had been arranged earlier.

Like so many things in the Navy there was an established procedure to be followed on reporting to barracks; it was known as the 'joining routine' and there was an established tradition that every man should drag it out as long as possible.

Following my arrival at HMS Victory, 'Pompey Barracks', I spent a lot of time enquiring as to the location of the sick-bay where I had to report for a medical and I was still trying to find it at the end of the day. Fortunately I experienced no such difficulty in finding the right place to put in my request for 'in from sea leave'.

L/S R.K. Grant (Shorty).

Before I set out to Yorkshire and home I had managed to get my station card stamped for all the medical requirements apart from dentistry and reckoned there was sufficient 'joining routine' remaining to take care of at least three days on my return from leave.

My life at sea had come to an end for the time being and there was a great sense of relief on my release from the hard, unyielding environment which had compressed the normal maturing period of years into months. I had yet to pass the various medical and mental examinations required by the Fleet Air Arm and it made my future uncertain but exciting.

The one thing I was sure of was that I did not want to go back to the life I had just left.

My heart was much lighter when I got home at the end of a week which had witnessed a dramatic change in my life. I was convinced that things could only get better from now on.

111

It was during the following week that my father arrived home for his tea just as I was leaving the table. It was Mary's evening off-duty and I intended to catch the bus at quarter past four in order to arrive in Bradford with plenty of time to walk up to the Nurses' Home.

The evening paper, the Telegraph & Argus, was still folded on the corner of the table. My father opened it and glanced at the headlines as he waited for my mother who was busy in the shop.

"Just a minute," he called me back as I was leaving, "What type of leave did you say you were on?"

"In from sea leave," I replied, wondering what had caused him to ask the question.

"Are you sure it's not survivors' leave? You might as well tell me, I won't say anything to your mother if you don't want me to."

He passed the paper to me with his finger on the 'Stop Press' column.

'The Admiralty regret to announce the loss of the frigate HMS Itchen, the Canadian destroyer HMCS St. Croix and the corvette HMS Polyanthus. The next of kin have been informed'.

"It is in from sea leave," was all I could say.

Our eyes met and we shared an involuntary silence; words don't come easily at such times.

"I'd better go or I'll miss the bus," I excused myself and left.

For the whole of the journey to Bradford I experienced a strange sense of detachment, similar to that which I felt when ships had been sunk near us. A feeling of unreality with no extremes of emotion; all around me life was continuing normally.

At the bottom of Manchester Road I got off the bus and headed up Little Horton Lane towards St. Luke's Hospital. As I was passing the Princes Theatre my thoughts turned to the lad who had taken my place at the eleventh hour - how had he fared? - how had any of the crew fared? - were there any survivors? - was Davey one of them?

"You there! Come here!"

There was no doubt that the barked command was directed at me; it jolted me back into reality.

The voice had come from within an Army uniform which displayed the skill of its maker rather than the character of its wearer. It needed several days more wear before it would adapt to his outline.

"Why didn't you salute? What do you think you're doing wandering around the streets and ignoring your superior officer?"

"Sir!"

I adopted the time honoured universal reply, the shortest possible and capable of so many interpretations, and I gave him the salute for which he craved.

"You salute the Captain of your ship, don't you?"
He was not to know how ill-chosen a question it was.
"Sir!"
Alec sprang into my mind. Alec who had returned from Dunkirk, exhausted and dishevelled. He had suffered at the hands of just such an officer. I thought of his disenchantment with the Navy and with the war which had denied him the return to civilian life when he had completed his twelve years in the summer of 1939. Was his war now over?

The officer was still tearing me off a strip and I had not heard half of what he had said. My eyes were fixed on his pristine Sam Browne belt; there was not a bend, crease, or crack to be seen.

A small group of onlookers had gathered on the pavement and their eyes darted constantly from the officer to me and then back again. One of the older ladies directed an occasional "Tut-tut" towards him and he realised it was time to end his tirade.

"Don't ever fail to salute an officer again. Let tonight be a lesson to you."
"Sir!" I answered.

I carried on up Little Horton Lane and met Mary outside the Nurses' Home, only this time, the usual good natured chaff from the other nurses failed to produce my customary responses. Less than an hour had passed since I had read the brief announcement.

We went to a cinema; there was nowhere else to go where we could avoid the unwanted attentions of bright-eyed young officers or other distractions. In the half-darkness we quietly reflected on our good fortune in being together and were humbly grateful.

My initial reaction to the loss of Polyanthus and my former shipmates was a numbed sense of detachment; a part of my life had been wiped out at a stroke, and in its place was a void. Fate had delivered a brutal reminder that life was determined by forces beyond my control or understanding.

I learned, as did so many more, that I must put the past, together with its memories, behind me, and accept whatever fate might hold in store for the future.

TWENTY

"Where do you think you're going? - and don't tell me you're doing your joining routine, because I won't wear it."

There was no doubt in my mind that the question was aimed at me but the voice lacked the hard edge of inescapable trouble. I turned my head to find Shorty Grant grinning at me from a doorway, wearing the crossed 'hooks' of an acting petty officer. He had left Polyanthus after all and had been given the task of chasing up the dilatory 'joiners' like me.

It was not difficult to spin out the joining routine at Pompey Barracks; clutching some document or other I moved around in a purposeful manner and it seemed to work very well. When the time came to present myself for dental inspection or for gas drill, a call of nature at the appropriate moment could postpone the event until after stand-easy or other suitable break in the day's routine, after which it was to the back of the queue once more and a further wait.

One of my messmates turned out to be Kerr, who had attained some notoriety in the boxing ring when we had been together at Ganges; he had been serving on a cruiser and his life in the Navy had, not surprisingly, been very different from mine. We found common ground in having come 'in from sea' together and the previous evening had agreed that prolonging the joining routine was far more demanding than normal duty.

"Only got the gas chamber to do and I'm on my way there now. This joining lark's too much like hard work for my liking".

Shorty had other ideas.

"I'm going to keep my eye on you my lad, from now on I'll see you complete your joining routine, don't you dare leave my side".

For the next two days I did as he asked; we found great difficulty in putting our thoughts and feelings into words.

Shorty was able to tell me what he had learned about the sinking of Polyanthus. By the time his relief had arrived the train for Larne had left Londonderry, the ship was ready to sail and he had helped to cast off one of her lines. Probably because his home was in Portsmouth and near by, he had been recalled from leave to check the list of the ship's company at the Records Office and therefore knew that Polyanthus had been sunk before the loss was announced in the press. He had been told there were no survivors, although he understood that an officer had been picked up only to be lost when the Itchen was torpedoed. Ernie Leach had arrived in Londonderry a day adrift but had caught up with the ship at Moville.

Once his story had been told there was very little left to say and we moved around the barracks sharing emotions which were too complex to understand, much less explain.

Now I could begin to understand why men spoke little of those experiences which affected them most deeply, why many of them bottled up their thoughts, their fears and their nightmares, until finally they cracked. Of all the men in the barracks, Shorty was the only one with whom I could share my thoughts and if I was unable to find the words for him what point could there be in telling the story to anyone else.

We exhausted our topics of conversation and I brought my joining routine to an end, leaving Shorty to continue his endless amble around the barracks alone.

When a team sheet appeared on the notice board for a game of rugby I could not put my name on it quickly enough. All the back positions had names already entered and I was obliged to put my name down in the forwards. It did not require a genius to realise that the 'barrack stanchions', men who would have us believe they were indispensable ashore, had first choice of the positions. The opportunity to get out on a rugby field again for the first time since joining the Navy was not to be missed no matter where I was to play.

My earlier experiences in 'coarse rugby' proved invaluable in my unaccustomed role as a forward; there was a wide spread of ability and I set out to have some fun even if the standard of play left much to be desired.

My companion in the second row of the scrum appeared to be equally unfamiliar with his position but soon displayed a remarkable flair in open play. In due course he suggested we should develop our own game and outlined some simple moves. We may not have provided our backs with much useful ball but we enjoyed ourselves.

When we came off the field I asked his name and where he played. He was an international Rugby League centre and told me he had never been able to get a game in the backs since he arrived in Portsmouth; the barrack stanchions saw to that.

The ordered life of HMS Victory contrasted vividly with my life aboard Polyanthus; the solid barrack blocks alongside the parade ground and the impressive main gates over which, it was claimed, the Drum Major of the Royal Marine Band had tossed his baton and caught it successfully at the other side as he led the band through, testified to the traditions of the Royal Navy. Most of

115

the ship's company was transient but it maintained the standards expected of Portsmouth Division.

I did my drills and fire-watching duties but found shore-leave less compelling when its future availability became constant and predictable. Much of my free time was spent in taking advantage of the facilities within the barracks.

In due course I was required to travel to Bristol for an aircrew medical, written examination and assessment along with three other aspiring aviators. One of them, a New Zealander and a rugby enthusiast, was at the time playing regularly with the New Zealand Services XV, the wartime equivalent of the All Blacks. His name was Herkt and I found his company enjoyable, quite apart from our common interest in sport.

Neither of us had any difficulty in meeting the requirements of the examining board, which had a far better approach and attitude than the one in Darlington. The psychologist did not sit with the board on this occasion however, but interviewed us individually. He had a rather haunted look about him, like that of a bewildered and lost soul. As he probed into my background I told him my father had been a chief cashier and he became obsessed with the word cashier, as if unable to disassociate it from its use in court martials and implied disgrace. Time after time he would return to it.

"What do you mean by cashier ? If it is a person, what does he do?"

There appeared to be no possible connection between his questions and the purpose of the interview, and his torment was not dissimilar to that suffered by some of my former shipmates. I felt sorry for him.

By the time we arrived back at Pompey, feeling very pleased with ourselves, 'Kiwi' Herkt, my companion from New Zealand and I were friends; when I eventually played rugby with him I felt sure that in times of peace he would have been an All Black, such was his ability and commitment.

My draft chit to HMS Daedalus, the Fleet Air Arm base at Lee on Solent, was issued with very little delay. I left the executive branch of the Navy behind and entered the air branch.

The wooden huts of Daedalus contrasted sharply with the solid blocks of Pompey Barracks and though the discipline and routine were little changed there was a different atmosphere; the traditions of the Royal Navy were built into the bricks and mortar of Pompey, it was no contest as far as the huts of Daedalus were concerned.

Now that I was considered suitable material for flying training my HMS cap ribbon had to be replaced with a white band; this signified a CW (commission worthy) candidate and marked the wearer out for more special attention in respect of his general behaviour, which was expected to be above average.

I found myself in a very cosmopolitan hut with a few more who had changed hatbands and an assortment of others, some awaiting the air-gunners course, some who had 'dipped' or failed courses and were awaiting re-muster and one man who was beyond hope of classification. The latter, from the East End of London, was barely literate yet loved to climb on a chair and declaim communist dogma as if he were at Hyde Park Corner. On his shore-leave he had only one destination - the dog track - and on every occasion he returned with a fistful of winnings, a feat which, in view of its unfailing regularity, was extremely suspect. His winnings were, we firmly believed, acquired by other means; such a steady accumulation of cash suggested a skilled and successful pick-pocket. We returned to the hut one day to find him gone and no one took the trouble to find out where.

Three New Zealanders who had dipped their course were in the beds adjoining mine. As they had volunteered specifically for flying duties only, they were awaiting transport home for their discharge, and in many respects felt discarded and unwanted. When it came to a game of rugby they were unable to obtain any rugby boots to fit them from the pool of kit but, undeterred, the three of them discarded their ill-fitting footwear and played the second half in their stockinged feet.

"That's how we learnt to play the game back home as kids", they told me.

The individual backgrounds of the 'white bands" was quickly sorted out as the older hands discovered the best 'skives' and quickly disappeared, leaving the more onerous or dull routine duties to be performed by the less experienced. A tall slim signalman with striking auburn hair displayed, for someone so distinctive, a remarkable ability to disappear. When he was no longer employed in evading routine duties, his laugh and constant chuckle could be heard from the midst of several newly-joined men as he entertained them with an un-ending stream of jokes and tales. 'Ginger' Hymers had been one of a select school of solo players who had found a remote pill-box on the edge of the airfield where they foregathered every morning; as a result of his growing band of followers the school collapsed from the sheer weight of numbers when they tried to join in. Ginger, together with his henchmen Jinks and Brunton, had to find another skive.

As with the joining routine at Pompey, the game of 'dodging the column' or skiving eventually became boring and pointless; it was pleasant to get well out of the way around the perimeter of the airfield where we could watch the take-offs and landings, but our presence was soon reported and the activity became too risky. A squadron of Barracudas was there at the time and I had an opportunity to study this strange, big, ungainly 'fish' at close quarters when one stopped at the perimeter fence. I remember thinking as an embryo pilot that it was a rather formidable and awkward-looking object.

From time to time, probably arising from undue demands on the accommodation, groups awaiting the start of their course were sent home on leave. Not surprisingly we lived in constant hope that we might be so fortunate ourselves and realised that should the opportunity arise we would have to be

117

around if called. The skiving was reduced dramatically and I became a main gate sentry with a first world war Lee Enfield rifle and a clip containing five rounds of ammunition, one of which had a habit of falling apart on inspection. Every duty I was told to be careful with the offending round because no replacement was available.

"Wouldn't make a ha'porth of difference, lad, whether you've three or five rounds on that gate, just so long as you let one off before you're killed".

Our class number, when it came over the Tannoy, brought us all running to the guardroom where we assembled fully expecting at least seven days' leave.

"For those of you who have not yet heard, I have to tell you that the First Sea Lord, Admiral of the Fleet Sir Dudley Pound, is dead. His funeral will take place in London and you will be part of the naval guard representing the Portsmouth Division. Tomorrow morning you will report here for transport to Whale Island for instruction in ceremonial drill. You are going to show all the other forces that the Royal Navy is not only the Senior Service, it is also the smartest and the most efficient. Heaven help any man who lets us down".

Whale Island was the place where strong men were reduced to tears if we were to believe all we had been told; where the gunners' mates swore and cursed officers with impunity, although they always showed due deference with a 'Sir' as they concluded any such attack. For some of our number the prospect was little better than a sentence to hard labour; in their minds Whale Island was the naval equivalent of Devil's Island. I found the prospect intriguing yet at the same time daunting.

In the event it proved to be hard work on the parade ground from the moment we arrived. The instructors were working to a very tight limit and had no time to spare for any awkward types - they were weeded out in quick time and dispensed with. Easily distinguishable by our white bands and anxious to avoid the ignominy of a rejection before we had even started our course, we gave an acceptable account of ourselves, fixing and unfixing bayonets, learning the ceremonial drill of 'rest on your arms reversed', marching and countermarching. For the officers who were in trouble with their swords the Commander in charge showed no mercy despite their humiliation being very public, and I found myself full of sympathy for them.

Number One suits were brushed and cleaned to perfection, boots shined as never before, khaki gaiters and webbing blancoed, bayonets and guns polished until they sparkled; then, in the early hours of the big day, we boarded the special train which was to take us to London.

Victoria Station was taken over to a very large extent by the Royal Navy that day. One of the largest rooms had been converted into a temporary canteen where we were all fed before being given a final review of the duties expected of us.

"Now empty your bladders and your bowels because you won't have another chance for quite a long time. Platoons will assemble in the positions allocated to them on the platforms or station forecourt five minutes before the time just given so that we are not waiting for anyone".

At the appointed time every platoon was present and correct, each platoon was called to attention in turn and every man, without exception, was inspected by the Commander from Whale Island, the man entrusted with the task of forming the ceremonial guard. With him were sailors equipped with clothes-brushes, boot-brushes, blanco and polish which they applied to any bit of uniform which failed to meet the Commander's standards. By the station entrance the scarlet jackets and white helmets of the Royal Marine Band brought a bold splash of colour to the great mass of navy blue as we stood easy awaiting the order to move off.

"Parade!"

The voice roared out, defying all the customary clangour and din of the station; with faces straight ahead, we looked through the corners of our eyes in the direction of the sound. The Commander was standing on a gantry that straddled the platforms, his three gold rings somehow managing to shine through all the smoke and steam, his head turning quickly and purposefully to the right and to the left as he assessed our reaction. He had bellowed across the parade ground of Whale Island, frequently into the face of howling winds, far too often to be intimidated by the enclosed space of Victoria station, and he gave a glorious demonstration of his abilities; the aid of a microphone and amplification was not for him.

"Parade ! .... henshon !"

And every manjack present moved as one, without exception, despite the actual word of command bearing absolutely no resemblance to what it was supposed to be.

Then came the succession of commands which had been drilled into us over the previous days, and the sharp sound of each one being executed was followed by a silence that testified to the manner of its completion.

"By the left ! Quick .... march!"

The drums of the Royal Marine Band burst forth with immaculate timing as the Drum Major led them out and on to the main road; the bugles blared to warn London that the Royal Navy was there. And our necks were stretched to give us an extra inch of height when 'Hearts of Oak' rang out, attracting the attention of all around. Suddenly there were crowds appearing and someone gave a cheer, then another until it seemed everyone was cheering as we marched to Whitehall where we were to line the route of the procession.

"Go on touch the sailor's collar dear, it'll bring you luck."

The nurses often touched my collar when I stood at the Nurses' Home at St. Lukes when waiting for Mary, but then it was a bit of fun. Here I was on duty, holding a rifle and unable to turn round or avoid the attention. I was sure the child

119

who was being held up and encouraged to touch my collar had sticky hands, and dreaded the prospect of being told off by one of the gunners' mates; what might bring luck to the child could have dire repercussions for me.

"Oh ! You lovely boy, how is it you're so popular?"

The feared gunners' mate appeared at my side and straightened my collar.

"I know he's nice but you must control yourself dear - leave him alone until this lot's over and then you can have him as far as I'm concerned."

Although I would have liked to join in the good natured banter I had to stand my ground, unlike the gunners' mate, who now returned to his station along the road.

In the distance the sound of the approaching procession prepared us for the command,

"Rest on your arms reversed."

We performed the drill like veterans despite the fact that none of us knew it existed a few days before; with my head lowered and the muzzle of my rifle resting on the toe-cap of my boot I completed the drill by placing the palms of my hands across the butt. Whereas my view had been restricted to straight ahead, it was now concentrated on the road immediately surrounding my feet. For a few brief moments my mind went back to a war that now seemed so far away, to the North Atlantic, to Polyanthus and the men who had been lost with her. Just a few yards away, out of my vision, all the pomp and circumstance of the day reclaimed my attention and when my curiosity eventually became intolerable I lifted my head slightly to sneak a quick glimpse; the gun carriage carrying the flag-draped coffin was in direct view and my head was never fully lowered again until the funeral party of dignitaries, from the Prime Minister down, had passed by.

When it was all over and our rifles had been returned to their normal position we awaited the order to 'fix bayonets'; the Royal Navy, we had been told, was entitled to march through the Capital with bayonets fixed and we were going to observe the custom for our return march to Victoria. It was the drill I was unhappy about, as I sometimes found difficulty in fixing the bayonet in position on the muzzle of the rifle and, sure enough, it failed to click into place at the first attempt. Visions of being the man who mucked up the drill before the Cenotaph in Whitehall were about to overwhelm me when there was a reassuring click to save the day.

'A Life on the Ocean Wave' filled the streets of London. Ahead of us, beyond the sea of shining bayonets and the white helmets of the Marines, the Drum Major was giving an inspired display. We drew ourselves up to our full height and beyond. A couple more parades like this one and I felt sure I would be as tall as Hymers who was our marker, the burnished tone of his light copper-coloured hair gleaming like a beacon below his cap.

At Queen Anne's Mansions the Wrens packed the windows, waving down to us, cheering and blowing kisses.

"Keep those eyes to the front", yelled the zealous gunners' mates as they moved back and forth along the ranks. Yet they too were revelling in the tremendous reception that London was showing and they were smiling, just as we all were, the solemn purpose of our presence soon forgotten. For a few minutes we enjoyed the illusion of being heroes. Carried away by the drums, the bugles, the band and all the trappings of a ceremonial occasion I almost forgot the stark, grim reality of the war on the North Atlantic.

On the train, as we returned to Portsmouth, everyone was in high spirits; some had managed to buy newspapers and the accounts of the day's events were read out again and again, particularly those most complimentary to the Navy.

"The Brigade of Guards were as impressive as always, displaying the discipline and precision we expect of them; the Royal Air Force contingents acquitted themselves very well also, but the day belonged to the Royal Navy. For this was our senior service at its best, they not only matched the Guards in their turn-out and their precision, they made them look wooden by comparison."

"If only we could have stayed in the Smoke for the night - we could have had all the birds we wanted - going crazy, they were."

"Where the hell did the Commander find that voice, stopped Victoria dead he did, he could get a station announcer's job after the war."

"He won't be needing a job after today, not after what we've done for him, his promotion prospects haven't come to any harm at all."

"With a write-up like that in the newspapers he's a dead cert for a gong, probably the DSO I reckon, a DSC for sure."

"Grow up, will you!, he'll be lucky to get anything more than a good report; any gongs that are going will be bagged by someone higher up the tree who just gave the orders and probably had no idea how to knock a crowd like us into shape."

The reflections and speculations continued throughout the journey and even interrupted the inevitable card games; someone always managed to secrete a pack of cards away somewhere, no matter what the occasion. The smug satisfaction of a job well done, of a pride in ourselves and in the Navy, was inescapable, yet we were the same men who less than a week before had been devoting most of our energies to the evasion of normal duties.

By the time we had handed in our rifles and equipment and reached our huts we were tired, extremely tired; it had been a very long and demanding day. We turned in for a well-deserved sleep, justifiably proud of ourselves.

The following morning I reported to the guardroom for duty as sentry on the main gate with the efficiency and drill of Whale Island fresh in my blood.

I was issued with a rifle and ammunition. I got the clip with the faulty round again.

121

TWENTY-ONE

HMS St. Vincent at Gosport and HMS Victory - Pompey Barracks, were built around the turn of the century along with countless hospitals, workhouses and similar institutions, including prisons. They all consisted of large austere accommodation blocks enclosed within a stout outer wall. Prisons could be recognised by the bars on all the windows and their solid gates, naval barracks by a tall mast alongside a large parade ground.

The first step to be taken by anyone starting his naval training to become a pilot was through the gates of St. Vincent. Along with 249 others I took that step at the end of November in 1943 and we became the 59th Pilots Course. Callow youths of 18 fresh from school mingled with slightly older undergraduates who considered themselves mature, and professional men of thirty who really were. Men who had forsaken their safe, reserved occupation and family to 'do their bit' struggled to adjust to a strange environment while younger men who had already experienced active service had no such problems.

It was a course with an unusually large complement of existing servicemen; six petty officers, a gaggle of TAGs (air-gunners) who were leading airmen, twelve Royal Marines and a bunch of 'fleet entries' who had been transferred from the 'Andrew' - the traditional Navy. All were volunteers who had been through a rigorous selection process and were of a required standard of education.

Along with the other fleet entries I was quickly installed in the building which was to be our home for the next three months. For the newcomers who were encountering such accommodation for the first time, the conditions were very basic, but for me, it was comparative luxury after the inescapable discomfort of a corvette's fo'c'sle. The messes were on the ground floor of the block and consisted of long tables with benches on each side, free from the overhead intrusions of hammocks, mess kettles and the assorted paraphernalia which I had endured in the past. A wide stone staircase led up to the floors above, where the washrooms and the large airy dormitories filled with two tier metal bunks were situated.

The draft from Daedalus was dispersed amongst the newcomers and I found Ginger Hymers had the bunk next to mine. Surrounded by a much wider audience and one containing so many new to the Navy, Ginger was in his element; his fund of anecdotes was shared with everyone, including those who were not interested. At times my bunk ceased to be my own as his audience grew and backsides found a resting place on my mattress.

"I was already in the RNVR when war broke out", Ginger was telling them.

"I took part in quite a few parades and because of my height I was always the marker - he's the only man who ignores the order 'Eyes Right' at the salute, you know. On one occasion, at the beginning of the war, I was on a big parade when the King took the salute. I was as proud as a peacock as we marched off, my rifle at the perfect slope and my arm swinging straight out from my shoulder. When the order came, 'Eyes Right', all the heads snapped smartly to the right, all except mine, I stuck my head up even higher and fixed my eyes straight ahead. It was all according to the book and even if I say it myself, we were bloody good."

An infectious chuckle preceded his conclusion.

"Suddenly, out of the corner of my eye, I caught sight of these cameras and I realised it was being filmed for the newsreels. I couldn't believe it and took a good look at them, 'I'm going to be on the pictures' I told myself; completely forgot I was the marker. Guess what? When the newsreels appeared, there's Hymers slowly turning his head and breaking out into a big daft grin right in the middle of the picture. I got a real bollocking for that I can tell you."

By this time Ginger was chuckling and laughing harder than anyone.

"The next thing I know, my mother has been to the local Odeon and seen the newsreel, she was so proud and excited she saw it through twice, nudging the people on each side of her, the ones in front and the ones behind, telling them 'That's my son there, isn't he smart?' She still thinks I was the smartest and best sailor on that parade even if no one else does."

I had already heard the story and was more interested in regaining control of my mattress.

"Give it a rest, Ginger" I called.

"What's got into you to make you so miserable, you old sourgut, when was the last time you had a laugh?"

"How can anyone not be miserable when they've heard the same story more times than enough? Even your variations lose their appeal, second time round."

Little did we realise it at the time but we were establishing a scenario we were to repeat so often that it would become part of our everyday life.

Archie Brunton and Jinks, who were only too happy to support Ginger, had not had very much time in the service beyond their initial training, and this applied to the greater part of the fleet entries. Quite a few had spent the previous six months on a 'crammer' course at college which was designed to bring them

123

up to the educational standard required. Those of us who had met that standard only to be rejected by our first selection board and had then become, by default, air-gunners or common sailors like myself, felt hard done by. It was obvious that very few transfer requests from men who were already on active service had been approved.

For those who were struggling to shrug off their civilian outlook and instincts, the classes on the traditional naval subjects helped in their transition. However, they tended to suffer most on the parade ground, the vast open expanse of tarmac that stretched from the main gate to the mast, immediately in front of the barrack blocks. Here we began and ended the day and at some point in every one of our days we spent some time at drill.

Gunnery, navigation, signals, W/T, ship and aircraft recognition, the theory and principles of flight, all had to be learnt and mastered in the three months before our proficiency would be assessed. At the outset this presented quite a challenge and made for a rather serious and sober atmosphere in the messes and dormitories. Excursions ashore were infrequent but there were one or two who were not to be put off, two of them being our undergraduates who had joined from Oxford.

Their names were Snodgrass and Marks, who was also known as 'Wacky', and they distinguished themselves with a remarkable exhibition following an evening devoted to the consumption of an awful lot of beer.

"Not any old beer, you must understand," Wacky informed us "but a very special brew which, when combined with Snoddy's guts, produces the most amazing results."

By the time the pair had arrived back in the dormitory several of its occupants had already turned in and did not welcome a noisy intrusion but their protests were of little avail. Snodgrass began to undress, somewhat clumsily in view of his inebriation and relatively new uniform, until, naked from the waist down, he stood at the foot of his bunk, grasped the top rail and bent over.

Wacky meanwhile had been fumbling in a box of matches. When he had finally extracted one, he stood, ready to strike it alongside Snoddy's backside.

"Ready, old boy?" called Wacky.

"Ready, aye, ready", answered Snoddy.

Curiosity overcame the annoyance of the early birds and they sat up or leaned out of their bunks, peering around a growing audience.

Snodgrass was obviously concentrating his mind and was going red in the face. Suddenly he yelled - "Now" - and with an enormous rasping roar, broke wind.

Almost simultaneously Wacky struck his match, pushed the flame into the path of the gale and jumped back.

A flash of blue flame appeared momentarily.

"Sorry old boy, didn't quite catch that one, do you think you could manage another if you searched your bowels thoroughly?"

Snoddy was still concentrating and building up the colour in his cheeks.

"Light the bloody match when I tell you and catch the fart when it's fresh." he called angrily.

For what seemed like an age we were silent and motionless, as everyone in the dormitory studied Snoddy's bare backside and Wacky's stance, with his match at the ready.

"Take your time, mate, don't spoil the ship for a ha'porth of tar."

"Give it all you've got, Snoddy."

The tension began to ease as we became aware of the ridiculous picture we presented when, in the middle of the laughter, we heard Snoddy's,

"Now!"

The match was struck and lit before the dormitory resounded to a triumphant trump, and we were treated to a fine spectacle of light and sound.

The quick flash started out a vivid blue, growing paler as it quickly dispersed. It really was a magnificent effort.

Physical fitness was encouraged and the opportunity to participate in most sports was available. One of our number was destined to become an Olympic swimmer and our division did well in water sports largely as a result of his example and encouragement. Ginger became an enthusiastic member of the waterpolo team; he played in goal, where because of his height he was able to keep his feet on the bottom for long periods. For the non-swimmers attendance at the swimming pool was compulsory during certain of the dog-watches until such time as they were capable of swimming two lengths of the baths partially clothed - the standard expected of all entrants. White 'ducks' (jumper and trousers) had to be donned for the test, they were usually heavy and cold following the test taken by a prior candidate and it was claimed that, by tucking the jumper into the trousers before diving into the water, an air bubble could be trapped inside the jumper which would aid buoyancy. The trick never worked to my knowledge. Unsuccessful candidates were regularly rescued by an attendant instructor stationed on the side of the pool with a long pole; and even the loss of shore leave, until the required standard of swimming was reached, failed to help some individuals through their tests. They never learned to swim throughout their naval service.

As a result of my friendship with Kiwi Herkt I enjoyed rugby at the highest level available until someone mistook my head for the ball. On my discharge from sick-bay I was told that any further concussion would jeopardise my future training and so I reluctantly gave up the game for the rest of the course.

"I was with a fellow once who got kicked by a horse."

My return to the dormitory had prompted one of Ginger's anecdotes.

"Caught him just under the eye - shattered his cheekbone, just around the eye socket."

125

Ginger's expression was serious, there was no laugh tucked away in the tone of his voice and the ready smiles of his followers quickly faded in response to his stare.

"Turned out to be pretty useful for him though. We were on the same working party when I first met him and we had a right bastard of a P.O. who was giving all of us a rough time but picking on this lad more than anyone. Suddenly the lad let out a hell of a moan and there was his eyeball, out upon his cheek."

Unable to maintain his serious expression any longer, Ginger started to chuckle.

"Then we all let out a moan, a couple passed out and I didn't feel all that good either. As for the P.O., he was shitting blue lights."

"How did it happen?" asked an incredulous Jinks.

"He told us that because of the accident his eye socket had been permanently damaged, leaving his eye none too secure. That sod of a P.O. got on his wick so much that he decided he'd had enough. Just popped his eye out - end of working party."

He peered into my face,

"That left eye of yours looks a bit slack to me", he chortled.

"Dry up, you long streak of copper wire", I retorted and normality was restored.

Although sport was encouraged, it was a spare-time activity with the exception of PT which appeared in our time table regularly two or three times a week. As with many activities it suffered badly in its popularity as a result of the compulsion factor: Lloyd hated PT and adopted many devious ruses to avoid it.

Another son of Liverpool, Lloyd was cast in the same mould as Barton of the 'Polyanthus'; an opportunist with a nimble and creative mind, he got 'lost' whenever PT appeared on the timetable.

Throughout the working hours of the day the ground-floor in the barrack blocks was the only one to be occupied, the dormitories and washrooms on the floors above were empty. During a routine inspection of our block the Divisional Officer was surprised, as he climbed the stone staircase, to see movement in the washroom ahead of him.

"What are you doing here ?" he barked, "You know very well that this is out of bounds at this time of day."

Lloyd stopped wiping the wash-basin, turned and came to attention.

"Excused PT Sir!"

His answer was prompt and smartly delivered.

"I thought I would just give the washroom a tidy-up before I started on some revision."

Faced with such a responsible and enterprising attitude, the officer was impressed.

126

"Good man - carry on."

He disappeared, leaving Lloyd to recover all his dhobying from behind the washroom door where he had hastily flung it after hearing foot-steps approaching. Any panic he might have felt when he saw the officer's cap coming into view on the staircase must have been short-lived, for he had recovered a white vest to use as a cleaning cloth.

For some time after the incident, Lloyd enjoyed the officer's favour and was regarded as an above average prospect. The sting in the tail was, that in having once distinguished himself, he was unable to fade into the background or get 'lost' on PT periods.

Everyone had to bear his share of the general duties, the sweeping, scrubbing, washing and polishing of our living quarters; these were activities that many of the course had never encountered before. My own early experiences in this respect were frequently brought to mind as I found myself, along with the other 'older' fleet entries, trying to impress on our fellow students the importance of performing such tasks thoroughly; tasks they considered so menial that, up to then, they had always expected to be done by others. Several embryo airmen were reminded of the difficulties they might have faced had they found themselves with a blocked toilet to clear on a small ship in a lively sea. There was very little chance that they could ever appreciate the enormous variations in the conditions within the Navy.

With the approach of Christmas the overall standards of the course were improving and our progress could be measured most readily on the parade ground. All but the most awkward and unco-ordinated of our number had by this time mastered the drill patterns and movements and were beginning to introduce pride into their contribution to the efficiency of their class and the course.

We were all sent home for seven days leave over Christmas.

Victoria Station in London became the gathering point for most of the course as we returned from leave. There was no need for me to study the destination boards in order to find the platform for my train when there were so many familiar faces gathered around the gates of the one I sought.

"I had a hell of job to persuade her not to come and see me off at the station, I hate to think of the envy it would have created amongst you lot."

"I said goodbye to mine at the foot of the stairs, she said she was coming to the station with me and then started to blub so much that she couldn't show her face outside the door."

The copper-haired one was where I expected to find him; clearly visible above the other heads that were gathered around, Ginger was making his usual contributions interspersed with his inimitable chuckles, apparently far less dispirited than the majority at the end of their leave. He had, after all, experienced quite a few sailor's farewells.

Rounds that night were later than usual and a large number of the beds were

127

already occupied by weary or pensive men when the Duty Officer made his appearance. His inspection followed the normal perfunctory lines for the evening as he walked the length of the dormitory and turned to make his way back to the door. Suddenly he stopped and returned to the bunk in the corner; in it the outline of a body in the top and a body in the bottom bunk could be seen, both with the heads at the same end.

"Waken that man," ordered the officer, pointing to the bottom bunk.

"Why are you sleeping with your head at this end of the bunk ? the standing orders are quite clear; everyone must sleep with heads at alternate ends."

Lloyd sat up in his bunk and blinked at the officer. "Sir" was all he could manage to say.

"Take that man's name, First Lieutenant's report in the morning."

When Sick Parade was called the following morning, Lloyd was first in line, asking for early treatment as he was on 'Defaulters' and was anxious to avoid being late. He was the first to be seen.

"It's my head, Sir, every morning I waken up with these terrible headaches."

"How long have you been experiencing these headaches ?"

"Ever since I started sleeping in my present bunk, Sir, it's the radiator I'm sure, right alongside my head. I waken up with a filthy mouth too, Sir."

"Well why don't you sleep the other way round, man, with your head as far from the radiator as you can?"

"I'm not allowed to, Sir, because of the standing orders on sleeping head to foot."

The doctor leaned across his desk for his message pad and scribbled a note on it.

"Well I'm giving you dispensation to sleep with your head away from the radiator." he said and handed the note to Lloyd.

"You have heard the charge, do you have anything to say?"

Defaulters was following the traditional pattern.

"I have dispensation from the doctor, Sir. I'm allowed to sleep that way because of the radiator."

Lloyd produced his trump card. The First Lieutenant glanced at it and presumably failed to notice the date it was issued.

"Why didn't you produce this last night, man?"

"I had just been awakened, Sir, I wasn't given time to collect my thoughts or say anything."

"Dismissed." The First Lieutenant sounded annoyed at the waste of his time by what he considered to be an over-zealous junior officer.

Lloydy had put another one over on authority.

Sunday morning divisions followed by the church parade had once again become part of my normal routine. Unlike Valkyrie where the OD's (other denominations) only had to step outside the gate for their service, at St. Vincent we were marched a fair distance. Our Padre was a very down to earth character who would mingle with us when we had broken ranks and were standing outside the church having a quick cigarette before entering. He enjoyed a cigarette with us.

"Is there anyone here who can play the piano or organ?" he asked. "I have a problem this morning, someone has just given backword."

The opportunity to play a pipe organ was too good to miss and I stepped forward eagerly.

"I played the organ before I joined the Navy." I volunteered.

"Good man, come along with me." The Padre led the way into the church, round the side of the pulpit and past the organ console.

I had fallen for the oldest trick in the book, the one beloved of music hall comedians since the First World War, only there was no piano to move this time.

"You'll know much more than I do about pumping the bellows," was the Padre's parting shot as he left me to it.

And that was where I spent an hour of every Sunday morning whilst I was at St. Vincent.

The end of the course, which had seemed so far ahead, eventually drew near. Out on the parade ground each one of us had taken his turn to be in charge of our class and had issued the orders necessary to satisfy the officer in charge of the parade as the class marched and drilled repeatedly, day after day. The nearer the end of the course, the more complicated the drill required.

"Divide your squad into three separate columns and place one before the wardroom, another facing it at the opposite end of the parade ground and the third facing you before the mast," was a test of the lungs as well as concentration when the parade ground was shared with other classes.

Misunderstandings and mental blocks compounded with confusion to create mayhem and, as we struggled with our orders, squads of classmates became obstinate and awkward. The satisfaction of successfully placing two columns in position would be rapidly destroyed by the sight of the third compressing itself against one of the barrack blocks, often with the face of its leader flattened on the wall, or, even worse, the realisation that one of the columns had disappeared completely, either around or into one of the buildings.

High pitched, despairing yells identifying the class followed by an even more frantic "Halt!" rang out frequently as demoralised men struggled to regain control of their wits and their squads.

Warnings abounded of what could be expected when the time came for the final tests. The ruses adopted by the officer in charge, an exemplary marine, were relayed by men who had completed earlier courses to others who had yet to undergo the ordeal.

"Just when Nobby thought he was in the clear he was asked how many windows overlooked the parade ground; poor old Nobby was trying to count the

129

ones in each block and do some rapid mental arithmetic when the major asked him if he'd mind keeping his squad in earshot as they were about to leave the parade ground."

"We reckon he's looking for a quick and sensible answer like 'sufficient'."

"He's testing your general observation as well, quite likely to ask you the price of petrol before the war. In case you haven't noticed there's an enamel sign on the gable-end of a building advertising R.O.P. petrol at 1/1d a gallon."

Mid-way through the course the few of us who qualified for the award received the medal ribbon of the 1939-43 Star and when the time came for my parade ground test in command of a squad I was wearing the ribbon. Whether it affected the severity of the test compared with the test set for the others is most unlikely but we thought it did at the time.

The squad moved off smartly as ordered; my next command was ready on my lips when I was asked

"Where did you serve before this?"

I just had time to answer "Newfoundland Escort Force, Sir!" before bellowing "B platoon, B platoon right wheel!"

Now my nerves were becoming taut as I brought my concentration back to the drill, hoping there would be no further distraction. The squad reached the appointed place in good order and I was about to relax when I realised a rogue column from another class was heading straight for my squad, probably beyond the control of its commander.

With the test nearly over my squad was about to be penetrated and there was nothing I could do about it; I stared across the parade ground filled with despair. Just when disaster seemed to be inevitable the leader of the column changed direction sufficiently for him to miss the rear rank of my squad. My immediate sense of relief was short-lived as I realised my examining officer had been speaking to me whilst I had been doing my hopeless and helpless act; I could only guess at what he had said.

Over the wall, beyond my squad, I could see the enamel sign advertising petrol.

"One and a penny a gallon, Sir." I ventured.

There was a faint smile on the officer's face.

"I haven't asked the question yet," he observed as he ordered me to stand the men at ease.

The test came to an end shortly afterwards and I have never known what was said that gave rise to my announcement on the price of petrol.

St. Vincent proved to be a well-organised and well-run establishment which did credit to the officers and staff responsible. None more so than the Master at Arms or 'Jaunty', Chief Petty Officer Wilmott; his presence and example were so powerful that everyone recognised the fact that he alone set the ultimate standard. Discipline was firm and strict, yet he enforced it with fairness and a benevolence which prevented it from being oppressive or harsh. Truly a man amongst men, CPO Wilmott was one of the Navy's greatest assets; few men command such respect that they are remembered by so many for so long.

Three months after we had walked through the gates we walked out of them, the majority of us wearing an anchor or 'hook' on our left sleeve. What the Royal Navy had failed to do in 16 years with Signalman First Class Alec Massie, St. Vincent had succeeded in doing in three months, we had become leading hands.

TWENTY-TWO

Westwood was a small hospital beyond the tram-sheds at Queensbury on the outskirts of Bradford. For the nurses from St. Luke's who were required to staff it, generally on a three-monthly roster, it was not a particularly welcome duty; remote from the city and exposed on a hilltop which could be wild, windy and bitterly cold in winter, it was not unlike banishment to Siberia.

When I arrived home on leave from St. Vincent, Mary was working at Westwood, on nights. Our meetings involved more travelling but as her time during the day was her own we were able to see each other frequently, usually for one or two hours in the mornings. Her first day's off-duty started on the day my leave ended.

"Would you like me to read your cup?"

During the quiet hours of the night the nurses usually had a tea-break and the question from the VAD, an auxiliary nurse a little older than the rest, was a welcome diversion. The patterns of the tea-leaves left in first one cup and then another were converted by the V.A.D. into various prophecies and fancies until she took Mary's cup.

"Do you know anyone in the air force?" she asked, seriously.

"Yes," said Mary, light-heartedly entering into the spirit of the occasion.

The VAD studied the cup for a while as if to ensure that what she saw was correct.

"He's going to crash," she warned, ominously, "on foreign soil."

The train to Manchester on which I travelled at the end of my leave began its journey at Bradford Exchange station; in order to see Mary that morning I travelled to Bradford and she rushed down from Queensbury when she came off night duty. Another member of my course, Bill Cook, hailed from Bradford and his girlfriend was with him on the platform. Together we leaned out from the carriage window and waved until the faces of our loved ones were lost in the distance; only then did we find time to speak to each other.

Mary never mentioned the incident with the tea-cup: I prepared myself for my flying training in Canada or the USA: she turned homewards for her two

132

days' off duty, wondering if she would ever see me again.

The course met up again at Heaton Park, Manchester, and on the next day we were herded on to a train bound for Greenock. On a cold, wet. pitch-black night we gathered in a dock-side shed before boarding a tender which was secured alongside. With all our gear jammed around us it soon became tightly packed, but a brightly-polished brass plate could be seen above our heads in the assembly area bearing the title 'King George V'. Many puzzled and worried lads were on the point of believing that this was the vessel on which they would be crossing the Atlantic, until we drew alongside the large hulk of an ocean-going liner. To their great relief we clambered up her side and embarked aboard the 'Aquitania'.

Where the rich and well-to-do had passed many idle hours in luxury we found rows of bunks had been erected and, since the ship was westbound, demands on the accommodation were not heavy. All the naval personnel were bulked together and I found myself with the three New Zealanders I had met at Daedalus who played rugby in stockinged feet. In all the time I had been at St. Vincent they had been kicking their heels as they awaited their passage home.

On each bunk was a blanket, mine was a lightweight of fine woven wool that probably had graced many a knee on the sun-deck in peace time. Lloyd, who was bunking quite near me, wasted no time in finding something to do; not all the bunks were occupied and Lloyd saw to it that one of them lost its blanket before we had left home waters. For the better part of the first day he beavered away on the edge of his bunk with scissors, needle and thread, oblivious to those around him. By evening he displayed a roll-neck jacket complete with two patch pockets and offered to make further copies to order for a price, blanket to be supplied by the purchaser. He was given orders for two that same evening.

The Aquitania ploughed across to New York at her own speed, free from the limitations of a large convoy. Conditions on board a large liner were so completely different from those I had experienced on my previous crossings that the tension I was expecting on encountering the North Atlantic once more never appeared. There were none of the violent movements I had known on Polyanthus and, with no duties to speak of apart from putting in an appearance for boat drill, I thoroughly enjoyed the experience.

In just over five days we gathered on the upper deck to view Ellis Island and the Statue of Liberty; ahead the skyscrapers of Manhattan passively awaited our arrival as tugs shepherded us up river to pier 4. That was as much of New York as we were able to see since one of our number had become ill during the voyage and been diagnosed as having suspected spinal meningitis. This placed the rest of us in a form of quarantine and did not endear us to the authorities in the USA who could not get rid of us fast enough. We were off the ship and aboard a train bound for Canada within hours of our arrival.

Our segregation from the rest of the world restricted us to the railway coaches

133

in which we travelled to Moncton in New Brunswick; the novelty of travelling on the combined day/sleeper coaches soon palled on the long slow journey northwards through snow covered countryside. Thirty-six hours after leaving New York we arrived at the RCAF's large transit camp at Moncton. We remained in quarantine and were plunged into a series of immunisation and inoculation sessions, each jab being recorded by a hole punched into a personal medical card. To add to our discomfort and frustration we were also treated to a series of medical films in the camp cinema which vividly illustrated the outcome of indiscriminate sexual activity. In due course, having acquired the requisite number of holes in our medical cards, we were left to our own devices and played innumerable hands of solo or games of liar dice in an effort to relieve the boredom.

Living conditions were substantially different from what we had known at St. Vincent, however; in place of the old large, draughty, brick and stone barracks we were billeted in new, well-insulated timber buildings with double windows and heated by a constant supply of steam from a central boilerhouse. Canada had not known the restrictions of rationing and the standard of catering was far higher than anything we had known previously.

Quarantine was finally lifted on the day of my 21st birthday. Along with Jimmy Gregson, another fleet entry and a couple of other lads I ventured into Moncton intent on a celebration. The night was cold and walls of packed snow between four and six feet high lined the streets; the shops were closing their doors before we had been in the town an hour and it became clear that Moncton was unlikely to contribute very much towards a momentous night of pleasure. Groups of acting leading airmen trudged round with hunched shoulders and lowered heads as they dodged in and out of shop doorways in an effort to avoid the icy winds, and as we trudged along the main street, a solitary figure came out of a jeweller's shop. It was John Howard who had been a class-mate of mine at St. Vincent. When we asked him if he had found any good eating places he was unable to help and confessed that, like most of us, he could find little pleasure in mooching round Moncton that evening. He declined our invitation to join in our party and headed back towards the camp.

My birthday party never took place; we sat, side by side, at the bar counter of a restaurant where we ate sausage and mashed potatoes accompanied by hot coffee. Outside it had started to snow and, acting on the advice of the waiter, we crunched our way along the sidewalks to a cinema. Apart from being dry and warm it had nothing to recommend it, both the seats and the film left a lot to be desired and simply added to a most disappointing 21st.

Our impressions were shared by our companions who had returned to the camp. For most of them it was their first encounter, apart from the train or camp, with North America and it fell short of their expectations. We had been back quite a while when John Howard appeared; he emerged from the washroom wearing a towel, a contented smile and a wrist-watch. As he walked past my bed he paused,

"This watch is absolutely waterproof," he told me and held out his wrist to show me the watch, a Rolex Oyster. "I had just bought it when I saw you earlier and I turned down your invitation partly because I wanted to be sure that it's waterproof. I've spent almost two hours in the shower and it hasn't affected it one bit."

"How on earth did you get the money to buy that?" I gasped.

"Tell you later old chap." Howard smiled conspiratorially and moved on.

The funds we were allowed to transfer upon our entry to Canada remained at the £10 maximum I had known in Newfoundland and most of us had changed that amount before venturing out into Moncton; it was of course hopelessly inadequate in relation to a new Rolex. I was most intrigued. Howard later confided in me that his first priority had been to call at the Canadian Pacific Railway Office with a letter which had been given to him by his father. It authorised the local managers to issue him with any money he might request during his stay in Canada. As his father was the President or Chairman or of similar standing with Canadian Pacific it was unlikely that he would experience any financial deprivation in the months to come.

Shortly afterwards notices appeared informing us of our postings. Kingston, Ontario, with the RCAF and Pensacola in the United States with the US Navy, were well established as the stations which trained pilots for the Fleet Air Arm and the majority of our course was allocated to them with Kingston claiming the larger share. During the previous year, however, in order to meet the Navy's greater needs, two stations in Western Ontario, Goderich for elementary training and Aylmer for advanced training, had been introduced into the programme and I was one of twenty-five who, together with five officers were consigned to Goderich.

Howard was allocated to Pensacola where his connections with Canadian Pacific were of no value; his purchase of the Rolex turned out to have been made just in time.

TWENTY-THREE

We left Moncton in a special coach hitched on the back of a service train. At various times and places during the next two days we were unhitched and hitched from one train to another. It was as slow as our previous train journey but it was far more comfortable than the one from New York. Where the track followed the St. Lawrence river the scenery became more varied and interesting and added to the general atmosphere of anticipation and excitement as we drew nearer to our destination and the chance to fly.

At RCAF Goderich the barrack buildings appeared to be even newer than at Moncton. In the two-storey buildings we found the usual lines of double metal bunk beds; outside, a vast area of virgin snow covered the airfield and on the edge, where a long stretch of concrete had been cleared, we could see some Tiger Moth aircraft lined up in front of a high bank of snow.

"Flying is restricted until the field thaws out," we were told when we gathered in the gymnasium for the CO's address. "This will not present a problem for the time being as you have to undergo various compatibility tests before being assigned to your flying instructor. During this time you will commence your ground school studies, draw your flying kit and familiarise yourselves with the station."

Goderich turned out to be a pleasant small town on the edge of Lake Huron. A deep gorge separated the airfield from the town and created a detour that lengthened the journey between the two considerably. Some of us attended the John Knox Presbyterian Church for church parade and were made to feel very welcome. The townspeople were still trying to adjust to the novelty of having British sailors in their midst and as a result we had several invitations to visit their homes. There was a club in the town that was run for the benefit of servicemen and it was not long before some of our lads were arranging dates with the local girls.

On our second weekend we were granted a 48 hour pass; it was the weekend before we started our flying training and most of us took the opportunity to visit Detroit on a special bus provided for the purpose. It was an articulated vehicle of dubious origin and negligible comfort but it managed to transport us there and back without actually falling apart about our ears.

Along with Jimmy Gregson I set out to savour the delights of Detroit. When I had been in Baltimore I had visited the burlesque theatre there and was quite willing to fall in with Jimmy's suggestion that we should sample the programme of its counterpart in Detroit. We entered the darkened auditorium rather self-consciously and sat down in the first seats we could find to watch the film. As the film ended and the lights came up, we sank down in our seats and looked around the audience. The first two rows were filled with blue naval collars, and in the centre was a distinctive head of hair; an unmistakeable chuckle and laugh when the strippers appeared and the audience began to sing their song "Take it off, take it off, cried the boys at the back!" left no room for doubt - Hymers was there. Had it not been for the support of the British Navy we realised the audience would have been as thin as the muslin brassieres worn by the strippers.

At the YMCA where we found beds, we had been told of invitations to visit various functions and homes that evening; we expressed interest and were duly collected by car and whisked away to a family party. To my surprise I found our hosts were music lovers; beside the piano was Grandma's harp, the party was in the basement but before long Grandma was playing the harp and I was playing the piano in the parlour, leaving the rest of the household below. Unfortunately some of our fellow teenage guests began to criticise the British presence in India during the journey back to the city; at the next road junction we thanked the driver and asked to be excused. As we closed the car door behind us Jimmy turned and in a quiet and very polite voice observed "You have a colour problem here, you know".

It marred what had been a very friendly and enjoyable evening and when we eventually found our own way back to the YMCA we reached the conclusion that Detroit was not worth the expense and the journey.

For my introduction to flying I was fortunate in being allocated to a steady, even-tempered Pilot Officer named Killaire and when the time arrived for my first-ever flight his calm approach and explanations guided me through my first turns, climbs and dives, leaving me with a very favourable impression of the man, an impression which was never to change. The airfield still had a thick coating of snow and the concrete apron formed our landing strip. A strong wind was blowing across the apron which meant we had to approach it sideways-on with the nose of the light Tiger Moth pointing into the wind. My apprehension increased with the buffeting as we neared the ground until I felt sure we would end up in the bank of snow. At the last moment the instructor swung the nose in line with the clear apron ahead and we bounced to a stop. In my log-book I made the entry for my first flight, it lasted 45 minutes.

In just over a week the temperature rose dramatically and the airfield was cleared of snow. The RCAF issued us all with khaki drill uniforms for wear on

137

the camp in place of our navy serge, and our naval caps became our only means of identification from the RCAF. When the field dried out sufficiently we were able to start on our landings and take-offs; most of us had never driven anything beyond a dodgem car at a funfair prior to our arrival at Goderich and the sensation of accelerating along a grass field, in control for the first time, was unforgettable. So too was the temptation to level out for landing much too early. After slightly less than eight hours' flying came my solo check with another instructor; after two or three circuits and bumps he said "Drop me off at the apron and take her round once yourself, I'll wait for you to pick me up when you come back."

As I sat in the cockpit on the edge of the field, waiting for the 'green' from the control truck, denied the reassuring presence of an instructor to yell "I have control", I felt very, very lonely. The flashes of green light startled me into action and I was bumping down the field, keeping her straight on the rudder until I began to ease the stick back gently and became airborne. The instructions were simple, like the instruments - 'needle, ball, airspeed' - they indicated if I was flying straight, was not slipping to the side and that I had enough airspeed to keep me flying. So far so good, now the down-wind check before turning for my approach and there was the 'green' flashing at me. The temptation to level off became greater and greater as the ground loomed ahead until I could not resist it any further; for what seemed like an age the plane floated on, then dropped and bounced back into the air for a short hop before it bounced again and I was down.

After another 'circuit and bump' with the instructor I was signed out for my first hour's solo flying during which I was expected to complete eight 'circuits and bumps'. Bumps was the operative word until the seventh landing; I had been given the green and was on my approach. The control truck was flashing a 'red' to the planes behind me, the field ahead was clear and then, just before I was about to touch down, I found I was being overtaken by a plane on my starboard side. Almost simultaneously when my plane hit the ground and bounced back into the air, the other plane turned steeply and crossed in front of my nose. With insufficient time to indulge in blind panic, I waited for my propeller to start tearing into the other plane and in the absence of anything better to do, opened the throttle and pulled the stick back.

In retrospect such action may seem to have been misguided because my plane did a flick-roll at about 15 feet, caught a wing tip and landed on its back.

With my head stuck through the canopy I heard all the panic sounds of ambulances and fire tenders as they raced towards me. I had however, managed to miss the other plane.

'Petrol!' I thought as I hung helplessly upside down in my straps; I could just reach the lever with my foot and turned the supply off. Since the fuel tank on a Tiger Moth is situated in the upper mid wing section it was of course below me at the time. My efforts were rather pointless.

"Don't move your head or you'll cut your throat!"

After my head had gone through the canopy, the remaining perspex had sprung back to form a very unfriendly jagged necklace, and before my head could be pulled back through, the hole had to be enlarged. One of the fire crew was attacking the perspex of the canopy with what appeared to be more enthusiasm than skill, and my throat and neck acquired more slight cuts and abrasions from his efforts than from the crash itself. One or two bruises were my only other injuries but I had to spend a day in sick bay under observation.

It was not, of course, an acceptable form of landing and my first solo resulted in the first endorsement in my log book. It read 'Stalled on landing causing aircraft to go over on its back, resulting in 'A' category crash, endorsed "Error in Judgement".

There were two flights at Goderich, and my visitors during my stay in sick bay told me the plane which had crossed my bows was from the other flight. In what was alleged to have been a 'dummy' approach the pupil was said to have 'frozen' on the controls and forced his instructor into a desperate struggle to recover control. A cloak of secrecy was thrown over the part played by the other plane and I never discovered the true story.

At such an early stage in our flying activities when everyone was full of the inevitable excitement and tension of taking to the air for the first time on their own, a crash was the fate feared by all. I became an object of considerable curiosity as I faced my next flight and, although I was not prepared to openly admit the fact, the prospect of flying again had lost most of its appeal. The alternative of a return to the North Atlantic, however, appealed far less and flying still had the edge.

Verbal and written reports had to be made which constantly reminded me of those dramatic few seconds and did nothing for my confidence despite the complete absence of any criticism of my actions. The support provided was mainly silent but unmistakable from all sides. When, after a compulsory flight check with the Flight Commander, I was told I had a natural 'feel' for the aircraft I felt a little better about things. With less than 11 hours flying I was told to take my 12 hour check flight and I realised that the instructors were doing all they could to help boost my confidence.

The moment I most dreaded had still to be faced. It arrived when P/O Killaire told me to go solo again. I collected my flying helmet and parachute and stood wrestling with my nerves inside the locker room; my thoughts turned to Polyanthus and the lads who had been lost with her. I had managed 6 months more than they had, was this to be my turn? Someone caught my arm, it was Killaire.

"Come on, boy, go out there and show 'em. You can do it. Come on and sign for the plane."

139

It was only with the greatest difficulty that I managed to walk from my locker to the desk where I signed for the plane. There seemed to be more people than usual around us yet there was much less noise and everyone was taking pains to look elsewhere. Feeling very much like a condemned man I strapped on my parachute and shuffled out with the ridiculous penguin-like gait it created by constantly banging the back of my knees.

There could be no going back, even though I was becoming more convinced that every short stride could be one of the last I would make. Even when my mind was occupied with pre-flight checks fears constantly tormented my concentration; I taxied round to await my 'green' wondering when the images of my past life would flash before my eyes - and then came the signal. I accelerated down the field and into the air.

An hour later, after one or two bumpy landings, all right side up, I returned to a welcome that surprised me; every move had been watched carefully by many of the instructors and by all of my class-mates who were not flying. Killaire, they told me, had rushed up into the control tower as soon as I had taxied out and had stood with binoculars at his eyes from the first take off to the last landing. Where quietness had reigned there was laughter, and our attention turned to the activities of the pupils who were out on the airfield as life returned to normal.

"I reckon you're our lucky omen, if you can crash on your first solo, walk away with hardly a scratch and carry on flying, what have any of us to fear?"

"That wasn't a crash, he landed upside down that's all, he doesn't know his arse from his elbow."

"Anyone who's done what he's done must have a hell of a lot of luck going for him; he can't help but bring us all luck, let's call him 'Crash' from now on. Is everyone in agreement?"

The verdict was unanimous. For the rest of my days in the Fleet Air Arm, like it or not, I was to be known by the unenviable name of Crash.

Each and everyone had his difficulties to face and overcome in those days. Ginger Hymers ran out of grass and completed one landing in the obstacle course between the airfield and Lake Huron; Freddie Farrow, an ex-air gunner, repeatedly hopped down the field like a kangaroo before he finally landed, his despairing instructor swore he would have shot him down had he not made

Canada 1944
"Lets call him 'Crash' from now on".

140

it when he did. Others never made it beyond their 12 hour check and were sent back to Moncton within the month to train as TAGs or be put on general duties.

Green, who had been in my class at St. Vincent, was really keen to become a pilot but was unable to overcome his airsickness; he managed to solo despite what must have been acute distress and every flight resulted in the appearance of a soggy brown paper bag as he left the plane. Aerobatics duly appeared in the flying training programme; they simply compounded poor Green's problems, yet he unflinching cleaned out the cockpit after each flight. His dogged determination won the admiration of instructors and pupils alike but he never conquered his disability. Finally and reluctantly he was dipped and sent home.

Steady progress had to be maintained in order to continue on the course. Those who found difficulty in meeting the targets were shown understanding and reasonable latitude in the early stages but as the 25 hour check approached we knew we would be bidding farewell to some members of our course.

For the 25 hour check we were expected to be capable of performing several aerobatics and able to cope with a forced landing. The engine would suddenly cut out and the pupil then had to carry out the forced landing drill, calling out each action as it was taken and selecting a field suitable for a landing. To stop the engine the instructor had to knock off the magneto switches or turn off the fuel which made the diagnosis of the engine failure pretty straight forward. With the switches or fuel returned to normal and the engine idling, the plane had to be put into a glide and flown so as to approach the chosen field into wind at the correct height. At about 15 to 20 feet the instructor would call "I have control" and take the plane back up before handing control over to the pupil once again.

The examiner for my 25 hour check followed the forced landing procedure according to the book until he took control. Instead of climbing away from the chosen field he landed and taxied to one corner where he turned off the engine and climbed out of the cockpit.

"Come on down," he called, "and have a cigarette."

With our backs to the fuselage and in defiance of all rules and regulations, we each smoked a cigarette in the warm afternoon sun before he told me to get back in. " Switch on", he ordered and then swung the propeller. It was so reminiscent of the attitude of the Canadian sailors I had known in Newfy, a symbolic defiance of authority and a dumb declaration of independence.

Our airborne abilities improved as we mastered loops and rolls and learned how to recover from a spin; sessions with a hood pulled over the cockpit to blot out any view of the world outside accustomed us to the art of flying on instruments. It was an essential preliminary to night flying, a prospect that increased the level of tension yet again.

Life had become a series of challenges, mountains to climb and bridges to be crossed, no sooner had we overcome one than another loomed before us. Taking off was not too bad but the art of landing could not be treated lightly during the day, how on earth would we cope with landing in darkness?.

"Get up, you lazy bastards, come on, you're night flying!"

The room filled with groans of disbelief as we awoke, startled by the din, and either sat up or rolled out of our bed.

"Come on, hurry up, Flying Officer Gordon's waiting at the flights and we all know what a bastard he can be if he's kept waiting."

Jinks had not had a happy time with his instructor. F/O Gordon possessed a quick temper and an earthy vocabulary which together kept Jinks very much on the hop, and Jinks was really hopping now. In a state of tremendous agitation he dashed down the line of beds, shaking every one as he passed.

It was one o'clock in the morning and we were not night flying.

Sleep was obviously impossible until Jinks had been silenced; most of his fellow pupils stared in disbelief, others stirred themselves into action. Jinks had the advantage of being already on his feet and mobile; he disappeared into the washroom at the end of our dormitory as we struggled to catch up with him. Round the washbowls and into the shower room, back through the toilets towards the entrance, he was a pied piper without a pipe. Our annoyance began to mount with our lack of success when he suddenly dashed through the door at the top of the fire escape and disappeared down the chute to the ground below. It was not an act any of us was prepared to follow.

We grabbed warm clothing and set out into the cold night air in hastily organised search parties. None of us had any success and after fifteen minutes of fruitless effort we returned to the dormitory.

Jinks was in his bed, fast asleep and snoring his head off.

He always disclaimed all knowledge of the event and his behaviour was regarded as a most unusual form of sleep-walking. Fortunately for him and for us, he never repeated it.

After the initial difficulties of night flying had been overcome, we had to face the challenge of navigation and flying across country. We each had a navigational aid strapped on the left thigh which enabled us to calculate the corrections to our plotted course. All we had to do was to fly on the heading we had plotted on our maps and identify landmarks as we flew over them. When one could be recognised it was possible to see, by reference to the map, how far from the required course we had travelled, providing the map had not fallen onto the floor of the cockpit by that time. The variation had then to be transferred to the navigational aid on the thigh in order for the drift and adjustment to our heading to be calculated, together with the changes in the ETA (estimated time of arrival). It will be realised that the pupil had found two hands hopelessly inadequate long before this stage had been reached and in the interests of sheer survival had retained his grip on the joystick and resorted to prayer.

Prayer usually proved to be more dependable than the navigational aids, but there were exceptions.

The cross-country route took us to Paris, easily recognised by the town water tower which had Paris emblazoned in great big letters around the bowl, then on to Kitchener where we had to land and re-fuel. It was the return journey from Kitchener where the problems arose.

Ginger Hymers became apprehensive. Nothing he could see corresponded with his map, the large regular-shaped fields all looked the same and the roads resembled identical lines on a grid. Below him a tractor could be seen crossing a great big field, heading towards some farm buildings. Ginger put the nose down, floated in nicely over the hedge and landed. By the time the startled farmer had driven up on his tractor, Ginger was out of the plane with his map and wearing an enormous smile.

"I wonder if you can help me ?" he asked courteously. "I'm afraid I'm lost; could you tell me just where I am on this map?"

Not only did he determine his exact position, he was also given a glass of milk before he took off successfully and returned to Goderich somewhat overdue.

It was yet another anecdote to add to his repertoire, the repertoire that, by this time, I knew almost as well as he did himself.

Bill Cook was less fortunate. He flew around searching for the railway line which we had been told was also our life-line if lost. The procedure was to fly along it until it reached Goderich. 'Cooky' found the line all right but turned the wrong way and eventually put down in the largest field he could find when he realised he was almost out of fuel. He eventually arrived back with his instructor who had to be taken out to recover the plane.

Wedding rings made of anything other than 9-carat gold were unobtainable in wartime Britain. With the benefit of the increase in pay following promotion to leading airman I had been

The only two members left from Aylmer course 108 J.W.V. (Ginger) Hymers and myself.

143

carefully accumulating enough cash with which to buy an 18-carat ring before I left Canada. The departure of the lads who dipped the course was a constant reminder that my own future was uncertain and so one weekend I took the bus to Kitchener along with Jimmy and bought Mary's wedding ring.

Ten weeks after arriving at Goderich, we who had survived the course so far, moved on to Aylmer for our advanced flying training.

TWENTY-FOUR

RCAF Aylmer was a much larger unit than Goderich in every respect. The airfield had a triangle formed by three double runways in place of the large grass field from which we had been flying; they served to emphasise our move from the relatively intimate atmosphere of a small unit to a more ordered and impersonal establishment.

Large hangars with heavy sliding doors faced on to vast concrete aprons and taxi strips, neat rows of single-storeyed barrack blocks and clean well-kept roads gave an immediate impression of an efficient and well-run station.

The facilities were of a high standard: a large sports hall, an assembly hall, a room for reading and study and a small outdoor swimming pool. It was a well-equipped, self-contained unit.

We arrived there at the beginning of June in sunny warm weather, set about unpacking our kit and put our swimming trunks on one side in anticipation of a quick dash across to the swimming pool.

"Do you see what I see?"

Ginger's eyes widened in disbelief, others gasped and Jinks almost drooled. Around the pool, several girls could be seen, some of them clad in two piece costumes and gorgeous tans. The station had even more attractive amenities than we had first realised, a complement of WD's., the Canadian equivalent of our WAAF's.

From the civilian point of view however Aylmer came a poor second to Goderich, the town would have been hard-pressed to qualify as a village at home in England. On our journey to the camp we had gained the impression that amenities for service personnel would be very thin on the ground and we were not mistaken. Our appreciation of the facilities on the camp was all the greater as a result.

One or two hearts had been left behind in Goderich where they remained for a few weeks; the first 48-hour pass enabled their owners to regain them. Distance, they realised, had not made the heart grow fonder.

From Tiger Moth to Harvard was a big step. In place of the light bi-plane with its basic, simple instruments in a small cockpit with ample visibility we faced the overnight adjustment to a much larger, heavier and more powerful monoplane fitted with a vast array of instruments and controls in a big deep cockpit. With a retractable undercarriage, variable pitch propeller, aileron trims and radio equipment to cope with, it was going to be quite a handful and I realised that a flick-roll at 15ft in a Harvard was likely to hurt much more than it had done in a Tiger Moth.

Wags on the course ahead of ours who were just coming to terms with the larger aircraft found great delight in telling us. "You're only allowed one fatal accident in the Harvard, after that you are taken off the course."

Our apprehension was too great for the observation to be thought in the least bit funny, nor did it boost our confidence.

All my efforts to mug up on the location and purpose of the instruments, together with all the checks to be carried out were of no avail when they were needed nor were the varied and often rude mnemonics we had found highly amusing; I was forced to rely on my new instructor to prompt every move.

Yet again we found that very few difficulties are insurmountable; the strange, confusing bank of instruments and the formidable controls proved to be straightforward and well within our capabilities. The R/T equipment kept us in touch with the ground and with each other as we put the powerful, raw, rowdy, Pratt and Whitney Wasp radial engine through its paces.

More than anything in those early days I missed my first instructor, P/O Killaire. His successor had a totally different temperament, and the relaxed relationship I had enjoyed at Goderich was missing. Each instructor had two pupils, my opposite number was Lt. Fison RN, an engineer officer, and fortunately we got on well together. There were two more engineer officers and two executive officers with us on the course, all RN, and though they lived separate lives in the officers' mess we were all equal where training was involved. My difficulties with the instructor were shared by Lt. Fison and we concluded that he was efficient but unfortunately dour and humourless. Before long we found more and more of our dual flying was with other pilots who displayed the disregard for formalities that I had come to associate with so many Canadians.

Aylmer's chief navigation instructor was an eccentric individual. The wings on his tunic were invariably obscured by the liquor permit which protruded from its top left hand pocket and probably indicated his order of priorities. One of our navigational classes took place in a twin-engined Anson and he was the pilot; as we made our calculations and adjusted our plotted course he suddenly asked:

"How many of you have flown over Niagara ?"

If one thing had been made absolutely clear it was the fact that the airspace over Niagara was out of bounds. Without waiting for an answer he announced

"We'll take ten minutes and go down there. Don't worry about your plots, I'll bring you back to this point so you can pick up where you left off."

Later in the course when we were engaged on night navigational exercises, 'Mad Mac', as he had become known, was told just before take off that his wife had given birth to a daughter. As the Harvard neared St. Thomas, Mad Mac took over control from Bill Cook who was the pupil allocated to fly with him that night. With the plane's landing light piercing the night sky he looped and rolled over St. Thomas at one o'clock in the morning for the benefit of his wife. Her views on his behaviour were never passed on to us.

Not content with his demonstration over the town, he headed out in the direction of an approaching train. Cook, who was by this time fighting a losing battle with his bowels, swore that the train came to a stop amidst a shower of sparks when the plane swooped up and over the locomotive with its landing light still on.

Despite his bouts of apparent irresponsibility, Mad Mac managed to give us all a good grounding in practical navigation.

Formation flying was introduced into the programme; the sky became a smaller place as we grinned at each other, separated by just a few yards. Formation flying could only be performed under the supervision of an instructor and one of them often demonstrated his release of control by holding up his joystick which, in the rear cockpit, was removable. He would then use it as a mock gun aimed at anyone who was not flying as well as he thought fit. It was

The Harvard
"We grinned at each other, separated by just a few yards."

not unknown for him to use it as a weapon to hit the pupil in the cockpit in front of him on the head.

Our training on instrument and blind flying was backed up by sessions in the

147

Link Trainer, a replica of an aircraft cockpit housed in a rather absurd mock aircraft perched on a plinth and linked to a control desk by an umbilical cable. All the actions and reactions of the pilot in the trainer were conveyed down the cable to a peculiar piece of equipment perched on the glass top of the desk. It moved around, crab-like, leaving a trail of red ink behind. An instructor issued orders through an intercom and monitored every movement.

It was a fine piece of equipment which saved a tremendous amount of time and expense, the pilot was enclosed in the dark cockpit by a canopy or hood, cut off from the outside world apart from the intercom. Everything he did produced the same result as it would in the air apart from one important ingredient, the adrenalin of actual flight.

The hours spent in the Link Trainer were probably more valuable than we recognised at the time; they were dull and boring, sometimes soporific. A group of us were waiting to change over when one of the mock planes began to move erratically before it came to rest at a grotesque angle on the plinth. The hood moved slowly upwards to reveal the face of Freddie Farrow, rubbing his eyes and blinking as he tried to adjust to the bright light.

"Are there any submariners about?" he asked, "My altimeter's reading 500 ft below sea level. I seem to have spun in."

Grinning, he sheepishly added "I'd better close the hood before the cockpit gets flooded."

Freddie got away with that incident but sadly he was unable to master the art of flying the faster Harvard at night and was dipped. He returned to his former duties as an air gunner and we lost a popular member of the course. Freddie always claimed he was a TAG before Pontius was a pilot.

The station, or camp as it was often called, had a very positive approach to all aspects of life. The role of physical fitness in a successful training programme was fully recognised and most forms of spontaneous activity were encouraged and supported more than the organised sessions of PT. Occasional games of soccer were played between the courses and some of us played a game of softball from time to time. Coaching was freely given by the PTI's during off-duty hours, perspiring would-be gymnasts worked out on high bars or other equipment, while hopeful athletes trained out on the field beyond the swimming pool where Romeo, the PTI who specialised in swimming, demonstrated the techniques of springboard diving. In the sports hall queues formed for games of badminton.

At the end of the counter in the mess hall a refrigerated, stainless steel container provided a constant source of cool fresh milk. The food was always plentiful and, for a service establishment, of a high standard. It was appreciated by all but the most fastidious on our course.

Bronzed by the sun, our bodies became fitter by the day and the better we felt, the better we looked. After the cramped, unhealthy conditions, the deprivations and often the downright squalor of a corvette's fo'c'sle with its abysmal standard of food, Aylmer was beyond my wildest dreams.

On the weekly parades which involved the whole camp, we became more aware of our increasing fitness. Our standard of drill had attracted favourable comments from our Master at Arms, C.P.O. Beasley, not to mention the envy of his counterpart, the Station Warrant Officer. It was enough to pump up our pride, with the greater pride came tighter discipline which in turn made for a happy course. Not one case of indiscipline by anyone on our course had to be dealt with by the authorities at Aylmer.

Not many bathers attempted the dives demonstrated by Romeo at the pool. One of the girls, who was something of a tomboy, believed in having a go at anything to do with swimming; she was working on a backward somersault off the springboard when the accident happened. Unfortunately she had failed to propel her body far enough out into the pool before she came out of the somersault; as her face came down it met the end of the board as it came up. She was carried to the sick bay, her white two piece costume spattered with blood, and no one showed any interest in the springboard for quite a while afterwards.

"Do you fancy a walk up to the WD's sick bay Crash?"

Jimmy Gregson's question took me by surprise.

"I've heard 'Sparksy' has lost part of her tongue, I just thought it would do no harm to ask how she's going on."

Jimmy had helped to get Evelyn Sparks out of the pool and to sick bay following her accident; although she was frequently at the pool it was doubtful if either of us had spoken to her before.

Our enquiry was warmly received by the orderly at the entrance to the ward. Through the doorway Evelyn could be seen along with several other patients, all of them were sitting up in bed.

"She's coming along just fine; why don't you boys go in there and say 'Hi'. None of you girls mind Sparks having two sailors call on her, do you?"

"Only if she doesn't keep them to herself, could I have the taller one for 5 minutes?"

Her tongue was still badly swollen but intact; it seriously restricted Sparksy's contribution to the conversation and the length of our visit.

Stan Austin was a late entry into the Navy; although short on service experience he was one of the oldest members of the course. As a married man he held strong views on relationships with the opposite sex.

"You should be ashamed of yourselves." he declared when he heard we had actually been inside the WD's sick bay.

"You're a married man Gregson, and you're engaged and almost married, Crash; neither of you has any business to be in female quarters."

Taken aback by such an unexpected outburst I was wondering how to reply when Jimmy gave me a nudge.

"We've had an incredible ten minutes, Stan," answered Jimmy, "Crash took

149

one side of the ward and I took the other. We enjoyed ourselves and all the girls were contented and ever so grateful."

Archie Brunton stared at us in amazement and Jinks rolled the plate of false teeth around inside his open mouth as his imagination took over.

"Did you actually have some slap and tickle in the ward?" they asked.

Even Ginger, who was already having difficulty sorting out the merits and affections of two WDs, showed signs of envy.

Jimmy's time at Aylmer came to an end shortly afterwards. Given more time he would have eventually got his wings but there was a tight schedule to be observed and Jimmy's progress had been falling behind. We walked up from the barrack room together, carrying his kit between us, and loaded it on the truck that was waiting to take him to the station at St.Thomas. He went back to his old duties as an AB and presumably lost his 'hook' together with the pay of a leading airman. We had enjoyed our brief friendship and recognised that we were about to follow different paths; I never saw or heard of him again.

Following Jimmy's departure I often spent a part of the evening in the assembly hall when it was not in use; it housed a piano and a harmonium which I had been called upon to play once or twice for the Sunday services. A WD from Vancouver came along too and to avoid one of us being denied the chance to play one of the instruments we played duets together. It was only when we met at the station dance that I realised she regarded me as her 'boy' and, although she was a very nice girl, I had no intention of forming a relationship of the kind she had in mind.

Sparksy, looking very fit and just back from sick leave, was my saviour. After I had one or two dances with Evelyn my musical partner took the hint and the danger passed; she never appeared in the assembly hall to play duets again and I found myself playing badminton with Sparksy and her friends.

On the evening of 'D' Day the whole camp was ordered to parade in the sports hall. Garbled reports had begun to circulate before we assembled for the C.O.'s address and the brief details he was able to supply clearly excited many and disappointed others who wished they could have been there.

The fleet entries displayed less excitement than the rest of the camp that evening, we were thankful to be out of the mess but sympathetic towards those who were involved. There was too, a feeling that our temporary domicile in Canada had allowed us to escape more urgent responsibilities in Europe, and as I thought of those whose war had ended that day, the memory of Polyanthus would not leave me.

Those of us who had spent some time on active service before starting flying training had an unusual relationship with our instructors, who, during the occasional idle moments, would question their pupils on the realities of fighting a war which seemed so strangely remote from Aylmer. They were eager to learn about war - we were trying to forget it.

With P/O Killaire the point had been reached where I found it possible to speak to him about my time at sea in general terms, but the enormous gulf between the conditions on a RCAF camp in Western Ontario and those on a corvette out on the cold grey wastes of the North Atlantic was far too great for me to describe adequately.

'Sandy' Harris was 30 and being the oldest member of our course was appointed class leader; he had just squeezed into the Navy for pilot training and must have been on the maximum age limit at the time he joined St. Vincent. The traditions of the Navy did not appeal to Sandy who had his own versions of the various 'pipes'. Our mornings began with his invitation to "Elevate and phosphoresce!" rather than "Rise and shine!" and Sandy preferred "Bother your deplorable lack of good fortune, my friend." to the more customary and crude comment on the state of one's luck.

In the early days at Aylmer, when we were all feeling demoralised by the apparent complexity of the Harvard, Sandy claimed he had reduced his instructor to a state of hysteria before he was half-way through his cockpit check.

"Before I eventually concluded the check he had expressed considerable doubts as to the morals and marital status of my parents."

Charlie Kelsall, a very serious and diligent lad, looked up from his book.

"That's nothing" he said, "My instructor swore at me."

"One of the instructors has come back without his pupil!"

Our first indication of the incident was a most unsatisfactory message from one of the groundcrews. An anxious time followed as we tried to ascertain more information, our enquiries eventually revealed that the pupil was Jinks and that he was on his way back to the camp by car. His return was awaited with growing curiosity.

"The plane started to do daft things," Jinks told us. "The instructor was playing hell with me and took control, then he went quiet for a while. 'Right, Jinks' he said 'Since you are having trouble with your flying we'll go through your parachute drill. Only this time I want you to perform the functions as you call them out'."

Jinks paused, he was having difficulty in believing what had followed.

"Next thing I knew I had released the safety harness and was out on the wing at 3,000 ft.; the wing dipped and I was falling. I pulled the cord and floated down on my 'chute."

Just as we had found previously when there was a significant incident, no one was prepared to enlighten the pupil pilots. There was no doubt that the rudder control cables had parted and that the instructor had ordered Jinks out because he could not be sure of the total extent of the problem. It was alleged that the cables had been cut through, leaving only a few strands to provide control before the plane took off. The point and purpose of any such sabotage

151

was difficult to understand; it was totally out of context at Aylmer.

Jinks rarely referred to the experience again.

Those of us who had been asked to look up relatives or friends of friends at home used our 48-hour passes in meeting those obligations. I had two, one in Toronto and one in Hamilton; when they had been met I visited Port Stanley on the shore of Lake Erie. It was a holiday spot for Western Ontario and Detroit and boasted a dance hall which attracted the big name bands from the States. Most of the houses offered beds at prices that were within our means, the days were spent on the beach or in the lake, the evenings dancing or simply enjoying the music.

Jones never missed the opportunity to travel as far as possible on every 48-hour pass. He had a compulsive obsession to undertake marathon journeys following his experience during a weekend in Detroit. Towards the end of the morning service in the church Jones had chosen to attend, the minister invited any strangers in the congregation to stand up, give their names and say where they were from. Jones found himself in a unique position, an English sailor with no competition to detract from the novelty of his presence. In the foyer after the service, many of the hands that were held out to him contained money. Jones found that his take was running the offertory a close second and he also had several invitations to Sunday lunch.

Most of the lads had turned in when Jones returned on the Sunday night at the end of his 48-hour pass and I was not pleased when, after the disturbance of his getting into the bunk above mine, his head appeared over the edge.

"I've been all the way to Chicago and back since Friday night," he whispered. "Hitch-hiked there and went to church this morning; did quite well, it was a pity I had to take the train back, I needed too much time to risk hitching. It could be worse though, I still have $2.35 more than I had when I left here on Friday."

"Go to sleep, Jones" I told him. "Flying a Harvard is as near as you're ever likely to get to heaven."

From time to time there were heavy thunderstorms when clouds would build up into giant cauliflowers, filling the vast blue skies with white cotton-wool after the rain had gone. Flying then took on another dimension and fascination as we chased each other in and out of canyons flanked on each side by restless mountainsides of clouds that rolled and curled around the plane when we accidentally flew into them. And when the clouds flattened out the sun beat down on the blanket they formed below, reflected back up and roasted us in our cockpits as we gained ever more experience in the art of flying.

Night flying was in complete contrast. Suspended in the depths of darkness with the fluorescent dials of the instruments casting a dim green haze around the cockpit I was cocooned in my own little world, free of the countless distractions of the day. Detached from the world sleeping below, I experienced a unique sense of peace, and yet on the nights when I could see the Plough, my thoughts would go out to Mary and she would unknowingly share my solitude.

With the departure of each successive course a batch of RCAF trainee air engineers moved in to take its place and the naval presence at Aylmer diminished. The day finally arrived when the penultimate pilots' course moved out from the other end of our barrack hut and we were the last representatives of the Royal Navy left on the camp.

Some time before this Ginger had eventually resolved his problem of taking out one girl while being pursued by another. His decision had not proved to be too difficult once he discovered that the one who worked in the administration office typed out the exam papers; it was no contest as far as the other girl was concerned. When Ginger confided his news to Jinks and Brunton they were beside themselves with glee and we all became aware of Ginger's hopes. But not even Ginger's charms could subvert her loyalties when he put them to the test.

An intensity of purpose gripped us as the final ground school examinations approached, there was very little light-hearted banter around as we applied ourselves to serious study. After the exams the last two weeks of the course were spent at the reserve airfield at St. Thomas where we practiced air-to-air gunnery and during this time our papers were marked and final assessments made.

The gunnery course was widely regarded as a waste of time because the guns fitted to the aircraft were old, badly calibrated and inaccurate. A drogue was towed over Lake Erie by a Lysander and was dropped on to the airfield after each series of attacks to be examined for bullet holes. Bullets with coloured tips were used, each aircraft having its own colour so that hits on the target could be allocated correctly. In the two weeks not one of us had managed to record a single hit on the target and so, on my last flight in Canada, I was determined to register a score; I would fly much closer to the drogue than our orders permitted.

At a distance of about 10/12 yards I peeled off from the attack and was almost immediately subjected to a tirade from the airgunner of the Lysander, blasting me over the R/T for reckless and dangerous flying. As I levelled out I was astounded to find the drogue draped over my port wing like a serviette over a waiter's arm. The air gunner in the Lysander had panicked and released the drogue because he thought I was about to fly into the tow wire. With no target to pursue, I turned and flew along the edge of the lake above Port Stanley feeling like a small boy who has just kicked a ball into a garden and is unsure if it will be returned. Of one thing I was going to be certain, this drogue would have some of my bullet holes in it. I fired a short burst from the gun which was covered by the drogue, and turned towards St. Thomas; the drogue began to move over the wing as the plane banked over and suddenly it was gone. Below me, the proof of my marksmanship floated down and disappeared into the lake.

My appearance before the gunnery officer did not last long and his reprimand was very tongue-in-cheek. I was just sorry I had been unable to keep the drogue

153

on the wing to bring back as a souvenir.

The lads all thought I had plucked the drogue off with my wing; I saw no point in telling them that it had hit me.

During our last week Aylmer did us proud. The RCAF held a station dance in our honour; a special dispensation allowed us to join the WD's in their canteen for a barn dance and the Canadian lads shared their beer ration with us before the dance.

A Canadian trainee air engineer walked over and offered a bottle to me.

"I see you're wearing the '39/43 Star, where did you serve."

"On a corvette with Newfoundland Escort Force", I answered.

"So did I; I've re-mustered from the Navy," he told me. "I was on the Morden, what was your ship?"

"Polyanthus, we sailed with Morden quite often."

He became enthusiastic. "Gee, just imagine that; when did you leave her?"

When I said it was in September '43 his expression changed to one of suspicion,

"But she was sunk in September, I know because we were right behind her, there was one hell of an explosion and a great ball of fire; when it cleared there was nothing left, no one could have survived."

When he heard how I had left Polyanthus he shook his head and my hand.

"Boy! how lucky can you get?, you must be the luckiest guy on this whole camp."

Many years were to pass before I discovered that the meeting had taken place exactly one year to the day after Polyanthus had been sunk.

Ontario was a 'dry' state in 1944; a liquor permit which was only granted to persons who were over 21 years of age was needed in order to purchase spirits. Early on in our training everyone who qualified obtained a permit and purchased his allowance of liquor each month; the cost was reimbursed by money from a common pool to which everyone contributed. All the bottles were handed over, unopened, to Lt. Fison to be held in readiness for our last night and the Wings Party. When the day of the party finally arrived he found himself in charge of a considerable stock.

The big event was held in the Grand Central Hotel in St. Thomas; it set out to be a very formal occasion, the senior officers from the camp were invited as our guests and we had printed menus, toasts and speeches suitable for an all-male gathering. The dinner itself was a success, not quite so grand as the name of the hotel would suggest perhaps, but we all enjoyed the food and the wine for the toasts, not to mention being waited upon. A short break allowed the staff to clear the tables and Lt. Fison to set up his bar in the bottom right hand corner of the room. We then got down to the serious business of 'enjoying' ourselves.

Throughout the course we had all been pretty abstemious, for one thing the saloons where we could obtain beer outside the camp were rather unattractive spots, the beer on the camp was rationed and Fison had all the hard booze locked away. Above all, we were far too intent on getting through the course. By the night of the Wings Party we were somewhat out of practice and, in the case of many of the younger lads, uninitiated. The mixture of wines for the toasts had released any lingering inhibitions and for the first hour Lt.s' Fison and Wright had a very hard time of it as they struggled to satisfy the thirst of everyone else.

Almost immediately I was led to the piano and instructed to play first one and then another of the fund of naval ditties and bawdy ballads we had picked up during our service. We, who had the broader service experience, contributed many versions of popular songs that were completely new to our Canadian guests and it became very difficult for me to escape from the keyboard in order to get myself a drink. After a couple of absences, the medical and dental officers became my personal stewards and ensured that my glass, on the lid of the piano, was never empty.

The time came when even the medical officer realised I simply had to 'go' again; I hurried, with a certain amount of difficulty, across a floor that was behaving very much like the deck of a corvette - or so it seemed to me - out through the door and up the stairs. The backside of a bent figure was coming down the stairs ahead of a slowly unwinding toilet roll - it was Ginger. Despite my pressing urgency I was able to follow the trail of toilet paper to its source, a bedroom door.

When I returned feeling more comfortable but just as unsteady the party had clearly lost a great deal of its formality; many inhibitions had been cast aside along with wits and senses. Here and there an odd body was draped over a chair or crumpled up on the floor, the closed eyes and open mouth of its owner testifying to his total oblivion. Others, wearing wide vacant grins, demonstrated their friendship by hanging around the shoulder nearest to them. Ginger was not hard to find,

"What's all this business with the toilet roll about then?" I mumbled in his ear. I found my arm had strangely found its way on to his shoulder.

Two eyes that matched the colour of his hair blinked and focused with difficulty on my face. Ginger began to giggle as he tried to put his mouth near my ear and almost ended up kissing me.

"I put the end of that 'bumff' under the door of a lovely, she gave me a great big smile as she went into the room, I'm just going to finish this drink and then I shall go and wish her good night." The chuckle that followed almost doubled him up but suddenly stopped as his eyes opened in disbelief.

"The rotten swine!" I followed his arm as he pointed through the open door. At the foot of the staircase the hotel manager was gathering up the last part of the toilet roll in his arms.

"Where the hell have you been Crash, let's have some more music; I've put a full bottle of rum on the piano for your use only so you can just keep right on playing without any more interruptions. Let's have that one about Rosie O'Neill again, come on lads, altogether - 'Rosie O'Neill had a bike with one wheel'."

The Medical Officer had been joined by his CO and they were both well on their way to enjoying their night out. There was no escape for the pianist.

Time lost all meaning, I wondered who had drunk the rum as I left the piano and staggered down to the bus that was waiting to take us back to camp; it took a long time to fill up. A very sad procession of acting leading airmen stumbled, staggered and sometimes crawled as they made their way out of the hotel and into the bus. A few collapsed into their seats and began to snore, others groaned and some continued to sing. Once the bus moved off, stomachs were stirred into revolt. For a celebration we had gone badly wrong - a sorrier, sadder lot would have been hard to find.

Three steps led up to the barrack room door, they presented a tremendous challenge, a challenge that almost proved too much as I found myself leaning backwards on the top step; at the third attempt, avoiding those who had fallen by the wayside, I made it.

Some time later I saw Hammond lying on his bed sound asleep and fully dressed, still wearing his cap. 'Better get undressed myself' I thought and found that I was. My uniform correctly folded, the trousers with seven neat folds, one for every ocean, was lying where it should be - at the head of the bed. It was morning - the morning of the Wings Parade and the last one I would spend at Aylmer.

My route to the washroom was an obstacle course over bodies lying on the floor beside beds that had not been slept in and through uniforms strewn around in untidy heaps. Naked forms in the shower room were slowly coming to life following a prolonged effort to achieve sobriety.

I returned to find several sad cases still in bed. Jimmy Jarvis, the ex-air gunner who had an 'oppo' in every ship or port, moaned as I passed by.

"My mouth tastes like a three-badge stoker's armpit."

Sandy Harris was not in a mood to indulge in his verbal fantasies and was finding the responsibility of getting everyone up and ready for the parade a daunting one. Jarvis was proving difficult to budge and was ignoring Sandy's pleas for him to leave his bed. In desperation Sandy grabbed the stirrup pump and bucket and stuck the nozzle into Jarvis's bed.

"If you don't get out of there I'll use this" simply resulted in more groans. Sandy had more than enough problems of his own without Jarvis - he pumped vigorously. The realisation that he now had a soggy mattress and bedding to hand in to the stores produced an immediate response from the hitherto immobile Jarvis; the girls in the stores would draw only one conclusion on the morning after the Wings Party. He began to sober up very quickly.

Those who were capable of making the journey walked slowly up to the food hall supporting others who were unable to manage it on their own. The plates of bacon and eggs were not greatly appreciated; Jinks in particular was so overcome by the sight of his that he fell face down into a soft-yolked egg. We cleaned him up and took him to the sick bay where an amused but understanding attendant produced a bottle of tablets, took a look at us all and handed us two each.

To the general amusement of the rest of the camp we struggled through the few remaining duties we had to perform, handing in bedding and the equipment issued to us by the RCAF and collecting our leave passes and travel warrants. As we gradually sobered up we became aware of Chiefy Beasley's presence; like a good shepherd he ensured that we completed our tasks and kept to our timetable. When the time came for us to line up for the final march to the parade ground he fussed around straightening our collars and caps and brushing our uniforms.

"You're like a bloody pregnant hen, Chief," PO Jack told him.

"Aye and you're my last brood of chicks," he replied.

To mark the passing out of the last naval pilots' course the RCAF band came to Aylmer. There was a short discussion between the Drum Major and our Chief before the band struck up 'Wings over the Navy'. Our pace as we marched on to the parade ground was not quick, nor was it slow, it was more that of a stroll. But our standards had been firmly established and it was an extremely smart squad that took up its place of honour before the rest of the camp - we simply took a little more time over our brief moment of glory.

We had made it! With our wings came promotion to acting petty officer and a rise in pay but there was no time for sewing new badges on our sleeves. All the energy we could muster was required to gather our kit and load it on to the truck which was waiting to take us to St. Thomas. Chiefy Beasley lifted the tailboard and pushed in the pins which secured it, then stepped back and looked up at us all - the Master at Arms is rarely a popular figure in the Navy but he was one of the good ones, that rare breed of men who represent the best of naval traditions and discipline. No one spoke, for a timeless moment no one moved; unable to express our feelings, we gazed back at him and took our last look at the camp. Hung over by the aftermath of the night before we became increasingly sentimental and I recalled the warning the Chief had issued on our arrival at Aylmer.

"The Aussies were here before the Navy arrived and they left some dirty linen - you'll leave here with clean sheets or I'll know the reason why. You're the last naval course that is planned for Aylmer so see to it that you're the best course they've ever had."

I glanced round at the solemn faces of my companions and suddenly realised how fortunate I had been to be part of Course 108, Aylmer's last pilots' course, for they were the best bunch of lads anyone could wish for. They had tried to come up to the Chief's expectations and as I looked down into his upturned face

157

I knew that he was proud of them.

A quiet "Thank you, Chief." broke the spell and we all chorused "Yes - thanks for everything, Chief."

As the truck moved off we sang "For he's a jolly good fellow" and CPO Beasley, Master at Arms - our 'Jaunty' - raised his arm tentatively in acknowledgement.

Then he brought out his handkerchief and blew his nose - hard and long.

TWENTY-FIVE

The Wings Party taught me that rum should not be drunk in large quantities: its strong and distinctive flavour is remarkably tenacious and stays with you for a very long time.

Aylmer provided us with a travel warrant for the journey to Moncton and a leave pass covering the next ten days; where and how we spent our leave was up to us. We made our way to London from St. Thomas that evening and by the time I had reached Toronto on the following day I was heartily sick of the everlasting flavour of rum, there was no escape from it; everything I ate or drank produced an immediate reminder of the Wings Party.

Our exalted rank of petty officer brought a welcome increase in pay; we bought presents for our families and loved ones and overlooked the fact that we also had to eat and sleep for the next nine days. The travel warrant would only take care of the last day's and night's accommodation and food.

Toronto presented no problem, the YMCA provided bed and food at reasonable prices and the stores offered a wide variety of goods that were unobtainable in Britain and therefore irresistible as presents. Two days in Toronto were enough to persuade me to move on before the money ran out altogether, it was disappearing much more quickly than the taste of rum.

Bill Cook had come to the same conclusion and together we made use of our warrants and travelled to Montreal where we bumped into two of our class who had gone on ahead; they welcomed us with open arms.

"This is a hell of a place to get a bed," they told us. "We've got a room with two double beds from an English bloke, he charges $6 a night for the room but doesn't mind how many sleep in it; how about sharing with us?"

The state of our finances assured our agreement.

It was in Montreal that the torturous rum from the Wings Party finally left me with an improved appetite to be satisfied from an impoverished purse. A service canteen was my saviour, its Spanish omelettes were a great bargain and became my staple diet for the rest of my stay.

Even in a large city such as Montreal we constantly encountered our former

159

classmates and although we were all hard pressed for cash some of them bought a pair of miniature boxing gloves and presented them to me. 'Jock' Hamilton had borrowed the shop owner's branding tool and inscribed them 'Crash, Montreal 1944'.

"You've brought us all luck throughout the whole of the course Crash, we want you to have these as a memento. We hope they will bring you luck in the future."

When Saturday night arrived, four petty officer pilots of the Royal Navy were wandering along Montreal's waterfront, almost cleaned out of cash and wondering how to pass the time until they could catch the Moncton train on the following morning. A couple of passing policemen stopped for a chat and on hearing of our problem suggested that the weekly dance at the nearby YWCA could be the answer to our problems.

"Admission's only 50 cents for servicemen and they give you a cup of coffee and a cookie."

It was a good dance and I thoroughly enjoyed the evening until the girl I had been dancing with said at coffee time, "I'd rather have a coke if you don't mind"; my cash reserves dropped to an all time low of 2 cents.

The whole class had an impromptu reunion at Montreal station where we caught the last train that would get us to Moncton before our leave ran out. Almost everyone was in the same state - flat broke; few days can have been more eagerly awaited than our first pay day after our arrival in Moncton.

We waited with impatience for the draft that would take us back home to Britain. Canada no longer had anything to offer and we were anxious to get home to display our new wings. The camp at Moncton was called upon to house and process vast numbers of men who were about to start their flying training or had just finished it, mainly Air Force personnel; we in the Navy felt rather like paying guests - not really where we belonged.

It was the fall in the Maritime Provinces and the local farmers were delighted at the chance of labour to pick their crops. At roll call in one of the large sheds each morning absentees' names brought forth loud shouts of "Apple picking!". We were never sent out on these duties but we often contemplated the opportunities for a good 'skive' that they presented as we faced the round of medical checks and inoculations that were the accepted routine of a transit camp. Our arms and our medical cards had more holes punched in them and we lined up with about two hundred others in the assembly shed for a 'short arm inspection'; successive lines of men dropped their pants and stood with them around their ankles until the MO gave permission for them to be pulled up again.

When our draft came we boarded a train for the short journey to Halifax; there we embarked on the Mauretania for Liverpool. Unlike the journey out to New York our return was aboard a ship packed with soldiers and airmen and we were relegated to a small area on a deck below the water-line where we had to sling hammocks. Many egos were badly bruised when newly-promoted naval petty officers discovered they had been allocated accommodation inferior to that of many airmen and soldiers of lower rank. Very few of our party had slept in a hammock and I was kept very busy helping all those who had not; much had happened since my first struggles with a hammock at Liverpool Destroyer Depot.

Eating arrangements suffered because of the congestion, the dining areas were in constant use, as one batch cleared the deck another followed almost immediately. Meals were restricted to two a day, breakfast and evening meal, with boiled frankfurter sausages appearing at almost every one. Groans and moans about the food and the accommodation provided an opportunity to let off steam; and I suddenly realised, as I joined in, how my own standards and expectations had changed; the conditions were still far superior to anything I had known on board Polyanthus.

Mauretania docked alongside the west wall of Gladstone Dock in the berth where I had once gathered oranges from the Union Castle boat. All the rails of the upper decks were lined with servicemen; for most of the Canadian soldiers this was their first sight of England. On the dockside an ambulance waited with two nurses standing at its side; their presence attracted whistles and requests for 'dates' from the soldiers who, aware of the rationing system and shortage of chocolate, showered them with gifts of Hershey bars and gum. The chocolate bars had hardly hit the dock before a horde of dockers swept out of the shed to scramble for all they could pick up. One of the nurses was knocked to the ground in the rush, the other was flattened against the side of the ambulance.

These were the same men, the brothers, fathers and sons of the mateys who had invaded Polyanthus and her sister ships demanding 'duty frees'.

Many of the rabbits I had gathered for my return to England were in preparation for the wedding that Mary and I were planning in the future, things that we would be unable to buy in Britain. I had a large box of cigars which was rapidly becoming an embarrassment; as a ship's postie I had the custom's procedure pretty well sewn up but this was going to be something altogether different. The customs men had come on board and established themselves in the assembly area; they were dealing with the men from each deck in turn. The duty on a box of cigars would be more than I had in cash and the possibility of losing my leave if I were found trying to smuggle it out was too great. An enforced sale leaves no room for negotiation - Ginger became the owner of a fine box of cigars for a pittance.

The ship gradually emptied and the Customs men put away their papers and closed their attache cases. When we finally disembarked we were put straight on to a special train and told we would have to clear Customs at our destination - a Royal Navy Depot at Bootle Station - way up in the wilds of Cumberland. The possibility of a Customs check in such a remote spot seemed highly unlikely

161

and Ginger's box of cigars became a greater bargain than ever.

"I will call out a number of names, if yours is one of them you will fall out and march over to the right. You will then form a squad where indicated by the Chief Petty Officer who is over there."

No time had been wasted after we had arrived at Bootle. A medical check had been followed by individual appearances before a Commissioning Board. As far as I was concerned the Board was a formality; when I made my request for training to the Captain of Polyanthus I had specifically stated 'for Petty Officer Pilot.' It was hardly likely that I would be seriously considered for a commission.

Now we were on the parade when we were to learn our future rank and I felt none of the excitement and anxiety that gripped most of the others. My destiny had never been in doubt from the very start. As the names were called and the class was divided into two squads I had difficulty in deciding which squad was which; I was even more puzzled when no more names were called and I glanced at those who remained with me, many of whom I would have considered certain for commissioned rank.

"Move to the left in threes, left turn, quick march," and we were away into the camp assembly hall-cum-theatre. On each chair in the front two rows was a book.

"File into the first two rows, face the front and remain standing at ease."

The CO appeared and bounded up on to the platform as we were called to attention.

"Pick up the book from the chair behind you, hold it in your left hand and raise your right hand..... Repeat after me."

It was only then that I realised I was swearing allegiance to the King.

"You have just been sworn in as officers in his Majesty's Navy, please be seated, gentlemen."

Our programme for the next few weeks was then outlined and we were told the type of training to which we had been assigned. It was emphasised that the selection process had been thorough and had involved a deep and searching analysis of our aptitude, ability and potential; it resulted in the three oldest members of the course being assigned to second line (non-combatant) flying and the youngest to fighters with the remainder assigned to TBRs (torpedo / bomber/reconnaissance). The proceedings were concluded with a short lecture on the conduct and behaviour expected of an officer and the steps to be taken with regard to the purchase of uniforms and equipment.

We emerged from the theatre and glanced around with uncertain smiles on our lips as we struggled with our private thoughts and reactions.

"So you're on TBRs too," I said to Ginger. "I had hoped to shake you off my tail."

Ginger assumed a distressed expression. "Obviously they didn't believe me when I told them of all your undesirable qualities - whatever is the Navy coming to when types like you become officers?"

The 'man from Gieves', the naval tailors, was ready and waiting for us with his tape measure and order pad and laid claim to a large part of our officers' uniform allowance within minutes of our becoming entitled to it. We were each issued with a form which notified anyone it might concern that we held commissioned rank and could be supplied with uniform. It only remained for us to be given our railway warrants and leave passes.

By the middle of the afternoon we were on our way home, there was no sign of a customs officer and no one was in the least bit interested in what we had in our cases as we passed through the gates.

Ginger had a box of cigars, a commission and a very big grin.

TWENTY-SIX

I arrived home with my cherished wings on my sleeve and a great desire to show them off. Unfortunately the opportunity to display all my finery and elevated status had to wait until I received my new uniform; I was no longer a petty officer and so I was forced to resort to my civilian clothes for the first few days of my leave.

Gieves were supplying my Number One (vicuna) uniform and greatcoat but the day after my return home I ordered my working (serge) uniform in Bradford. O.S. Wain were the military tailors there and received the majority of their orders from Army and Air Force personnel; I was measured in the company of a dummy clothed in an Army uniform complete with Sam Browne belt. My mind went back to the time, just over a year before, when I had stood facing just such a uniform and had been subjected to the ridiculous tantrum of its wearer. I vowed never to become so obsessed with my new rank of (Temporary/Acting/ Probationary) Sub.Lieutenant (A) RNVR

When the parcel arrived from Gieves, I examined the contents carefully before putting them on to admire the result. It was not until I was about to show myself to the world at large that I became uncomfortable and self-conscious; for a short while I was the one taking evasive action when I spotted another serviceman in the vicinity. My embarrassment was short-lived, I met Bill Cook who had just received his midshipman's uniform and together we strolled around Bradford, returning with assumed nonchalance, the salutes we were given.

St. Luke's Hospital found itself caught up in the aftermath of 'D' Day; as the offensive moved forward through France the wounded were sent back to Britain for treatment and St. Luke's received its quota of Allied soldiers; it also received enemy wounded from the field hospitals which had been over-run. Mary was one of the nurses assigned to the care of the casualties.

It was a time of considerable pressure for the nurses when a hospital train arrived. Every patient had to be examined for the course of treatment required and a priority list for surgery drawn up; the most urgent cases had then to be prepared for theatre and treatment given to the less urgent cases before their even more unfortunate companions returned to the ward.

We kept our fingers crossed and hoped that there would be no more hospital trains during my leave.

Nurses were rather like sailors during that time - greatly appreciated when they were needed and then forgotten just as quickly. Their monthly pay was usually the equivalent of the normal weekly pay of the workers in the factories and offices who were engaged on 'war work' and who held passes entitling them to priority travel on the buses at peak times. Nurses had no such passes nor did they wear their uniform when off-duty; all too often Mary found herself unable to get a place aboard the bus to take her home or to meet me because all the seats and standing room had been taken by the 'workers'.

Comparisons between the German and Allied wounded who were housed in adjoining wards simply brought home to the nurses the futility of war. The Germans had received inferior medical attention and treatment and some were suffering from gangrene, often very severe and requiring immediate amputations on arrival. A large proportion were young and generally undernourished; every scrap of food they were given they devoured eagerly without complaint, unlike some of the Allied wounded who did not always greet the food with enthusiasm.

It was the insignificance of the differences however that stood out; they were all men and boys with families and loved ones, with hopes and aspirations, who cried for their mothers as they suffered the pain of separation along with the pain from their wounds.

On one of Mary's spells off-duty Bill Cook and his girl friend shared afternoon tea with us in Collinson's cafe; Bill was only too happy to recall the event that had earned me the name of Crash. Mary listened to the story quietly and intently and I sensed her discomfort. The prophecy made after the reading of the tea-leaves, and her conviction that she would not see me again when I had left for Canada, could not be ignored but she was afraid to tell me of the prophecy then, or at any time until I had ceased flying.

The men who returned to Bootle were no longer quite the same as before. The course had now been split up in too many ways, some were still petty officers and others had stepped over the demarcation line to become officers; added to this was the split between fighter courses, the TBR courses and the men who were destined for second line duties. Course 108 from Aylmer was integrated with pilots from other courses, men who had trained at Kingston or on earlier courses at Aylmer.

Lt. Fison overheard some gossip concerning my matrimonial plans; with great enthusiasm he announced his intention of loaning me his full dress uniform, complete with sword, for the wedding.

"I had to wear all the trimmings for my wedding so I'm damned sure you will

165

do the same if I'm anywhere near when it takes place."

My relationship with Fison had always been excellent on the rating/officer basis but I found the adjustment to an equal footing difficult to overcome. To his great amusement I found myself constantly addressing him and his fellow RN officers from our course with an automatic 'Sir'. They had all proved to be first-class officers who were worthy of respect, I might not have found the 'Sir' rising as readily to my lips had they been otherwise.

Before embarking on our conversion courses to operational aircraft we were sent on a refresher course on Harvards that was intended to brush up our flying following our lay-off, and help us adjust to the flying conditions in Britain. Some of us were sent for a week to RAF Errol near Dundee where we were divided into two parts, those pilots who were destined for training on fighter aircraft stayed at Errol and those who were to be trained on TBR aircraft were sent to RAF Tealing - the next aerodrome to Errol. I found myself at Tealing, billeted along with eleven others in a Nissen hut, about three-quarters of a mile from the officers' mess and, more importantly, the ablutions. Each one of us was issued with a bicycle of doubtful age and origin for use as personal transport.

A sub-lieutenant wearing pilot's wings welcomed us to the camp and informed us that he was the naval liaison officer in charge. The sight of the '39/43 ribbon obviously made him feel uncomfortable as his eyes constantly flickered from Ginger's uniform to mine and then to that of 'Stripey' Hurley, another fleet entry who was on our draft. We in turn had grave doubts about our 'senior' officer when we discovered his role was strictly administrative and that he did no flying; to be 'grounded' and assigned to an RAF camp such as Tealing could hardly be regarded as a vote of confidence in his ability.

The area had a generous covering of snow and the location of our billet coupled with a lack of fuel for the iron stove gave us a reasonable idea of the degree of interest in our welfare taken by our liaison officer. Cycling in three or four inches of snow was more or less impossible, particularly on the return from camp to the hut which was situated on higher ground and approached by a rough track. A total absence of plugs for the sinks and baths in the washroom caught us unawares, while visits to the toilet required careful advance planning with adequate safety margins in terms of time. Although there were grumbles a-plenty, they were not accompanied by any offers to make a complaint and it was left to the 'old hands' to broach the subject.

"It's the Italian prisoners of war who 'nick' the plugs. They're employed in cleaning out the washrooms and carrying out the general duties around the camp. Not a lot I can do about it."

The subject had been introduced as casually as possible by Ginger and myself; the liaison officer dismissed it just as casually.

We followed it up with observations on the location of the hut and the impractical means of transport given the condition of the track.

"You must realise that you are no longer in Canada; the huts are dispersed on purpose, this is an RAF camp and they determine where you will live and how you will get there. You had better make the best of it because the arrangements are not going to be changed, nor am I prepared to tolerate anyone who tries to make trouble. Let me remind you that, regardless of your length of service, I am your senior officer and I shall be submitting a report on each and every one of you when you leave here."

Ginger's eyes met mine - words were unnecessary.

Only five members of the course at Tealing were survivors of Aylmer's last pilots course - Brunton, 'Pif' Grant, Ginger, Jinks and myself; we soon discovered that not all of our new companions observed the same standards of behaviour and trust we had previously enjoyed. Far too many small personal items were 'lost' in a very short space of time and the bland excuses of our liaison officer "It's those bloody Eyties again" did not help at all. The atmosphere in the hut deteriorated as the losses continued and tempers shortened.

"Where did you get that watch?"

The angry shout silenced us all; there was no mistaking the accusation in the question.

"What the hell's it got to do with you? I bought it in Canada, if you must know."

The accused was a Londoner, an aggressive 'smart Alec', who immediately went on the offensive. None of us could remember him wearing such a watch before.

"Do you think I'd be wearing your watch in full view of everybody if I'd nicked it?"

His dismissive sneer was intended to put an end to the matter, the tone almost a challenge to anyone prepared to dispute it.

The 'loser' complained to the liaison officer, who agreed with the accused that no one would wear a 'nicked' watch.

Ginger, Stripey and I held a council of war and declared our intention of a full-scale search if anything further 'disappeared'. Everyone was in agreement, apart from a well connected and wilful, upper-class brat and the Londoner.

There was no more petty theft in the hut afterwards but our senior officer, who appeared to be cultivating the connections of the brat, had obviously been told of the development and became even more resentful of the presence of the fleet entries.

The widespread condemnation of and readiness to attach blame to the Italian prisoners of war were put into perspective when the POW detailed to clean out the ablutions after dinner one evening was found to be still there after 10 o'clock, his teeth chattering with the cold. In his hand was a safety razor which someone had obviously left behind when preparing for dinner; the man had been

167

too scared to leave in case he would be accused of stealing.

The Harvards at Tealing were painted in drab matt camouflage instead of the bright and cheerful, shiny yellow of those at Aylmer and their appearance epitomised the difference between the two camps. From the efficient and purposeful atmosphere and the bright sunshine in which we had last flown we were plunged into the cold, dull, uncertain weather of a Scottish winter, going through the motions of flying on a course which became pointless after two or three flights.

The RAF instructors could hardly be blamed for a lack of enthusiasm and mine spent most of our dual flying time concentrating on 'wheelies' (tail-up) landings instead of the 'three-point' landings I had been doing previously. In view of the fact that all my landings in the future would of necessity be 'three point' it was all very interesting but rather futile.

For the greater part of our time at Tealing we mooched around the bare Nissen huts of the flights on the edge of the airfield, trying to keep warm in between visits from the NAAFI van which brought mugs of hot tea and doughnuts to relieve the boredom. When we were told one day of the availability of fresh milk at a farm just off the side of the airfield, we really lived dangerously as we deserted our posts and the NAAFI van for the hospitality of the farmhouse.

Two elderly ladies had set out a row of mugs on a pine topped kitchen table that had been scrubbed until it was spotless, their hands rested on large pitchers filled with milk and ready to pour.

"Please come in."

We looked at the flagstones of the kitchen floor, they were as spotless as the table-top, and we looked at our flying boots caked with the mud they had collected during our passage across the field.

"Our feet are too dirty, we would make a terrible mess of your floor."

As we excused ourselves, the brat pushed his way through and into the farm kitchen leaving a trail of muddy footprints in his wake.

A voice was heard from the back of the kitchen

"No one visits my home and is left standing outside the door." It was the 'Master'. "Come in, gentlemen, come in and enjoy the warmth of my fire."

To have ignored the invitation would have been ill-mannered. We tried to avoid making too many marks on the floor and stood around feeling self-conscious and embarrassed by the thought of all the scrubbing facing the old ladies after our departure.

The brat was dismissive of our recriminations when we returned to the flights.

"They're not farmers, simply farm labourers," he declared, "they know their place and they accept it."

The brat was from a Scottish family and I was quite taken aback by the realisation that the 'master of the house' displayed an identical feudal attitude towards the old ladies.

We never visited the farm again, we were too embarrassed by the thought that we would create more hard scrubbing.

Our flying programme was now much less predictable given the changeable weather and exercises were cancelled or curtailed as conditions suddenly deteriorated. A general recall of all aircraft was transmitted one afternoon and the visibility was just about nil by the time the majority of the planes joined the circuit at Tealing. After landing we parked our planes and dashed through the driving rain into the shelter of the flight huts where we took stock of the situation. We were one short - Stripey Hurley had not landed.

The slave speaker in the hut was switched on so that we could monitor the R/T traffic and almost immediately we heard Stripey's voice appealing for instructions from ground control, followed by their reply instructing him to proceed to one of the airfields to the East which were still operational. There was no acknowledgement from Stripey and we realised his set was not receiving for some reason.

Overhead the unmistakable sound of the Harvard's Pratt and Whitney Wasp engine emerged from the impenetrable clouds as Stripey flew round and round and transmitted more appeals for help until he eventually fell silent. Meanwhile the sound of his engine provided a certain amount of reassurance as we waited anxiously and helplessly.

The speaker began to crackle again and a weary, resigned voice called "Hello Darkie! hello Darkie!"

Stripey had switched over to the universal emergency channel - 'D for Darkie'. There was a pause and the call was repeated.

"Hello Darkie! hello Darkie! ..... Darkie, you little black bastard ...... is you there?".

And in response the dense clouds began to break up as they were driven across the sky by the strong wind; blue patches appeared and Stripey, to his great relief and that of the rest of us, landed safely. The transmit switch on his R/T set had not been cancelling fully when he released it and had prevented him from receiving any signals.

It was during my spell at Tealing that I received a letter from Mary containing the news that we had been given tenancy of a small house and could now go ahead with our wedding plans. On completion of the course at Tealing there was to be a break of about a month before our conversion to Barracudas and I knew that during this time, apart from a week's instrument flying course at Hinstock, there would be an opportunity for some leave. We made plans to be married whenever that leave came along.

Tealing's shortcomings receded as the end of the course drew nearer, and as our spirits improved we became aware of the sad state of the flights which had received little attention from anyone other than the fleet entries during our stay.

169

The remainder of the course had quickly assumed that they had no responsibility for menial tasks now that they were officers.

"This place is like a shit-house."

Stripey's voice was filled with shame and disgust as he surveyed the scene on our arrival at the flights; it was a miserable morning when there was little likelihood of flying.

"Come on! everyone get stuck in, let's get things swept up and ship-shape."

Within a few minutes there were five of us working, everyone else had disappeared. I busied myself cleaning out the very temperamental stove, sorting out the dross and ash from the grate and the surrounding floor before setting and struggling to light the fire. It gradually caught and I joined the others to finish the cleaning.

The sight of smoke from the chimney was the signal the absentees had awaited, they emerged from their various lairs out in the cold in search of warmth, grabbing all the available chairs and enveloping the stove to the exclusion of those of us who had made the place habitable again. One man - the brat - had ensured that he had the best place, others in the pack had been bounced against the wall or knocked to the floor as he succeeded in positioning himself in front and with his legs either side of the stove. He grabbed the iron poker and lifted the lid on top of the stove, then flicked open the door at the bottom before sticking the poker inside and stirring the contents.

Within a very short space of time the stove was surrounded by an extremely annoyed and complaining group of officers arguing over the brat's behaviour and the fact that the stove was already showing signs of expiry following his interference.

My own annoyance got the better of me and I pushed through the chairs and their occupants telling the brat exactly what I thought of him. As I told him to get out of my way he pulled the poker from the stove, jumped up and swung it across my face, hitting me near my eye.

Wresting the poker from him with my left hand I managed to put him in a head-lock with my right arm and dragged him kicking across the room. My first concern was for my eye and I blinked and checked that I could still see as I squeezed and twisted his head against my side. I moved my left arm to tighten my grip still further.

"For God's sake don't smash his face, Crash."

It sounded like Ginger's voice as several hands grasped the brat and dragged him away from me.

I went outside and grabbed a handful of snow which I stuffed over my eye and cheek.

Fortunately the poker had not been red-hot but I sported a very red weal and a bruise on the cheek-bone below my right eye which could not be hidden. I tried to explain it away by saying I had stumbled over someone's foot and fallen against the hot stove; no one was prepared to contradict the story, nor did anyone believe it. The resident naval officer decided it was evidence of my disruptive behaviour which would be included in his report and I have no doubt similar observations were made about Ginger and Stripey.

My leave became an exciting race against time from the moment Mary and I were able to fix the date for the wedding; I obtained a special licence because of the short notice,

"Is a Sub/Lt. a commissioned officer or a non-commissioned officer?" the lady registrar asked.

"A commissioned officer," I replied importantly.

"In that case the fee is two guineas," she replied, "it's seven-and-six for non-commissioned officers and other ranks!"

Mary and I were married on a Monday morning in January 1945.

On the following Saturday I reported to the Naval Advanced Instrument Flying School at Hinstock, in Shropshire. Apart from one numbing flight under a canvas hood in the open cockpit of a Tiger Moth, I spent a week flying in twin engined Oxfords. At the end of that week, on the Saturday afternoon, I was scheduled to take my test flight with Commander Flying. The weather was terrible and heavy rain was falling from the dark clouds that were closing in all around; as I reported for the test I fully expected flying would be cancelled. Commander Flying displayed a remarkable disregard for the conditions beyond urging me to run out to the plane if I wished to avoid getting wet through.

We taxied out and I began my cockpit check prior to take-off; no sooner was it complete than I was under pressure.

"Come on laddie, hurry it up or they will have cancelled flying before we get into the air, as soon as you have her lined up let's go."

I did as I was told, few people argue with Commander Flying. The last thing I wanted was to be rushed into a take-off with just over six hours flying experience on a twin-engined aircraft; I was still uneasy about balancing the throttles yet here I was, trying to line the plane up on a runway that disappeared into a thick, menacing mist.

"Keep her steady on that heading until you reach a thousand feet."

Buffeted by the gusting winds, the Oxford lurched and lunged further into the clouds; there was no question at all about this being a test of ability in instrument flying, the only source of comfort was the presence of my completely unconcerned superior.

One by one I carried out the various manoeuvres involved in the test and my thoughts turned to the problem of landing just as a general recall came over the radio.

"We'll just carry on and finish the test." C/F clearly had no intention of going

171

through all we had done for a second time.

The buffeting increased and the glow from the instruments grew stronger as the darkness deepened. Suddenly, all was transformed by a flash of lightning and the world seemed even darker immediately after it had gone.

We picked up the signals from the beam approach landing system and were entering our descent when instructions to divert to another aerodrome came over the radio.

"You didn't hear that; carry on with your beam approach," Commander Flying ordered.

I continued my descent following the radio beam on the instruments with growing apprehension.

"Don't worry my boy, you're doing well; I'll take over for the actual landing."

The altimeter fell below 100ft, a level which my stomach told me was unacceptable; with very little flying experience on twin-engined aircraft I was almost down to treetop height and smothered by an impenetrable dark grey blanket of mist and rain, unable to see a thing ahead or around me. There was every possibility that Mary's marriage would not survive a fortnight.

"80ft Sir" I ventured with difficulty; my voice sounded rather strange.

"You're quite right lad, almost down now ... I have control."

Dim lights suddenly leapt at us out of the mist and we bumped and lurched down the runway, turned off and taxied back towards the flights.

"It's my fifty-fifth birthday today and I have a celebration drink laid on, there was no way I was going to miss it. It would be a poor show if I couldn't land a kite on instruments now, wouldn't it?"

"Congratulations and many happy returns of the day, Sir."

I replied in a far more normal voice than I had been able to find for some time.

Despite an understandable lack of enthusiasm under the circumstances, I left Hinstock with a satisfactory assessment and returned to the relative isolation of Bootle and a Cumberland gripped in an unusually severe winter.

TWENTY-SEVEN

On our return to Bootle the survivors of Course 108 tended to keep together as we gradually adjusted to the new or less familiar faces around us. A small group appeared to find integration difficult and we discovered that none of its members had been in the Navy more than a few weeks. They were RAF pilots who had re-mustered and been transferred when the RAF could not find anything useful for them to do. Some had found themselves on the footplates of railway engines for a spell and, if we were to believe what we were told, had become reasonably proficient drivers.

Once assembled we set out in bad weather for the Royal Naval Air Station at Crimond, between Fraserburgh and Peterhead. It was a journey punctuated by frequent stops, delays and changes of trains; when we eventually arrived at Glasgow we were told that our connection for Aberdeen had been cancelled until such time as the line could be cleared of heavy snow. After sampling the warmth and comfort of several places of refreshment our small group managed to get seats in the stalls of the Glasgow Empire. The entertainment was the one redeeming feature of the whole experience.

To the north the countryside was deep in snow and when the Aberdeen train eventually left Glasgow late that night the snow was falling heavily. Before long we had plunged into a blizzard and progress became more and more difficult. After a series of stops the train entered a cutting and became firmly stuck in a deep drift of snow; the heating system packed up and by the early hours of the morning we were huddled together with chattering teeth and feeling thoroughly miserable.

"If only we had our flying kitbags we could get into our flying suits" was heard from the midst of the greatcoats.

Jinks disappeared down the corridor and made towards the guard's van, he had worked on the railways in civilian life and claimed superior knowledge of the system. Within minutes he was back looking crestfallen, the guard had locked the van containing our kitbags and was not prepared to open it for anyone, not even a railway employee on active service.

A couple of snowploughs, a relief engine and many hours later the train arrived in Aberdeen. Someone had shown some initiative and booked rooms for us at one of the hotels in the city and we enjoyed a warm bath and an hour's rest before breakfast. About 36 hours after setting out we eventually arrived at Crimond with little interest in anything but a good night's sleep. Before that could be enjoyed, however, we had to find our respective huts and beds, drop our gear and then report for our introductory talk.

The truck dropped off our trunks and kitbags outside a Nissen hut and we went in to be greeted by a small bouncy Wren orderly.

"Good afternoon, gentlemen, I'm your orderly and I shall be looking after you during your time here. Everyone calls me Addie."

We quickly sorted ourselves out by taking the first available bed we came to; I took the second up from the door, on the right side of the hut. Addie looked towards me and her eyes began to fill with tears before she quickly turned away.

"What's wrong ?" I asked; others too had noticed her discomfort.

"I'm just being sentimental and foolish, take no notice of me." Addie tried to escape towards the door as she answered but there were too many trunks and cases in her way.

"Come on Addie, if anyone has done or said anything wrong please say so."

"No one has done anything wrong," she blurted out. Her distress became more obvious. "It's just that the last two gentlemen who slept in that bed were killed and I can't bear to think that you might be the third."

Addie raised her head and her tear-filled eyes looked straight at me, the hush in the hut was deafening until it was broken by one of Ginger's chuckles, it was however a slightly nervous and uncertain chuckle.

"You don't have to worry about Crash, he's our lucky mascot, he's got nine lives and so far he's only used two of them."

Later that evening, immediately after dinner, as the others gathered around the wardroom bar I returned to the hut and exchanged my bed for the one next to it, which happened to be Ginger's.

"When are you going to get into bed, Crash? Not frightened by our sentimental little Wren, are you?" It was Ginger again.

"I'll tell you what, I'm pleased I'm not sleeping in that bed and you can call me superstitious if you want." Addie's outburst had obviously got through to Stripey.

We were turning in for the our first night's rest at Crimond and feeling very unsure of our future. The chatter and gossip we had picked up in the few hours since we had arrived had been less than inspiring. The C.O. had not been there long; his predecessor had been only too glad to rid himself of the responsibility for the initial operational training unit for Barracudas. There had been a number of fatal accidents on the squadron before our arrival, the number and nature of which we had yet to determine. Not surprisingly, the accounts were varied and not always capable of reconciliation, but disturbing none the less.

Ginger came over and put his hand on my shoulder,

"Don't worry, Crash, when they auction off your kit I'll make damn sure that all this lot will pay top price for it, I won't see your widow penniless."

"I'm not worrying, Ginger," I replied "I changed the bed so I'm not sleeping in the jinxed one."

"You old devil." Ginger giggled, "Who's got it now then?"

When I told him "You have, Ginge." his big grin dissolved in shock.

"That's a bloody lousy trick to play on anyone." he blurted out to the delight of all.

So began the travels of the restless bedstead as one after another surreptitiously exchanged it and thereby ensured that everyone in turn slept dangerously.

"You will be given a short familiarisation flight at the outset" we were told.

"An instructor will take two pupils per flight, one will occupy the observer's cockpit and the other the airgunner's."

We walked out and had our first close-up view of the Barracuda. It was not a pretty sight.

Everything about it was ungainly and clumsy, an assembly of incompatible parts from the big straddle of its undercarriage to the high wings with their dive brakes and numerous appendages; beneath the wings a large perspex observation window bulged outwards on each side of the fuselage.

Conceived as the replacement for the Swordfish and Albacore bi-planes, the original design had been allowed to gather dust whilst all the efforts of the aircraft industry were concentrated on the production of planes for the RAF. When the prototype Barracuda eventually appeared the Admiralty introduced all kinds of modifications and additions: the folding wings were raised to provide a better view for the observer at the expense of the undercarriage design which became extremely complicated; it added even more weight to an aircraft that was already heavy and cumbersome. Subsequent developments were hung on to the Barracuda somewhere or other until it became widely known as the Christmas Tree.

Following the guidance of the instructor pilot, two of us climbed up on to a wheel, then on to the horizontal section of the undercarriage. Using the handholds and footholds provided we clambered up on to the wing and then dropped into the cockpits. As an introduction to mountaineering a Barracuda had a lot to recommend it.

The instructor started the engine and taxied out. As he went through his cockpit check, his running commentary came over the intercom but was of limited value because we, the pupils, were unable to see any of the controls. Pif Grant occupied the observer's position behind the pilot but on a lower level,

175

down below the wing, I was further back and on the same level as the pilot. We took off, flew round the circuit and came in to land. The plane touched down and gently dipped to starboard. The starboard leg of the undercarriage folded and as the wing tip dug into the soft ground alongside the runway the plane spun round. We climbed out to find the side of the plane covered in hydraulic fluid; I took one look at the instructor and decided he was not in the right frame of mind to answer questions.

The prospect of my first solo flight in a Barracuda an hour later was not enhanced by the experience nor did it improve the confidence of any of the other lads despite their own introductory flights being uneventful.

Of my first solo flight in the Barracuda I have no recollection beyond a nervous apprehension; it was a simple 'circuit and bump' - a take off, fly around the field and land. I was preoccupied with the basic essentials; the detailed appraisals came soon enough when I became better acquainted with the plane's shortcomings.

There was no fault to be found with the Merlin engine, it had already proved itself to be powerful and reliable in various aircraft; the Barracuda simply demanded more than could be reasonably expected of it. Not even the outstanding contribution of Rolls Royce to the war effort could overcome the aircraft's inherent lethargy.

There was a marked lack of enthusiasm to be found following our initial solo experiences, and the permanent residents on the camp did not help. Morale was not particularly high following the recent loss of several pilots, generally claimed to be seven, who had found it impossible to pull out of a dive without a wing. The problem had been cured, we were told, by replacing the locking pins that held the wings in the extended position; someone had decreed that these pins could be made to a cheaper specification but the relatively small savings cost the lives of many pilots.

The hydraulic system on the plane gave rise to further misgivings because of frequent failures arising from the high pressures involved; particularly dangerous were the fractures and bursts that occurred in and around the cockpit which could very quickly fill with poisonous fumes. Quite apart from the havoc caused by such failures within the cockpit, the pilot had to overcome the loss of control of the relative equipment and hopefully get the plane down safely. Many were unable to make it.

One of the functions of the Barracuda was as a dive-bomber and a large part of our initial training was in this role; there was a problem with aircraft availability directly related to the loss of pilots and life for the ground crews was an unending struggle to maintain serviceability. The point was reached where a standing order was issued concerning loose rivets in the wings of aircraft engaged in dive-bombing exercises - no aircraft was to be considered unserviceable due to loose rivets unless the number of such rivets was in excess of 100 in either wing.

It was with considerable trepidation therefore that we approached our first attempts at dive-bombing. I heaved the aircraft into the air following a long-drawn-out trundle down the runway and raised the undercarriage. There was an unmistakable improvement in behaviour as we became airborne and started our climb up to 10,000 ft.; it took about 20 minutes. The procedure was to fly over the target and position the aircraft so that the target was in the corner formed by the root of the port wing's leading edge and the fuselage; once there, the aircraft was flicked over to port and into a steep dive, with its nose directed at the target. Pilots were spared distractions, such as bombsights.

With the stick pushed hard forward, this was one situation where the Barracuda could build up speed, I concentrated on holding the aircraft's nose on the target and let the airspeed take care of itself. I released the practice bomb at 2,000 ft. and then it was stick back to pull her out of the dive: this created the 'G' force and the blood left my head to drain into my legs and arms making them too heavy to move. Red images appeared as my sight returned to normal and limbs became manageable again, the horizon was where I hoped it would be and there was still a wing on each side of the plane. Several of my contemporaries claimed they could see rivets 'popping' along the surface of the wings as they recovered from the black-out but I never managed to check, my immediate priorities were always the horizon and the instruments.

Another slow and dreary climb back to 10,000 ft. was followed by another dive and then it was back to the airfield, obtaining clearance to land from the tower before dropping the wheels. The heavy undercarriage fell out of the fuselage and wings with an almighty thump and the aircraft sank like a stone. It now had the aerodynamic attributes of a Glasgow tram as the enormous drag of the landing gear upset the airflow. After opening the throttle to maintain airspeed and check the rate of descent all that remained was to ease the ungainly lump down and land as gently as possible.

And afterwards, when we had time to think, we remembered those who had never made the return landing and wondered if their end came before the end of their black-out. We ate our meal and repaired to the bar, I sat down at the piano and we sang the ditties we had learnt in the service. For many of the permanent company the songs that Ginger and I brought from the lower deck were new, and we became popular. We in turn learnt new ditties peculiar to Barracuda pilots none of which were in the least bit complimentary to the aircraft and at some point we invariably sang the ditty of all aircrews -

'Pour me a glass of steady, let's drink to the boys who fly.

Here's to the dead already - and here's to the next man to die.'

Addie proved to be a tremendous lass, she mothered her eight 'gentlemen' and kept our quarters tidy. Each morning she came into the hut with a cheerful

177

smile and the demand that we should be up and out of our beds when she returned five minutes later - we rarely were. Ginger was one of her greatest trials and was frequently the last to rise; he was obviously one of her favourites and she always rose to his teasing.

"Sub/Lt. Hymers, sir, if you don't get out of bed this minute I shall strip the bed-clothes off your bed."

"Don't you dare Addie, I'm warning you, I'm not wearing any pyjamas."

Poor Addie never summoned up enough courage to call Ginger's bluff.

The attraction he had always held for the ladies was even more pronounced now that he was an officer. One Wren became so infatuated that we encountered her each time we attended our lectures and classes, she was usually painting the stones at the road edges, frequently the same ones, up to three or four times a week. As we passed by she would jump up in front of Ginger, "Sub/Lt. Hymers, sir, hello."

I think he had taken her out one evening; as we mimicked her cry repeatedly, I rather think he wished he hadn't.

On our free Saturday a few of us took advantage of a special bus that was provided as transport to Aberdeen for a return fare of 2/6d. The others decided to visit the cinema in the afternoon but I preferred to explore the 'granite city'; it was a cold, clear afternoon and by early evening I was enjoying an early dinner in the Royal Athenaeum Hotel. By this time, in an effort to counter profiteers, the maximum charge for any meal was limited to 5/- and for this amount I had a magnificent meal with a main course of roast venison before returning to the camp.

A group of fellow officers greeted me at the bus,

"Where have you been ? we've been looking all over for you. We met some RCAF pilots in the town and one of them was from Goderich, his name was Killaire, asked if any of us knew you."

My first instructor, who had taught me to fly, was now on Air Control at Dyce, a reserve airfield outside Aberdeen. I telephoned him at the first opportunity and arranged for those of us who had trained at Goderich to drop in for a quick unofficial visit when we were next night-flying together. If the landing lights were switched on as we circled we could land, if there was any hitch the lights would not be switched on.

Jinks, Brunton and I flew down to Dyce in due course and instead of circling decided to go straight in and 'beat up' the tower. By the time we realised the lights were not being switched on it was too late. A senior officer of the RAF had decided to visit Aberdeen and was in the officers' mess at the time. He was told it was impossible to identify the aircraft in the dark and the Mosquito Squadron at Banff got the blame.

P/O Killaire and I never met again. I was now flying an operational aircraft and he was still waiting for that opportunity.

178

It was not long before we settled down to flying the Barracuda, none of us had any experience on any other operational aircraft, apart from Doug Cartledge who had flown Swordfish and Walrus bi-planes whilst on second line duties in the West Indies. It became a challenge that we had to face and cope with like so many things in the war. For some the challenge proved to be too much and they fell by the wayside, some were left behind for other reasons. Archie Brunton was taken ill and was admitted into the local cottage hospital. Jinks decided to let him know he was not forgotten and tried to cheer him up with a 'fly past' at low level. He lost seniority and his place on our course.

There were few opportunities to play rugby in the Navy, but games of soccer, hockey and netball were frequently available and I took part in them when possible. At Crimond I was given the chance to play in a rugby match which had been arranged with RAF Banff; it was played on an exposed piece of ground in driving sleet and no one was sorry when it came to an end. There were several 'other ranks' in the teams and arrangements were made with a pub in the town for a private room where we could all join together in the evening and avoid the segregation imposed in the camp. It was a great party which more than compensated us for the disappointing afternoon we had spent on the rugby field; inter-service rivalry disappeared, only to be replaced by argument as our hosts insisted on paying for everything. A compromise was reached - a member of each team would sing in turn a verse of 'The Ball of Kirriemuir' and the team that knew the most verses could pay for the drinks. I had been churning out the usual ditties on the piano for a while and entered into the spirit of the thing quite happily; twenty-four verses later the RAF found themselves unable to provide another verse whereupon our senior officer, a 'two and a half ringer' triumphantly sang three more verses to our great delight. We put our hands into our pockets and paid the bill with great satisfaction.

About halfway between Banff and Crimond it suddenly occurred to us that the prowess of our 'two and a half' had not done us any favours, we were almost cleaned out.

By some strange chance I found myself down to do some formation flying with another pilot who had played at Banff and with the 'two and a half' as leader. Our only instruction was to "keep it bloody tight, I want the wings really tucked in."

And at one point in the flight we flew straight down the airfield at Banff at 50 feet in tight formation.

The next day three Mosquitoes did the same at Crimond but we were confident that their formation was not as tight as ours.

Crimond reduced our numbers but we avoided the fatalities of our predecessors. Deck landings were to be our next hurdle.

The Barracuda

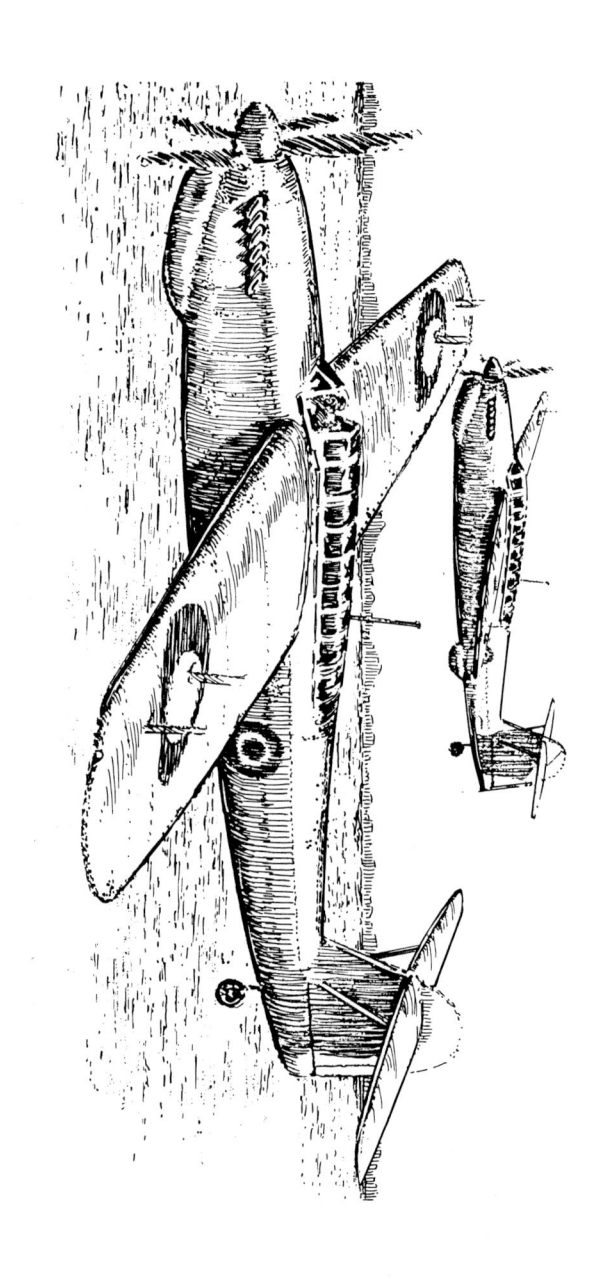

TWENTY-EIGHT

We left Crimond and moved on to the Navy's Deck Landing Training School at Easthaven, near Carnoustie, for our second stage of operational training.

Following our elevation to the status of officers and a higher rate of pay we became liable for mess bills. These were not too much of a problem to us because our basic pay was supplemented by flying pay. Nevertheless it came as something of a shock when we found that our mess bill at Easthaven was to be almost double what we had paid previously. It did not take long for us to realise why. At no time, including my time in Canada, did I eat as well as I did in Scrine Wardroom, Easthaven; at every meal there was a choice of dish and my acquaintance with venison in various guises was developed with considerable pleasure. To enquire how this was done in the days of such strict rationing was unwise, we simply paid our money and made the most of what it bought.

We joined a squadron that was tight and efficient, with a CO from New Zealand who had earned the respect of his resident pilots. During some rather boisterous exchanges on our first evening in the wardroom, he appeared to be taken aback when he heard one of his new pilots had acquired the name of Crash.

"When he heard the sound of your name he blanched," Geoff Stockall told me.

"He's away to check his aircraft availability," volunteered another voice. "He looks a very worried man."

"Spoilt his evening completely, you've obviously put him right off his beer, Crash."

Before long a couple of the resident pilots had quietly worked their way into our party.

"That's an unfortunate name to carry around with you," one of them remarked to me.

"There's nothing in a name," I answered. "What's important is being able to walk away afterwards."

Ginger quickly realised what was afoot; our two friends had joined us with a definite mission in view - to assess the extent of the hazard I might represent.

181

With a quick sly wink to me he took on a serious expression, gently clasped the arm of my questioner and drew him to one side.

"I wouldn't advise you to raise the question of his name too much." Ginger turned his head away in a conspiratorial manner and shot sharp, shifty glances in my direction as he continued,

"Crash was on corvettes on the North Atlantic you see, now I don't know if you realise this but corvettes have very little in the way of armament and even less in the way of speed; in fact, about the only thing they can do is ram the enemy. We know that Crash's ship was sunk and that's all, no one wants to open old wounds."

As he bent his head lower, Ginger's expression became even more serious, his eyes widened and his voice dropped to little more than a whisper.

"Now old Crash is OK, he's a pretty good pilot actually, just as long as he's not crossed or threatened. There was an instructor in Canada who upset him so much that Crash tried to ram him. He'd have made it too if it hadn't been on his first solo. As it turned out he missed and crashed. He improved a lot with time, in fact he became so good that when he was on air-to-air firing, he rammed the drogue; took it off as clean as a whistle. If I were you, to keep on his right side, I would stand him a drink."

"Don't believe a word he says," I broke in as I moved over to join them. "If you must know I have this incredible urge to do slow rolls at about 30 feet, I just didn't make it the first time I tried, that's all; I know now to go into them faster and with more power."

Whatever report was given to the 'Old Man', from that point on I was aware of his steady gaze whenever we met; he was determined not to forget me. I do not believe my name caused him to treat me any differently, however, and he quickly earned my respect as a thoroughly dependable and even-handed CO who regularly took his turn with the 'bats' and could as a result make his own assessment of our progress.

It was a well organised and administered station in all respects and we set about our training enthusiastically, knowing that it would be rounded off with the thrill and excitement of flying on and off a carrier.

Following the near disaster of my first solo flight in a Tiger Moth I had been constantly aware of the danger and futility of sudden and violent handling of the controls. I became very sensitive to any change in the engine note and the feel of the controls to the point where I almost flew 'by the seat of my pants'. The Chief Flying Instructor at Goderich had been a 'crop duster' between the wars and had been obliged to fly in that manner a great deal of the time. He had encouraged me in the days after my crash to develop this feel and although I found the Barracuda to be difficult and unresponsive, I still persevered with my attempt to achieve some measure of affinity with the plane.

It was during my time at Easthaven, as I struggled to master the techniques involved in deck landings, that I concluded the Barracuda and I were not compatible.

The end of each runway at Easthaven was painted with eight white lines which represented the arrester wires on the deck of an aircraft carrier; our objective was to land the aircraft in a three- point position on those lines. It is in the three-point position that an aircraft loses all interest in aerodynamics and finds the shortest route to the earth. Provided it is put in this position within close proximity to the earth, it will usually display good manners and float along until it gently subsides and eventually makes contact. This does not, however, permit the degree of accuracy demanded for deck landings.

In order to overcome this lack of accuracy the approach procedure had to be changed; we rounded off our approach at a height of 30 ft. or thereabouts and the aircraft assumed the normal landing attitude and airspeed. It was a situation in which the Barracuda was poised to exploit any weakness in its pilot, its manners took a decided turn for the worse and it assumed the characteristics of a stone. To counter this we had only one answer - the Merlin engine. We opened the throttle and regulated our rate of descent by the thrust of the propeller until the Barracuda was above the white lines; once there, the throttle was cut and the plane achieved its objective - it fell out of the sky.

To assist us in this hairy task was a batsman who positioned himself alongside the lines and using his bats, guided us down as we approached to land. He could indicate the need to change the attitude of the aircraft in relation to the ground, to increase/decrease the rate of descent, or to fly faster or slower.

For the training exercises the class would assemble at the end of the runway and observe the efforts of three of their number who were involved in the actual flying and practice landings. The leading aircraft would take off and climb up to 70 or 80 feet as it flew in a tight circuit around the field. The minimum height was laid down at 200 feet but anyone who observed that ruling was soon in trouble for taking too much time on the circuit. As the first aircraft entered the down wind leg the second would take off followed by the third when the second turned down wind. By this time the first plane would be on its approach to land under the guidance of the batsman and as soon as it had touched down the pilot would open up the throttle and take off once more, jinking his plane to starboard as he raised the undercarriage in order to clear the runway of his slipstream for the second plane. After eight landings each pilot handed the plane over to another until everyone had flown.

I was constantly being told to reduce speed, or go higher, when the rudder pedals were already ineffective and the joystick was like a spoon stirring a pudding. It was a situation that was far too reminiscent of the seconds immediately preceding my crash, when the controls told me I was on the point of stall and, as far as I was concerned, a case of 'once bitten, twice shy'. I decided to fly with one hand for the Navy and one hand for myself; so long as 'my' hand told me I was in control of the aircraft then the other hand would do whatever the Navy required - but my hand always had priority.

Following these sessions our individual progress was recorded and it came as no surprise to me to find that my assessments fluctuated between average and below, and were more often the latter. One criticism was constant, I did not respond quickly enough to the batsman's commands. I must have been a most frustrating pupil because despite my reluctance to follow the batsman's instructions slavishly, there were very few occasions when I failed to put down within the marked area.

Although I would have liked to achieve better assessments I consoled myself with the knowledge that I was managing to satisfy the requirements of the course without any mishaps while others were not always so fortunate. From the side of the runway we had a close-up view of each other's efforts to land and the final contact was never gentle, more often than not the aircraft would literally drop the last few feet out of the air and crash down with an almighty thud. None of this was of any comfort to the next pilot to take over the plane. Inevitably these heavy landings took their toll, oleo legs on the undercarriage would capitulate and transform the Barracuda into a lame duck. In the pitch black of the early hours during a session of night ADDLS (Assisted Dummy Deck Landings) a plane thudded down and with a terrific 'whoosh' something flew past our group of bystanders, the dim outline of the plane became hidden in a brief shower of sparks as it lurched towards us and ground to a halt minus the port wheel of its undercarriage. The wheel was eventually recovered when dawn broke - it was near the control tower, more than a mile away.

Whenever there was a mishap I developed a very cynical attitude towards the outcome - I was convinced that it would always be 'Pilot's error of judgement' and I was rarely wrong. The batsman appeared to be inviolate. My determination to keep one hand for myself grew stronger than ever.

There are certain conditions or situations that create difficulties for particular people and flying certainly had something against Stripey Hurley. An incident at Crimond closed the airfield until the runway had been cleared; several of us, including Stripey, were airborne at the time. Upon our return to the airfield we were refused permission to land and instructed to fly on 'economy settings'. The airwaves, which had been extremely quiet as we stooged around above the airfield, suddenly came to life with a request for an emergency landing; Stripey announced that he had switched to his reserve fuel tank and it was almost empty. Now that the airfield had another emergency the rest of us had even longer to wait before we could land; we mentioned our displeasure to him when we finally got down.

His 'doomie' followed him to Easthaven and struck again in the middle of an ADDLS exercise. He had made one landing and as he opened up the throttle the plane climbed up and over the trees at the end of the runway quite normally;

suddenly the roar of his engine began to fade and his Barracuda sank down beyond the trees and out of sight. Stripey discovered that belly landings do not endear pilots to their commanding officers.

At the top left-hand corner of the instrument panel in the pilot's cockpit was a small red knob, known as 'the tit'. When pulled it activated an additional super-charged boost to the Merlin engine; it was intended for use in emergency situations only, and even then for a very limited time. Whenever the tit had been pulled the fact had to be reported and the engine was then checked and overhauled if necessary. None of the Barracudas I had encountered at Crimond had been capable of attaining the performance attributed to the aircraft and I found the same applied at Easthaven. Aircraft appeared to lose an enormous amount of performance within two or three hours of a major service being completed and the over-taxed engines were invariably sluggish and dull; the suspicion that some of our number were prepared to utilise the extra boost without reporting the fact could not be ignored, particularly after Stripey's experience.

Dive-bombing practice continued to play a big part in the build-up of our flying hours as did formation flying. Great emphasis was placed on the tightness of our formations, and the wings had to be tucked in as if the planes were interlocked, it was regarded as a form of one-upmanship over the RAF and became an enjoyable part of our 'working up' as our ability and experience improved. People out for a Sunday morning walk along the cliffs near Arbroath would look down on a tightly-packed formation of Barracudas skimming the sea below and within the hour farmers with their families would gather at their doors as the same formation swept over their heads and on between the foothills.

Forming up tended to be a rather slow and tedious business with the lethargic Barracuda's inability to get much beyond 130 knots airspeed. Instructors became irritable and impatient as they staggered along and waited for us to catch up. When we had completed an enjoyable session of formation flying and could indulge in a spot of line shooting we all confessed to one uncontrollable reaction as we were forming up. Our struggle to catch up seemed never ending until suddenly the leading plane appeared to slow down - we were closing far too quickly and in danger of overshooting. At that point, no matter how hard we tried to resist, we found ourselves applying the brakes. It stopped the wheels from going round in the wings but little else. Geoff Stockall found his own solution. As he drew level with the leading plane he yanked the stick back, and when the plane was almost standing on its tail, he would let it flop back down. It was a most dramatic manoeuvre that reduced his speed very effectively and scared the rest of us to death each time he attempted it.

Night-flying in wartime Britain was not a great deal different from our earlier experiences in Canada. Although everything was blacked out below us as we flew over the Scottish coast and lowlands, the vast and sparsely populated areas

185

of Ontario too had been largely unlit. Purely by an accident of birth I found myself blessed with exceptional eyesight, particularly night vision, and this probably contributed more than anything else to my enjoyment of night-flying. There was a feeling of peace and solitude which detached me from the rest of the world in a cockpit scarcely lit by the dim glow from the instruments. The land below was silhouetted against the waters of the rivers and of the sea; they twinkled and glistened in the moonlight with the beauty of nature. There were opportunities to gaze yet again on the Plough and let my thoughts dwell for a time with Mary. Even dive-bombing at night had a fascination for me as I placed myself down-moon so that the target stood out boldly in the beam cast by the moon along the water.

Pif Grant failed to return from night dive-bombing - he had been unable to pull out of his dive in time to miss the sea. Some fishermen abandoned their night's fishing to rush to his aid. They were able to get him out of the sea and put him ashore quickly. Their duty done, they slipped back to sea just as quickly, without fuss.

Pif was whipped into hospital near St. Andrews where, by good fortune, an eminent surgeon just happened to be visiting. Pif's severed ear was successfully re-attached and so, not only was his life saved, he was spared what might have been severe disfigurement.

Alec.

The following day at low tide his Barracuda was clearly visible in the estuary with nothing in front of the cockpit; the engine had been torn completely off the fuselage leaving the controls sticking out into space. And we could only wonder how Pif could still be alive and how he had escaped without damage to his legs and arms.

Although we never thought of it at the time, Ginger and I had never been separated since our first meeting at Daedalus, now we were the only two members left from Aylmer's Course 108, all the other pilots on the deck-landing course had started their flying training before us.

Scrine wardroom held a party for each course which passed through. It was an occasion for feasting and drinking on a higher level than was normally considered possible. The imposition of higher mess bills clearly contributed greatly towards this junketing

186

and we determined we would get our money's worth. One of the resident officers was considered to be something of an expert on wine and spirits and he certainly ensured we had a superior standard of bar stock. He was also an expert at mixing punchbowls; 'Scrine Special' was his masterpiece, its ingredients were highly secret and its taste was delightful. And by the time it was found to be lethal the senses were irretrievable.

The spectre of the Wings Party rum still haunted me and inhibited my drinking habits. No doubt it was due to my being perpendicular without any visible means of support that a Wren steward asked me if I would mind having a word with the duty petty officer who was at the door. He was looking for the duty officer in order to do rounds.

Stripey Hurley was coming through the door as I arrived.

"I've just put the duty officer to bed." he confided. "He's been on these Scrine Specials."

He looked enquiringly at me and I returned his look; neither of us spoke.

Stripey sighed deeply, pulled a coin from his pocket and said "You call."

I lost the toss.

The petty officer had remained impassive and expressionless throughout. I donned my greatcoat and we set out in the squadron 'tilly', the utility pick-up, to do the rounds of the camp and the airfield.

"Are you a regular?" I asked as we drove off.

"I'll have done my twelve come next September, Sir"

I sighed inwardly with relief, his manner throughout had suggested he was one of the Navy's mainstays and it seemed I was right. He carried me on the rounds as only such men can.

When I got back to the wardroom my CO was standing just inside the door. He seemed to be grateful for the support provided by the back of a chair but his eyes were still clear and his steady enquiring gaze was as firm as ever.

"Damned cold night to be going out for a walk when you could be enjoying yourself in here isn't it?"

"I'm funny that way, Sir." I answered and returned his gaze as best I could.

Good commanding officers know what is happening in their squadron and the really good ones know when to emulate Nelson. The victim of the Scrine Specials was excused his unfortunate lapse, Stripey was very thankful to win the toss and I consoled myself with the thought that I had avoided what could have been a much bigger hangover.

Our big day duly arrived and the first flight of three set out for an escort carrier which was at the mouth of the Firth of Forth. Successive flights followed at intervals and as they returned the pilots collected their leave and railway warrants, packed their bags and departed. We who had yet to fly out never had a chance to speak to them.

As things turned out the carrier was unable to accept all of us on the first day;

187

someone, we were led to believe, had been unable to select an arrester wire which was to his liking and had used the crash barrier as a buffer. Ginger and I set out in a group of four the following day. It was only a short flight and we were soon circling the carrier in line astern making our identification signals. Three planes were ranged on its deck, the previous flight to ours was still aboard and everything looked extremely small.

I flew the leading aircraft and found my excitement was contained to a large extent by the activity; in no time at all I found myself turning into the approach and facing the batsman. One of the planes took off and from the corner of my eye I saw the other two follow. I was getting very close to the deck when the crash barrier suddenly sprang up; it emphasised the restricted area on which I would have to land - not much more than a third of the deck.

Our first approach, we had been told, would give the batsman an opportunity to judge our reactions before waving us round to come back in for the actual landing. I had the throttle firmly in my grasp ready to open up when I was waved round. With senses that had never been more finely tuned, I concentrated on the batsman.

His outstretched arms whipped inwards across his body and I reacted automatically to the signal to cut the throttle. The aircraft bumped down squarely and quite gently on to the deck and immediately came to an abrupt stop; my head shot forward and the harness dug into my body. Everything had happened so suddenly that I was totally unprepared for the shock of the rapid deceleration when the hook caught the arrester wire; in the space of less than 2 yards we had come from landing speed to a halt. The arrester wire began to recoil on to its hydraulic drums and I felt we were going into reverse. The wire safety barrier crashed down in front of me and figures appeared as if from nowhere. One of them was waving his arms frantically indicating that I should taxi over the barrier and that there was no time to waste. I responded without hesitation, the shock of the unexpected landing was occupying most of my thoughts and my reactions were simply automatic. The aircraft rolled forward; when it seemed it was in danger of rolling off the flight deck I was given the signal to cut the engine and climb down.

Everything felt unreal; I released my harness and turned as I stood up in the cockpit. Another plane was coming to a stop hard on my tail and I could see Ginger's face peering down at the deck party, it displayed a shock which was just as great as my own and the bewilderment of disbelief. Behind him the barrier was raised, the third plane was landing and the fourth was turning to make its approach.

By the time Ginger had climbed down to join me on the deck all four planes were down. We walked towards the bridge island with our parachute and dinghy packs over our shoulders, trying hard to appear nonchalant.

"It was a hell of a shock when I realised you had landed. I was certain I would be sent round again because I was so close behind you on my approach."

Ginger had not yet lost his look of bewilderment.

"I was calling the batsman all kinds of names for not sending me round before it was too late when the barrier shot back up and I was on the deck. I can't remember cutting the throttle."

We stopped by the bridge and looked at each other. I began to laugh.

"Now I know why the others were packed off on leave before we had chance to speak to them, all that business of a dummy approach was all my eye. Each one of us felt sure we would not be landing the first time round - they've put one over on us but at least we know we can do it."

It was decided that we should split into pairs for the rest of our landings and when we had successfully done seven of them Ginger and I were able to relax and observe the efforts of the others. A bunch of RAF pilots were aboard on some kind of information exercise; they had no hesitation in declaring us to be mad to forsake the space and stability of an airfield for the small deck of a carrier. We gathered behind and below the batsman in 'Goofer's Alley', the walkway at the side of the flight deck. There, with our eyes almost level with the deck, we witnessed the critical moments of the landings, when the arrester hook, dangling down beneath the fuselage, hit the deck too soon to catch the first or second wire, bounced over them, did the same with the third and fourth. All eyes concentrated on the hook, the suspense caught our breath and held it until the hook finally caught and the plane stopped.

When all the landings were completed and we gathered ready for our departure I was called over by the Deck Control Officer.

"We have a petty officer and a rating who have to be put ashore, are you prepared to take them with you?; I'm not ordering you to take them because this is your first time on the carrier."

"If they're prepared to take the risk then so am I, Sir." I answered, at the same time asking myself if I would be prepared to trust someone who a couple of hours before had never taken off from a carrier's deck.

When my passengers appeared they had their full kit with them; how they stuffed it all into the cockpits I have no idea but it was only then that I gave a thought to the fact that I was taking off with more weight.

With the brakes hard on I opened the throttle wide; the aircraft shuddered and began to edge forward as the brakes slowly lost their struggle with the thrust of the propeller. A signal from the flight deck officer and I was away, raising the undercarriage just before the end of the deck and jinking to starboard at the same time. For a brief moment we dipped slightly before the airspeed began to build up and we were able to climb away.

It was generally accepted amongst us that there was a 'black book' in existence in which notes were kept on our behaviour while we were at Easthaven. Stripey claimed to have seen it when we returned from our carrier

189

landings. He had found it in the hall porter's small office as he was leaving and had managed to get a quick glance at some of the contents; a photograph of each member of the course was in the book with a space for comments at the side. He never told us what was against his name but he gleefully reported that against Ginger's photograph was entered "Observed kissing the hall porter at 07.35 hours."

It is only fair to mention that the hall porter was a Wren.

All that remained now was for us to collect our leave passes and railway warrants, gather up our trunks, cases and flying kitbags, and find transport to the railway station. I was setting my case down alongside all the other gear when the CO appeared. As he tried to negotiate the heap of trunks and kitbags I became the object of his gaze for the last time.

"So you are back in one piece I see, and looking forward to your leave no doubt."

"I am indeed, Sir," I answered. "Landed first time, the batsman on the carrier didn't bother with a dummy approach."

He made no comment and carried on his way. After a few steps he turned.

"Enjoy your leave . . . and good luck." - And I do believe there was a twinkle in his eyes at that moment.

Responsibility for the training of raw Barracuda pilots in the art of deck landings was no sinecure but he did his job well; I felt sorry that I had not made things a little easier for him.

The train was rumbling across the Forth Bridge when one of the two ladies with whom we were sharing our first class carriage asked if we would mind lowering the carriage window.

"I just want to throw a coin out for luck," she told us. "Are you going to do the same?"

We managed to scrape a few pennies together between us and followed her example; it broke the ice and we were soon engaged in conversation.

"We left the carrier out there in the Firth earlier this afternoon." we told the ladies, there was little point in mentioning the short time we had been aboard.

Ginger was about to launch into one of his amusing anecdotes when a remark by the younger of the two ladies took us aback.

"We too only landed a very short time before this train left."

They were very well dressed and seemed to us quite old; having tossed this unexpected piece of news to us they were keen to exploit our amazement.

"It was rather a cold flight and not terribly comfortable" one of them continued. "There are far better ways of travelling than in the bomb bay of a Mosquito."

Now they really had us well and truly hooked.

"We left our Embassy in Stockholm this morning, the RAF sent a Mosquito for us - it's so much faster than anything else they have available. I'm very pleased it was, because in spite of all our blankets we were still jolly cold."

The train was almost into Edinburgh and we gathered our things together; as it came to a halt we handed out the two small cases which was all our travelling companions had in the way of luggage and said our farewells.

Ginger and I watched them disappear down the platform.

"And I thought I could shoot a good line," he said.

TWENTY-NINE

There was a sense of achievement and satisfaction in completing our deck landing course and in having actually worked from a carrier. Our pride did not allow us to be too boastful however, that would reveal our limited experience to the world at large, instead we waited and hoped someone would ask us what it was like to land on an aircraft carrier.

Crewing up was the next stage to be faced and as my leave came to an end I thought more and more about the men who would shortly become my crew.

Our orders were to report to RNAS Ronaldsway on the Isle of Man and so I set out once again for Mona's Isle. It came as no surprise to find that we were in company with a similar number of men wearing the upturned wings of an observer on their sleeves; as they appraised us we assessed them. Our exchanges were unusually polite and very much at arm's length.

Ronaldsway housed two squadrons of Barracudas and each one had its own camp adjacent to the airfield. Yet again we were billeted in Nissen huts with a Wren steward to keep both the hut and our uniforms clean and tidy.

At Crimond we had been mothered by Addie, a lovely gentle girl who was inclined to be sentimental. Balasalla gave us Agnes Gordon, a strong Scots lass who would stand no nonsense and who, contrary to all outward appearances had a heart of gold. We took up the beds in the same position in the hut as those we had occupied at our two previous stations, it simplified life and kept our changes to a minimum. Geoff Stockall took the first bed on the right by the door, I took the second, while Ginger and Stripey occupied the third and fourth; the pilots stuck together and so did the observers, we had eight of them in the next hut to ours.

A different atmosphere from the one we had left behind at Easthaven soon became evident, there was a more informal air about the wardroom and the resident pilots and observers were friendly yet did not appear to be altogether relaxed. We 'new boys', pilots and observers alike, trod carefully as we tried to slot into their midst. '39/43 Star ribbons were to be found on the breasts of one or two of the observers' uniforms and we learnt that the owners had been airgunners, men who had been unsuccessful when they first volunteered, like myself.

The Squadron CO and his senior pilot eventually made their appearance. They stood against the bar, dispassionately surveyed their new charges and raised their eyebrows in expressions of mock despair; those of us who were wearing evidence of previous service were regarded with barely concealed disdain. I looked at Ginger and Stripey; any welcome there may be was unlikely to be extended to fleet entries.

There was no mistaking the origins of our senior pilot; even without his RNZNVR shoulder flashes the sound of his loud voice with its heavy accent revealed all. We were quickly put in our place when both he and the CO repeatedly referred to us as 'Pups', their abbreviation for pupils, and we were most relieved when they adjourned to the 'senior officers' club. This remarkable form of segregation left us in no doubt as to our place in the order of the camp's priorities.

Our first few days were littered with unfortunate incidents that did little for our confidence. On my first flight at Ronaldsway I found my airspeed indicator and altimeter were not working, and had to fly round and land by the seat of my pants. My displeasure was even greater when the senior pilot accused me of not carrying out my cockpit check correctly before taking off. He was clearly cast in a very different mould from that of his fellow-countryman at Easthaven. With no thought of the consequences I immediately asked him how I should check the altimeter and airspeed on a stationary aircraft; this relieved my feelings at the time but did nothing for good relations.

Geoff Stockall was a well-spoken fellow; he had a decidedly plummy accent which could be rather off-putting on first acquaintance and his manner of speaking clearly upset our superior from 'down under'.

There was some difficulty in obtaining clearance for take-off on one of Geoff's earlier flights and it brought him into direct contact with the senior pilot, who gave him a telling-off for delaying the flying programme. The manner of the telling off and the language used were unnecessarily strong; it got under Geoff's skin.

"Before carrying on at me like that, kindly have a word with your minions in the tower, because they are responsible for the delay, they are the ones upon whom you should vent your displeasure."

According to Geoff, he would not have been surprised to have found the SP's eyeballs on the floor as the kiwi raged:

"Don't you try taking the piss out of me you cocky bastard, just you watch your step Mr La-de-dah, or I'll have your guts for garters."

And so Geoff became another of the many victims who were to suffer at his

193

hands.

Whatever the process adopted for the selection of crews it was not revealed to us; we flew with various observers and no one asked any of us how we felt with each other. Without warning the names of individual crews were posted on the notice board and we all set out to find our new partners. Sub/Lt. Ashton became my observer and Leading Airman Craddock my TAG; we had not flown together before.

'Jan' Ashton was an ex-TAG and we had no problems from the moment we joined forces; he was an even-tempered, steady type and so was Craddock. Whoever drew our names out of the hat did us a great favour and I considered myself to be very fortunate in my crew. Our relationship was a happy one without being too close, each one of us did our job without fuss and amazingly there was never a cross word between us.

We worked away at our programme and quickly settled into a sound, if undistinguished crew; we kept our heads down and tried not to draw attention to ourselves. Geoff was not so fortunate, true to his word the senior pilot was not prepared to forget his Mr La-de-dah and was constantly getting at him. Matters finally boiled over late one night and from then on I also attracted more of the New Zealander's attention.

The day had contained a full programme and we had all turned in; most of us were asleep when the lights of our hut were switched on and the shouting began. I was jolted to the surface by the row to see an unsteady figure struggling to remain upright and holding on to the wide-open door for support. A blast of cold night air snatched at my breath and brought tears to my eyes.

All around me voices were raised ordering the intruder in most explicit terms to shut up, get out and close the door. My eyes cleared and I recognised our senior pilot, both he and his uniform looked sadly worse for wear.

"What a pathetic lot of sods you all are," he was yelling. "Where in hell did they drag you all from? - a bloody girls' finishing school I wouldn't wonder."

He staggered into the hut towards the iron pot-bellied stove in the middle, grabbed the stove pipe and let out a stream of curses as he burnt his hand.

"C'mon rise and shine the lot of you, we're having a party and I'm going to see that you join in; I'm ordering you to get out of bed and get dressed, you can all buy your betters a drink and we'll show you how to really live it up."

"What a ghastly fellow," Geoff muttered as he slipped back down into bed.

At that moment the pest recognised his favourite prey, pushed past my bed and grabbed Geoff.

"I'll have you out first, you fancy fairy."

Geoff sat up in bed and with a big shove knocked him off balance; he fell backwards and on to my bed.

I had been denied sleep far too often since joining the Navy, to me the 'silent' hours were inviolate and I was in no mood to stand any more of the moron; his body was across the bed with his head and shoulders coming down at the far side. I gave them an added push to maintain the momentum and he crashed down on to the concrete floor. Without a moment's hesitation I was out of bed with a knee on his head before he could recover. It all happened very quickly; the shouting stopped abruptly and for a long drawn out moment so did time.

My prisoner had not yet gathered his wits and was probably wondering where he was and what had happened.

Five minutes earlier I had been asleep in my bed, now I was kneeling on the head of a senior officer whom I had just thrown on the floor. I was well aware of what had happened and was wondering how to avoid the consequences.

I got back on my feet to find the rest of the lads had gathered round; a voice from behind compounded my worries with the observation "Now you're for it Crash."

The experience had completely unnerved our intruder; he struggled up surrounded by a silent audience. No one offered to help him.

The bravado had gone. His eyes wide with alarm, he stumbled and swayed to the door and out into the night air. Soon we heard the unmistakable sounds of a stomach in open revolt; Geoff closed the door and climbed back into bed,

"He's laid out on the path and for all I care he can stay there all night," he told us. "I think we should register a complaint about this."

Ginger had been carefully weighing up the situation:

"Listen everyone, if we make a complaint we could drop Crash right in the proverbial. If anything is said, which I very much doubt, we must all stick to the same story, our friend out there burst into our hut and awoke us, then he attacked Geoff, that puts him firmly in the wrong. All Crash did was restrain him. Agreed?"

"And he broke in at a quarter to midnight," added Stripey.

Nothing was heard or said afterwards but the battle lines were more firmly drawn. No one had to warn me to watch my back and walk very straight in my shoes from then on.

Aircrews in the Fleet Air Arm were required to carry out dinghy drill at regular intervals, usually at the municipal baths nearest to the camp. A harness would be rigged above the high diving board to which a parachute harness could be attached. We jumped off the high board wearing the harness in turn and when we were about three or four feet above the water we hit the release button and dropped in. Then we were required to swim a couple of lengths before capturing and climbing into an inflated dinghy. The last part of the exercise could become a problem due to the dinghy's behaviour as it often displayed the properties of a wet bar of soap and shot out of the hands of anyone who tried to board it.

At Douglas baths we had our first dinghy drill as a crew and Jan's previous service as a TAG was a boon. Not only were we expected to climb into a one-man dinghy, we were also required, as a crew, to do the same with a larger circular dinghy. Jan briefed us on the procedure he had picked up, we had few problems and were out, dry and dressed long before many of the others. The drills were not a popular part of our training but it was reassuring to know that we could function as a crew with as much success out of the aircraft as in it.

Several weeks elapsed before I came into conflict again with the senior pilot and it involved the serviceability of the aircraft, just as it had in my first brush with him.

About twenty minutes of a navigational exercise had elapsed when Jan called up from his 'office.'

"Something's just fallen down from under the starboard wing, it looks like a long strip of metal and it's bouncing and swinging around a lot, it's about a third of the way along."

I looked out along the wing, from Jan's description the problem was almost certain to be the locking pin handle and sure enough the top of the locking pin could be seen moving slightly up and down in the wing. The actual mechanism of the locking system had never been fully explained to us, all I knew was that the locking pin was withdrawn by means of an arm connected to its lower end and housed under the wing. Being only too well aware of the Barracuda's malevolent nature and remembering its tendency to shed wings at Crimond I tried to sound as unconcerned as possible.

"Can you work out our position and give me a course for base Jan? I'm going to make a gentle turn to port and I'll fly on a reciprocal bearing."

Where I had flown in the past by the seat of my pants I was now flying by my finger tips, mesmerised by a bobbing piece of metal. From the moment Jan had reported the problem my brain had gone into fine pitch as I tried to cope with my immediate priorities and prepare for what might well be a major emergency. Faced with the task of making several decisions in double-quick time I was far too busy to panic. Should I gain height to give my crew a chance with their parachutes or should I go lower and hope we could ditch ? - there was little to choose between the two. Pif Grant had got away after hitting the water at Easthaven and we had practised our dinghy drill - I decided to go down to the water.

"Signal base with our position and tell them we're returning with a suspected fault in the locking system of the starboard wing. I'm going down so that if there are any signs of bigger problems I can ditch her quickly. I don't think it will be necessary but be ready to ditch, just in case."

The movement of the locking pin appeared to be variable but within reasonable limits for most of the time. My eyes rarely left it.

For the rest of the flight back the accounts we had heard at Crimond occupied my mind, stories of an alteration to the specification of the locking pins and of their substitution by ones made from cheaper metal; of fatal crashes attributed to 'pilot's error of judgement' before the new locking pins were recalled to be replaced by ones to the original specification. Wings had been torn off, we had been told, because a locking pin had snapped, pins had been found to be cracked. Had the locking handle become dislodged by a faulty pin? I found I was sweating profusely.

The island came into view, I put the plane into a gentle climb and joined the circuit, obtained clearance to land and set her down with extreme care. As we taxied round to dispersal Jan called me and in a very relieved voice said:

"You frightened me to death there Crash, when you turned off the runway I was still waiting for us to touch down, I thought we were about to spin in."

As we climbed down from the aircraft the squadron 'tilly' drove up and the SP climbed out.

"What the hell do you think you're doing, abandoning an exercise just because a handling arm is loose?"

He seized the opportunity to belittle me in front of my crew, the Wren driver and the ground crew.

"Even a newly joined 'sprog' knows that the pin won't come out in flight, the air pressure on the wing will keep it in place."

My last twenty minutes had taken their strain. I swung my harness with its parachute and dinghy from my shoulder and offered it to him.

"If that's the case, Sir, please get in the plane, just as it is now, before anyone touches that wing or the pin, take it up and land it."

My harness was pushed back in my face.

"I'm not here to play stupid bloody games with scared pups." he snarled. He jumped back into the tilly and drove off.

'Would the air pressure prevent the pin from coming out?' I asked myself, 'had I in fact panicked?' The ground crew had not moved.

"What are you all grinning at, get on with your work." I snapped.

"Well, we're not laughing at you, Sir, that's for sure." replied the boldest.

I turned towards the crew room. There was no suitable answer that I could think of.

Transport arrangements on the camp were a great improvement on those we had endured at Tealing. For our journeys back and forth between our camp and the airfield we travelled in the back of a three-ton Bedford truck, protected from the elements by a canvas top. We concluded that our Wren driver must have been off sick at the time when the purpose and use of the clutch pedal were explained; her working day was spent in crunching cogs as she did battle with the truck's gear box. On one of the early journeys Doug Cartledge had made a dash for the spare seat alongside the driver and, following one of her noisy attempts to strip the teeth from the gears, happened to refer to her as 'Sossidge'. As time went on we realised that she had taken this to be a term of affection and Sossidge became part of our everyday lives. Doug also found himself an admirer.

197

Ronaldsway co-operated with Ginger, as had every other camp to my certain knowledge, in providing him with female companionship; only Ronaldsway excelled. It provided him with a cracker of a Wren, a dark-haired beauty whose lovely eyes turned his knees to water. I soon recognised a change in his behaviour and attitude towards his new girl-friend and apart from dinner and retiring to bed I rarely saw him in the evenings. Spring was given its chance to work its spell and by the time summer was upon us Ginger was well acquainted with all the delights of the surrounding countryside as were several other 'pups' and Wrens.

On the weekends when we were free there was a mass exodus into Douglas aboard the unique Manx railway which chuffed along at a speed calculated to please pre-war holiday makers. It was a speed that encouraged high spirits too, the absence of corridors proved to be no obstacle when the coaches were fitted with running boards or steps along their sides. The sight of a figure making its way along the outside of a coach was commonplace until a particularly foolhardy individual tried it near a bridge with fatal consequences.

With more money in my pocket than during my previous spell in Douglas I could afford a few of the luxuries that had been out of my reach. Rationing was still less severe than it was on the mainland and food in the cafes was of a higher standard.

A visit to Wilson's cafe became a ritual for several of us whenever we visited the town. It was as if time had left the place behind, tiled walls, tables with marble tops on metal legs, bentwood chairs and all had a newly scrubbed look. On the left of the entrance was a glass-fronted display counter containing white earthenware plates. Pieces of steak, ham, bacon, fresh eggs and varieties of fish were set out individually on the plates by the proprietor who watched over them with dignified pride. The waitresses were of an age in keeping with the overall atmosphere and they had a soft spot for 'the gentlemen who flew for the Navy'.

Our ordering procedure formed part of the ritual.

"Steak, egg and chips, please."

"And the same for me too, please."

"Better make that four, four steak egg and chips, please"

And on each occasion the dear old waitress would tell us most respectfully, "I'm sorry, gentlemen, but you can have steak and chips or you can have egg and chips," after which she would smile sweetly and expectantly.

And we would then smile back and in unison say "Yes that's right, steak egg and chips, thank you."

Her smile then showed signs of bewilderment and she would retire in confusion to consult the proprietor. Their discussion would be interrupted by several glances in our direction until a decision had been reached. Bearing four plates, each with a piece of raw steak and a fresh egg, the waitress would then return to seek our approval before taking them into the kitchen to be cooked.

"Mr. Wilson asks you not to tell anyone outside about this but he is doing it as a special favour and as a gesture of appreciation to you."

And we, in turn, greatly appreciated his special favour and exploited it regularly and shamelessly.

I could not return to Douglas without visiting Hawarden Avenue and Ma Smethurst. On my first two visits there was no one at home and then we almost bumped into each other near the place where we had first met. I invited her to have afternoon tea with me in her favourite cafe but, although she was delighted to hear all my news and to learn that I was now married, the former warmth was replaced by a sense of reserve. There was no invitation for me to revisit Hawarden Avenue. As a young sailor I had been made more than welcome in her home but a naval officer was a different being altogether; it was the most poignant reminder that for some people 'clothes maketh the man' and I was saddened when I realised that, in her eyes, I had changed so much.

There were many instances of the restrictions that a commission can create. I was confronted quite unexpectedly by a former class-mate from my days at Valkyrie, who had been well established in a banking career before he had joined the Navy. His ship, the frigate Lagan, had been severely damaged in the same action in which Polyanthus had been sunk and now he was back at Valkyrie with the ribbon of the DSM on his chest. Our meeting delighted us both as we had so much to say to each other, unfortunately we were unable to fraternise openly because officers were not allowed to mix with other ranks. His wife and baby were on the island and he was on his way to meet them. We arranged a rendezvous out on the rocky beach by Onchan Head where there was less likelihood of our attracting attention. As far as his medal was concerned he told me he had simply remained at the RDF set after the ship had been hit 'because there was nowhere else for me to go.' The torpedo had blown Lagan's stern off and she had been taken in tow before Polyanthus had been hit; he could not supply me with any information about her. It was a most enjoyable afternoon, marred by the discomfort of the rocks and the furtiveness of our meeting. He was an intelligent, educated and responsible man but because we were wearing the uniforms of a leading seaman and an officer we could not mix socially.

Takings in the bars and pubs of Douglas felt the benefit of our weekend visits. By the time we arrived at the Strand Palace where we hoped to dance what was left of the night away, our inhibitions had been left far behind and we made the most of our time before we caught the train back to camp.

Someone at sometime had discovered that a Wren's cap was a perfect fit for the light-fitting in the carriages of the Manx railway. That is why no lights were visible in many compartments of the last train on a Saturday evening to Castletown and why it was known as the 'Passion Wagon'.

Excursions into Douglas were not possible every weekend. Our flying

199

programme became increasingly intensive and as a result we found fewer opportunities to move out of the camp. Drinking in quantity was discouraged whenever we were down to fly within around eight hours and with a heavy schedule of night flying the mid-week consumption of alcohol was negligible. Those of us who were not harassing the Wrens could indulge in an odd game of billiards or play cards when we had finished writing our letters home but there was little or no provision for active sport. Apart from one or two scratch games of soccer in which the senior observer and some of the resident aircrew participated there was a complete lack of interest on the part of our superiors.

Our wardroom had a piano of reasonable quality and singsongs became a regular feature of our gatherings after dinner. Several derisory jingles had been cobbled together concerning the Barracuda and could be relied upon to muster an enthusiastic choral gathering. They added to an extensive repertoire of ditties which I had built up over the previous years and since most of them were based on well known music hall song tunes and even more on the traditional hymns of childhood I could vamp out an accompaniment to all of them with relative ease.

Monologues also featured in our home-made entertainment, many of them accompanied by actions and usually reserved until all the Wren stewards had gone off duty. Some songs called for communal action and could get out of hand on nights when our drinking was not inhibited by flying duties; one concerned tom cats - round a fire-side sat - all round a bucket of charcoal, and produced a crocodile procession which culminated in an empty wardroom leaving me alone at the piano.

My services were usually demanded at some point on most evenings but there were times when few people were about and I could play for my own pleasure. On one of my forays into Douglas I bought a copy of Beethoven's Pathetique Sonata which was a particular favourite of mine. Very few of my contemporaries were interested in anything beyond popular jazz and blues but there were one or two souls who were sympathetic towards my efforts and one in particular, a resident observer called Chisholm, thought the second movement of the sonata was absolute bliss. So much so that one evening he absent-mindedly removed a chrysanthemum from a vase that was on top of the piano and with a far-away look in his eyes slowly ate its petals. Those of us who were around were fascinated and amused to such an extent that arrangements were made for a vase of chrysanthemums to be placed on the piano at all times. Whenever Chisholm appeared there would be the request,

"Play the Pathetique for us, Crash - just the slow movement."

The diet never appeared to do Chisholm any harm although he got through a good number of flowers.

When the resident officers decided to throw a party, in marked contrast to the similar function at Easthaven, we pups were excluded. The senior officers and their ladies gathered in the senior officers' club and left us to our own devices in our own den. Several of the resident aircrews who normally spent their evenings with us made it plain that they would have preferred our company and so none of us felt at all put out by our exclusion. We spent a quiet evening following a heavy day's work with the prospect of a similar workload in the morning. I was about to make for my bed when one of the resident pilots came into the mess and invited me to join Commander Flying in the 'other place'.

"Things are a little dull and he asked me if I could get hold of the chap who plays the piano to liven things up for them."

"Can't you tell him I've turned in," I pleaded.

"No chance my lad, he could hear you playing when he sent me down."

It was not an invitation I could refuse.

Following him reluctantly, I joined the party. It was the first time I had been in the place and I was taking my bearings when my squadron CO confronted me; he was not pleased.

"What are you doing here?"

Before I could tell him a hand clapped my shoulder and I turned to face Commander Flying.

"So you're the chap who's going to liven things up for us are you?" he asked. "Don't hang about then, get on to that piano there and give us a tune."

Turning to his nearest subordinate he demanded

"Get the fellow a drink."

Of all the people in the room he had dropped on my adversary, the senior pilot. Not only was I putting up sufficient 'blacks' with my senior officers through my own efforts, now I had the help of Commander Flying.

As far as I know my contribution was appreciated and most of those present enjoyed themselves. Everyone in the hut was asleep by the time I could get into bed.

Generally speaking the ability to knock out a reasonable tune was an advantage; my companions would keep the supply going for the pianist rather than have a lull in the proceedings and I was waited on hand and foot. This was one night when I would have been much better off with no musical inclinations.

VE day burst upon us when we were mid-way through our working-up programme and we celebrated at the Rushen Abbey, the nearest thing we had to a 'local'; in one of its rooms there was a very old and distressed piano. It was an entirely impromptu night and the room was packed, the celebrants burst out into the passages and through the open doors and windows. A 2/6d kitty was enforced and crate after crate of Castletown's red and blue bottled ale was piled high in the middle of the room. At 6d a bottle everyone could have five bottles, some had less, but some had more, much more. Crates were exchanged for others containing full bottles and no one asked who was paying for them.

The singing grew louder and louder as the crowd grew and the level of ale fell; the discordant sounds from the piano failed to detract from our jubilation. Someone decided it deserved a drink and poured the contents of a bottle through the open lid; then we had no alternative but to remove the front to give it air and a better chance to dry out.

A lovely Wren who was married to an observer had entered into the spirit of the occasion with an enthusiasm that was rather out of character; she was normally a quiet, retiring girl. Suddenly she jumped up, climbed on to the piano and proposed a toast

"Here's to the girl in the little red shoes,
who smokes my fags and drinks my booze
and then goes home, with her mother to snooze,"
And everyone yelled the response in unison at the top of their voices
"Bloody liar."

The walls and windows of Rushen Abbey shivered and rattled, even the piano joined in.

Back at the camp the celebrations continued and a game of the tom cats with the bucket of charcoal raised a procession of stumbling officers that swayed its way around the camp. At one point it passed through a static water tank from which the participants emerged dripping wet and perhaps slightly more sober. It ended when the leader became over ambitious and tried to take his followers up and over a nissen hut; one of them fell heavily and broke an arm.

It was a tremendous joy and relief to know that Germany was defeated at last. Now there was no question about our future - it would be in the Far East and the Pacific. Japan was the last enemy.

THIRTY

Shortly after VE day Mary wrote to tell me she was pregnant. It made me even less enthusiastic at the prospect of going out East.

Within one small area of the dispersal point we used at Ronaldsway, the broadcasts of the Japanese propaganda service could be received very clearly on our R/T frequency and though we regarded their news flashes as pure propaganda they made us seek reassurance from the BBC bulletins when we returned to the mess. It was a remarkable phenomenon which we attributed to the radio waves bouncing down on that precise point of the earth's surface and it added further emphasis to the direction of our training.

More flying was being crammed into 24 hours than at any time previously which caused some of our former RAF lads to question the practice. They maintained that we were being required to fly within the minimum rest period laid down, but in the event no-one was prepared to raise the question with a higher authority and no explanation was given for the concentrated hours. Then it was noticed that a couple of the doctors on the camp were always present at mealtimes and eventually we concluded, rightly or wrongly, that they were monitoring our behaviour for the first signs of cracking up.

Every aspect of operational flying was practised repeatedly both night and day in five-day periods which left our weekends free for recuperation. Someone suggested an alternative motive for the new procedure - our flying programme was being arranged so that the staff could enjoy a five-day week.

Now that we were flying with a crew our aircraft were Barracuda Mark 111's instead of the Mark 11's we had flown before. The main difference was in the additional equipment fitted in the later model, a radar set. The antenna of the set was housed in a large perspex bubble situated two-thirds along and below the fuselage. It was a most useful piece of equipment in an area so prone to sea frets and sudden changes in the weather but it did not enhance the outward appearance of the aircraft. The Mark 111 resembled a pregnant newt.

For our bombing practices we had two bays on the island that were overlooked by quadrant huts. These were 'manned' by Wrens who took sightings and plotted the fall of our practice bombs; they also estimated our angle of dive. On at least three occasions I was credited with an angle of dive of over 90 degrees. These figures were discarded as being erroneous, as indeed they were, but the equally inaccurate assessments of dives indicated in the 60 degree bracket were accepted as correct when I and my crew knew full well that they were around 75/80 degrees. Similar discrepancies arose from time to time between the fall of bombs reported by Jan and confirmed by Craddock, and the subsequent plot issued by the shore based plotters. Our confidence in the value of the recorded results dropped and we relied far more on what we saw for ourselves. And on the sunny days, when the off-duty Wrens lay sunbathing on the grass beside the quadrant huts, we saw more than the bursts of practice bombs; our airgunners began to load messages in bottles, which they dropped through the smoke-float chutes in their cockpits as we passed over the girls, "Could I see more of you?" was one of Craddock's efforts. Fortunately the prank was nipped in the bud before anyone was hurt.

Expense limited our torpedo exercises. To compensate, the Navy had erected a large spherical chamber in which we could practice our torpedo work much in the same way as we did our other flying in the link trainer. This was a far more sophisticated piece of equipment however; the lights could be adjusted to represent total darkness through to twilight as the outlines of ships were projected on to the wall of the sphere along with the sea, the horizon and the night sky.

Our performance as pilots of aircraft carrying out torpedo attacks on the ships could be monitored and assessed and as far as we knew the sphere fulfilled a very important need. Our sessions in the sphere were quite enjoyable, Geoff Stockall was particularly enthusiastic about them and even more so about the commissioned Wren lovely who controlled operations; he was a most attentive and industrious student but it got him nowhere.

At the appropriate stage in our programme we flew with practice torpedoes. Such practice was essential because the additional weight made a big difference to the handling of the aircraft, which required a much bigger 'heave' to persuade it to leave the deck. As an extra safeguard a wire strop was passed around the torpedo after loading; this had to be released before the torpedo could be dropped. During a night exercise when we were carrying a torpedo one end of the strop became unstuck for some reason; the free end swung down under the torpedo before it finally struck and shattered the observation dome of the observer's cockpit. Jan suddenly found himself surrounded by shards of perspex and a blast of cold night air; it was quite some time before he realised that his helmet was loose. One sharp lump of perspex had sheared neatly through his chin strap and had lodged in his 'Mae West'. He got away without a scratch but I had a severely chilled crew.

I was duty officer that night and so, instead of joining the mad scramble to climb aboard the truck, I dumped my flying gear and returned to the aircraft; I was anxious to find the cause of the strop coming loose. Everyone else had but one thought - to get back to the mess for an early breakfast and bed.

"The truck's ready to go, Sir - they're waiting for you."

The petty officer was anxious to get the squadron put to bed and me out of the way.

"I'll take care of everything, Sir, and report to you once the men have been stood down. It's the usual procedure."

Although I had little fear of my immediate superiors dragging themselves out of bed for a spot check I was determined not to leave myself open to criticism; the PO was no doubt a sound and capable chap and there was always a chance to learn something quite apart from the problem of the strop.

"Tell the driver to carry on without me, I haven't finished down here yet," I ordered.

Barely concealed groans could be heard from the group of ratings partly hidden in the darkness behind me.

"We've got a right pusser bastard tonight."

Before I could get back to the aircraft I had flown earlier it was moved off along with another towards the torpedo section for the torpedoes to be off-loaded. Thoughts of bacon and eggs with hot toast and coffee did not improve my outlook as I stood around with little more to do than watch a cold, dark dawn creep furtively over the horizon. When no more aircraft had moved for some time I asked one of the leading hands the reason and was told there were only two men who were allowed to taxi.

Shortly afterwards the two 'taxi-drivers' returned, the PO being one of them. Within a few minutes I was briefed on the routine and adjustments were agreed. With my help the aircraft were moved far more quickly and the attitude of the ground crews changed. After a couple of runs I overheard the petty officer call

"Give the galley a shout and tell them we'll be up for our breakfast early."

A subsequent and unexpected bonus was the frequent appearance of a petty officer at my side when I signed out for an aircraft - he made sure that I signed for a good one.

Our efforts in the air were backed up by lectures from our 'instructors'. It was difficult for them to retain any credibility when their prepared script contained such gems as instructions to observers to stand up in their cockpits and face aft during dive bombing. This, so it was claimed, would enable them to report the fall of the bombs as the aircraft came out of the dive. For men who were experiencing the immense 'G' force created when pulling out of high dives every day, such instructions were ludicrous. Serious doubts arose in our minds as to the type of person responsible for the programmes in which we were involved.

Progress was being made as we gained experience in flying the Barracuda but it had become increasingly clear from the outset that we were being driven from behind; there was no one leading from the front, no one setting an example. At Crimond the personnel had shown signs of being demoralised by the losses, both in aircraft and, more importantly, in pilots. Easthaven had been different in the absolute dedication of the Chief Flying Instructor to his deck landing training programme. His self discipline, energy and enthusiasm was outstanding and commanded respect.. His task was to train us to land successfully on a carrier and that he did; sadly his interest did not extend to the general part of the training programme at Easthaven. There was no escaping the fact that the Barracuda lacked the power to inspire anyone, it was simply accepted by those who found themselves without an alternative.

When it was announced that the King and Queen intended to visit the island we were told they would fly out from Ronaldsway at the end of their visit. Preparations were immediately made to present a smart and efficient airfield for the King's inspection and since the extent of that inspection was not known we were all ordered to carry out formal drill practice. Our squadron CO decided he would personally drill the pups.

This was a time which called for leadership, a time when with a bit of luck he might even be presented to, and perhaps speak with his Sovereign.

Unfortunately the CO's knowledge of drill was much less than he believed it to be when he embarked on the exercise and things did not go at all well. His performance became more and more reminiscent of our early efforts on the parade ground at St. Vincent as he struggled with half-remembered unfamiliar orders. He became increasingly aware of the fact that two members of his squad were controlling the exercise far more than he was and the knowledge did not help his growing frustration.

For Ginger and me the drill routines involved had been firmly planted in our memories back at Whale Island. We straightened our shoulders and our backs and held our heads high; this was an area where we had no doubts as to our competence.

We were completing one element of the drill when the CO finally lost control. Ginger was the marker as usual and had, on reaching the appropriate spot, faced the front and smartly stood at ease; other members of the squad followed but their movements were hesitant and lacked definition. I took my place and emulated Ginger's smart movements.

"What do you think you are doing? Who gave you the order to stand at ease?" The CO was desperate to demonstrate his authority and control before the parade became a complete shambles.

"Sir," I answered, hoping he would let the matter rest.

"Answer my question, who gave you permission to stand at ease?"

"The drill book, Sir." It was the correct answer but unfortunately it challenged his position.

"Stand to attention until I tell you otherwise; I am giving the orders here. If you are so sure of yourself bring the drill book to me afterwards."

When our practice drill was over I sought out the regulating petty officer and asked him for a copy of the drill book. He handed it to me already open at the appropriate page; from my days on the lower deck I should have realised that the news would travel ahead of me.

"You are quite right, Sir, I know that, you know that, and the CO probably realised that after he had opened his mouth. Could I suggest that you forget it and let it die a death."

One of the common traits attributed to Yorkshire folk is a stubborn nature and I proceeded to demonstrate that I could carry that trait to the point of stupidity.

"My orders were to show him the drill book."

"What do you want?" the CO looked up from his desk knowing full well why I was there.

"The drill book, Sir, you ordered me to bring it to you."

"Did I ? Well now you can take it away again."

And my thoughts were filled with the memory of Alec Massie who had been such an example and help when I was learning to cope with life on the lower deck. I was very much aware of my failure to follow his advice.

I became more and more aware of the difference between our present squadron and the tight, firm and efficient squadron we had left at Easthaven. Our instructors as a whole were perfectly good men and it was significant that they mixed with us socially from the senior observer down; if we had differences with them these were of a minor nature and acceptable.

The King and Queen did not visit Ronaldsway, it was covered in mist at the time and so they left from the RAF aerodrome at Jurby in the north of the island.

Navigational exercises were monotonous and boring for pilots; we simply flew the courses advised by our observers and became their drivers; we called them lookers. Unlike its American counterpart (the Avenger) the Barracuda was not fitted with 'George' - an automatic pilot - and the plane was quick to take advantage of any lapse on the part of the pilot. Flying a steady course on a pleasant summer afternoon, the more rarefied atmosphere of 10,000 ft. could become very soporific. In order to keep alert under these conditions we opened the coop-top and stuck a hand out of the cockpit; the slip-stream would blow hand and arm back against the edge of the coop-top immediately concentration began to slip. Despite all the weird and wonderful appendages and additions to the Barracuda's basic design, its pilot had to resort to some very primitive devices when it came to aiming bombs and keeping awake.

Navigation exercises at lower levels could be far more interesting for a crew. On a headland near Kirkcudbright was a firing range: We were flying at 5000 ft and just above the top of a blanket of cloud when a piece of the cloud appeared to burst in front of me. Almost immediately another burst off the starboard side.

207

"That's ack-ack." yelled Jan very positively.

"I've just seen the 'Lizzie' - Starboard 60 about 1000 yards, she's in and out of the clouds - she's got her drogue streamed." Craddock was equally positive.

Our flight path had brought us from light cloud over St. Bees Head across the Irish Sea towards the Solway coast and I knew the cloud layer was not too deep. I put the plane into a steep dive.

"I'll give the Radar operators brown bloomers." I called to Jan. "Until we come out of the cloud they'll think we've been shot down."

"I was wondering if we had been." came the reply. "Pray don't hang back on my account; I've just given Craddock a warning signal to transmit to the rest of the squadron. There's no point in sending one by R/T until we regain some height."

Beneath the clouds Kirkcudbright was waiting and inviting our closer inspection. Identification and appreciation of landmarks involved quite a lot of discussion and resulted in some strangely feeble efforts on my part to gain height until we had negotiated most of the inlets and bays from Gatehouse of Fleet to Kippford. Because of the disturbance we had caused to the peace and tranquillity of such a delightful area we agreed there and then that we must return after the war to make our apologies.

There was every likelihood that someone would have taken our number and that a complaint would be made but we believed we could claim justification. There was a complaint and investigation already in progress following an exercise which took the squadron over the Lune estuary. On that particularly fine afternoon a surprising number of Barracudas reached the Lancashire coast south of their landfall and were obliged to fly past or over Blackpool, hopping piers and flying above the promenade, their crews waving to all the folks who were fortunate enough to be on holiday. We all hoped that ours would not be one of the planes which had been identified.

Following my brush with the CO I was determined to make sure I did not jeopardise my already unfortunate relationships with my senior officers still further. It was not to be.

The aircraft I had signed for was nowhere to be found on the apron and we were part of a formation flight; all the other crews were ready to climb aboard their planes.

"I think it's the one that's jammed in, they're having trouble with one in front of the hangar over there, Sir." The fitter was being very helpful even if his information was not.

We struggled across towards the hangar with our parachutes and dinghies and all the various paraphernalia peculiar to observers and TAGs. There, in the corner of the hangar apron was our chariot for the day, blocked in by the starboard wing of another aircraft. Two fitters stood idly by, giving their own interpretation of 'It's got nothing to do with me mate'.

To my sharp demand for an explanation I was informed that the engine had failed to start, the starter unit had expended all its cartridges and the PO had gone to find some more hands to help them push the plane out of the way.

"I see the starboard wing's half ready to be folded, if it was folded I could taxi my plane out." I looked around; there was no sign of the PO nor of any spare hands.

"Grab the handling rail," I ordered. "I'll unlock the wing."

It was something I had never done before and as I was soon to discover, it was something I should not have been doing then.

"Ready" I called and moved the handle of the locking pin slightly in order to get the feel of it. Not only did I get the feel of it, I withdrew the pin.

Along at the wing tip a startled fitter grabbed the handling rail as the wing began to fold back. His mate stood by looking mildly surprised and motionless. The wing tip thudded into the tail plane at a greater speed than it should have done; the locating pin on the wing was bent back as it entered the socket on the tail plane but no other damage was apparent.

More than a little dismayed I wriggled my aircraft out of its corner to carry out the formation flying with our frustrated fellow crews. On our return I went to the crew room and wrote out a brief and factual report of the incident of the folding wing which I then handed in at the office.

The CO wasted no time in sending for me. He was sitting behind his desk, carefully studying my report, all six lines of it. His senior pilot stood to his left, just behind his chair. After a significant pause the CO raised his head and looked at me with a serious expression of theatrical quality.

"Have you anything to add to this? Are you putting the ratings on report?"

The CO inclined his head towards the SP and raised an eyebrow as he asked me the question.

"No, Sir."

"In other words, you are taking the whole of the blame for this stupid accident yourself."

"I believe my report is correct as submitted, Sir and I stand by it. As far as I am aware the damage is only minor."

"I am not concerned with the nature of the damage, that is for others to assess. Your behaviour does not surprise me in the least; you, and one or two more like you, display more affinity with the lower deck than with the standards of the wardroom. Your interference in the routine following night torpedo exercises did not go un-noticed; the movement of aircraft when flying has been completed is the responsibility of the ground crews. As an officer your responsibility is to ensure they carry out those duties - nothing more. You most certainly do not perform those duties for them. You have displayed a similar attitude today in taking on the task of a handling crew. Have you ever folded the wing of a Barracuda before?"

"No, Sir." I answered bleakly as I became increasingly aware of my total lack of escape.

"So you blithely take on an operation of which you are completely ignorant and create trouble not only for yourself but for everyone on the squadron?"

"Sir."

"I consider you have shown a complete lack of discipline and responsibility and will make a decision on the action I should take in due course. Dismiss."

Not only had I been careless and foolish in my haste to get away on the exercise, I had presented my seniors with an opportunity to redress the balance on our earlier encounters; I left the office feeling extremely annoyed with myself.

In all his previous dalliances, Ginger had carefully prepared escape plans for use in emergencies or other contingencies; it was not uncommon for him to start putting them into effect very shortly after a liaison began. His behaviour at Ronaldsway gave cause for concern when, after several weeks, there was no sign of the various ruses and excuses in which I was often asked to play a part. To the contrary, he was displaying alarming signs of settling down with his one and only girl since our arrival on the station. He drew me to one side as we were about to go to dinner one evening towards the end of our course.

"Would you do me a big favour, Crash, will you come with me to the telephone?"

The lad was distinctly nervous and on edge.

"You don't need me to come with you, Ginger, all you have to do is put in your tuppence and wait until someone answers, then you press button A ."

"Stop messing about, Crash, this is serious. I have to ring Pat's father - I want to ask for his permission - you see Pat and I would like to get married - and wipe that bloody stupid look of surprise of your face because it's nothing like that."

He really was agitated and in a state with himself.

"Mr Smith? - this is Vernon Hymers," Ginger's voice cracked and moved up the scale a couple of tones, "I believe Pat has told you about me."

"If your voice gets any higher he'll be wondering what he hasn't been told about you." I whispered.

Ginger however was past caring.

"I would like to ask for Pat's hand in marriage." he blurted out in a fine falsetto.

I was beginning to see why he had insisted on my presence, at his present rate of progress something was bound to blow soon; but a slight change at the corner of his lips heralded the broad grin which gradually spread across Ginger's face and his high colour began to subside along with the pitch of his voice. My first aid was not about to be called for after all.

"You're O.K. to go solo now, Ginger. You have control."

I slowly walked away. Ginger caught up with me before I reached the dining room.

"Since I'm the first to congratulate you can I kiss your intended?"

"Can you hell as like, I'm not going to let anyone near Pat and least of all a married man."

Communications from above improved as we neared the end of our course. With the end of the war in Europe our sights were turned firmly towards the Far East; the thinking behind the wide variety of the exercises we had been undertaking and their intensity was explained. There was a possibility, we were told, that we would form a squadron aboard an escort carrier that would operate independently from the main fleet in a diversionary capacity by attacking secondary targets. The theory was that such tactics would draw some of the enemy's resources and so weaken their resistance at the main targets which would be the responsibility of the main task force. It all sounded too hare-brained for most of us.

Our prospects were further enhanced by lectures from a Surgeon Commander RN who was also a pilot, a very basic and down-to-earth character who preferred Anglo-Saxon to Latin when referring to any medical condition. His favourite seat was the pot-bellied stove in the corner of the lecture hut. Wrapped in a grubby and seasoned duffle coat and with a Mae West across his knee, he advised us on the survival techniques we should employ if we were forced down in the jungle or into shark-infested tropical seas. His lectures always concluded with the advice:

"If you come down in the jungle you have several problems, snakes and Japs being two; if you come down in the sea you

*"Take the small knife from your Mae West."
With S/Lt Panter.*

211

have other problems, sharks and Japs being two. Don't waste time worrying and messing about when you are faced with any one of them, take the small knife from your Mae West, the one with the pointed end here."

He pulled one of the knives from its pocket on the front of the Mae West and held it up for all to see. It had a short double-sided blade with a sharp point.

"You stick it in your neck here, under your left ear, very firmly and keeping it well in, pull it sharply round to your other ear where, if you feel so inclined, you can then pull it out. Do not, I repeat, do not waste time making little cuts around your Adams apple, they will only help you to breathe more easily. Do it once and do it right."

I do not recall anyone displaying the least bit of enthusiasm for flying Barracudas in the Far East.

Having left all our earlier contemporaries behind, Ginger and I were somewhat isolated from their activities. Odd snippets of news filtered through from various sources, not always good, sometimes of fatalities. The other squadron at Ronaldsway had its share of misfortune but we managed to avoid any serious incidents during our time there. The two squadrons were on different timetables and when a new course appeared at the other camp it included Jinks and my adversary from Tealing, the brat. Although we shared the same airfield and objectives, there was very little socialising between the two squadrons; we confined our off-duty hours on the station to our respective camps and met up briefly in Douglas as and when we could get there.

The weekend before we completed our course a rating from the camp was drowned in Douglas harbour. We were told he had been given a lift by a pilot from the other squadron and the car had run over the harbour wall, the driver of the car was safe but his passenger had been trapped. It transpired that the car was an official navy vehicle which had been taken without permission by the brat, who was reported to have been drunk at the time. When a life is lost it affects everyone on a ship or a station; with an incident such as this feelings ran much stronger, particularly amongst those of us who had prior knowledge of the perpetrator's character and temperament. He was under close arrest when we left the island and Jinks had been appointed 'prisoner's friend' - not an enviable position under the circumstances.

"Your flying log-books will be available in the wardroom after lunch, the CO's still signing them at the moment."

Trunks, suitcases and flying kitbags were already packed and waiting for our departure, the course was at an end and we were now classified as competent crews ready to become fully operational. My thoughts were firmly fixed on leave, on Mary and home, there was no room for the realisation that I had finally achieved what I had set out to do when I first volunteered for the Fleet Air Arm - to become an operational pilot.

The time for departure drew nearer and our log books had still to arrive; we loaded our gear into the truck and stood around impatiently in our greatcoats muttering:

"Come on, come on, the boat won't wait for us."

The squadron tilly appeared and one of the instructor pilots climbed out and carried our log books into the wardroom. We were into them before they had settled on the bar top, flipping open the pages when we found our own, for a quick check on our assessments.

"What have you got, Crash?"

Ginger had seen my face change as I opened my book.

"Below Average for Day, Average for Night."

Now it was Ginger's face that changed.

"But that's bloody ridiculous."

His voice rose with annoyance, one or two of the instructors turned to see what had brought about the disturbance.

"If Crash here is below average, heaven help the rest of you. I haven't met a pilot I would rather fly alongside anywhere, he's the one man you can depend on to keep his station, no matter what anyone else is doing. I'd fly with him, any day, anywhere, before I'd fly with any of you - and that goes for the CO and the senior pilot."

The instructor who had delivered the log-books broke in

"I think you'll find the answer at the back of your log book, there's an endorsement."

Somewhat incredulously, I turned to the back of my book. There was the endorsement describing the incident when I had pulled the locking pin and caused the wing to fold. It concluded in bold red ink:

(A)Day (B)Land (C)Taxying - Degree of responsibility Negligence.

My foolish experience with the folding wing had been manipulated into an endorsable incident by stating it occurred whilst the aircraft was 'Taxying'.

"But I was never in the bloody aircraft, it was incapable of being moved at the time, much less taxied."

The instructor was sympathetic.

"Yes it's a pretty rough trick, slapping that on you without warning and just as you're about to leave."

"I'm the first one to accept I was a clot and if the damage warranted punishment then I must accept it but it has to be fair and appropriate, not twisted and misrepresented."

The rest of the lads seemed to find the whole business to be so ridiculous as to be amusing.

Geoff Stockall took a couple of paces back and intoned a solemn announcement in his most plummy voice:

"The Commanding Officer and the Senior Pilot would have been here to say their goodbyes and wish you well, gentlemen, but they had reason to believe their pink gins had already been poured out in another place. In their absence and since there is a vessel awaiting, I suggest we all get to blazes out of here as quickly as possible."

It seemed like a good idea at the time, so we did.

THIRTY-ONE

Leave at the end of July in 1945 provided a wonderful break and a time for rest, above all Mary and I were able to be together in our own home.

On leaving Ronaldsway we had been given orders to report to RNAS Maydown in Northern Ireland when our leave came to an end. From there we could expect to join an escort carrier. Although I tried to put the future on hold, and to a large extent succeeded in doing so, my imminent departure to the Far East was ever present; it was a dark cloud lurking in the background and ready to envelop me all too soon.

On the day when Ginger married Pat I sent them a telegram from the small local sub-post office. The sub-postmaster was beside himself with curiosity.

The telegram read 'Report PCSWT 2400 hours, happy landings. Crash.' (Position, Course, Speed, Wind and Time)

The day of departure for Maydown arrived far too quickly. With all my gear I needed a taxi to take it and me to the station and I had ordered one for one o'clock. We had decided that we would say our farewells at home.

As the time drew near our feelings inhibited our small talk until we hardly knew what to say to each other. Although there was not much doubt about my future destination it was a subject I had avoided as I was determined not to let anything drop which would increase Mary's worries and fears.

One o'clock came but no taxi. I turned on the wireless to check the time just as the one o'clock news bulletin began. It was the bulletin which told of the first atomic bomb being dropped and of the fearsome devastation it had caused.

We had barely time to embrace each other and share the relief we felt before the taxi arrived and we had to part. It was a relief so great that I hardly gave a thought to the horror and destruction involved.

Once more I made the circuitous and dreary journey up to Stranraer, across to Larne and along the Antrim coast. But my heart was much lighter than it had been before when I had travelled those, by now, familiar miles.

Maydown was in a state of suspense. No one was sure what should be done and attempts to follow a normal daily routine were half-hearted to say the least.

215

We had lectures on the use of sono-buoys in conjunction with the aerial acoustic bomb, all still highly secret. Exercises for us to practice the use of the equipment were doomed to failure by our ability to discover faults in our aircraft which made them unserviceable. A target submarine was based at Larne and we were supposed to be working with her; we formed the opinion that her crew shared our lack of enthusiasm for anything in the least bit energetic until the overall war game was resolved.

Londonderry now housed a large flock of surrendered U-boats and we had an opportunity to board and inspect them. It was a unique experience for me, as one who had sailed out of Londonderry, to be aboard one of the U-boats we had opposed in the Battle of the Atlantic. They were moored at Lismahally where Polyanthus had also once moored.

One of the submariners came round from Larne on an exchange visit and for a flight in a Barracuda. I was asked to take him and it was decided that Jan would take Craddock's place in the TAG's cockpit, leaving our guest with the much better views provided in the observer's 'office'. As it was to be a straightforward 'flip' there was no point in trying to avoid it by looking for faults. We flew out to sea, then over Larne before returning along the coast. He saw his sub' and we made one or two passes at it. I made a steep approach as I came into land with the object of putting the wind up him, and it did.

I landed at Maydown to find that the second atomic bomb had been dropped and all flying was suspended for fear of pilots going berserk. For the Barracuda pilots of RNAS Maydown, flying was the last form of celebration we would think of.

My Lords Commissioners of the Admiralty had many decisions to make and our fate was not high in their list of priorities. I was able to visit Londonderry and look up my friends Mr and Mrs Bell, but the Longwell family were on holiday in Portrush. I found it hard to reconcile being in Derry as an officer, it was almost as if I were another person from the A.B. I had been when I had left Polyanthus there in 1943.

Arrangements were made for advice on release and resettlement to be available during our enforced idleness. Tables were set up in a long, glass-fronted building which might have been a conservatory at some stage and we attended in batches at appointed times. It was a hastily-organised affair which provided us with some useful information but the venture was limited for obvious reasons and we spent quite a lot of our time browsing around rather aimlessly once we had discovered the things that interested us most.

One or two educational types moved about behind the row of tables and with the help of some Wrens did all they could to stir up interest. I sensed that I was under scrutiny, a Wren was appraising me with a steady gaze; her face was familiar but not one that I could place readily.

Slowly she leaned back on her chair, her eyes, unfaltering, never left mine as she tapped her teeth gently with a pencil. And then the faintest trace of a smile crept into the corners of her eyes.

"Well hello, Polyanthus." She spoke softly, in a voice as smooth as Irish cream.

Then I remembered; I had last seen her in Captain 'D's' signals office in Derry. I stood, open-mouthed, captivated by her smiling Irish eyes.

She eventually broke the silence: "So you made it."

Spellbound, I continued to stand, oblivious of everyone in the room apart from this girl whose name I had never known, the girl who, two years earlier, had handed me the signal that had saved my life.

"Yes." I answered quietly. "Yes, I made it."

Japan formally surrendered on the 2nd September, 1945 and the war came to an end. It was the Sunday of Cleckheaton Feast.

APPENDIX

ICEBERG. The location of the iceberg by Polyanthus merited a mention by the C. in C. Western Approaches in his Daily State as 'An example of the tremendous value of RDF equipment for navigational purposes in peacetime'.

WEATHER DURING THE WINTER OF 1942/43. It was reported that between October, 1942 and February, 1943 the winds in the North Atlantic reached Force 7 or higher (i.e. gale strength) on more than one hundred days (over 65% of the time)

During January 1943 over 30% of the escort vessels available to Canadian Operational Command were rendered unfit for operational duties: eight merchant ships floundered, four went aground, forty were severely damaged by weather and a rescue vessel capsized under the weight of ice on her superstructure.

CONVOYS ONS18 and 0N202

Following the heavy losses suffered in May 1943, Germany withdrew its U-boat packs from the North Atlantic. At the end of August they returned in force equipped with the new, top secret, Acoustic Torpedo and on September 19th located convoys ONS18 and ON202.

On September 20th H.M.S. LAGAN had her stern blown apart, and H.M.C.S. ST. CROIX was torpedoed twice, after being struck by a third torpedo an hour later, she sank. H.M.S. POLYANTHUS had gone to her assistance and was herself torpedoed. The survivors from H.M.C.S. ST. CROIX, and one officer from H.M.S. POLYANTHUS were picked up by H.M.S. ITCHEN the following morning.

When H.M.S. ITCHEN was sunk in the early hours of September 23rd only two men from her crew and one man from H.M.C.S. ST. CROIX survived from the three ships.

The action was spread over four days and involved nine ships of the Royal Navy, seven ships of the Royal Canadian Navy and three Free French ships along with sixty-seven merchant ships of various nationalities and three squadrons of Liberator aircraft.

Three escorts and seven merchantmen were lost; two escorts were damaged.

There were twenty-one U-boats involved; three of them were sunk and one was badly damaged.

Acoustic torpedoes were responsible for the losses of the escort vessels.

OUTWARD BOUND '43.

Long ago we sailed the Foyle, saw its waters churn and boil.
Our propeller thrashed - a final spree - and then was still
    - by Derry's Quay.

And Derry saw our tired face, clasped us in a warm embrace,
Our refuge from the restless sea, we nestled snug
    - by Derry's Quay.

Saddened, weary, age-old men, suddenly were boys again
who laughed and danced - and some maybe found true love
    - by Derry's Quay.

How short the time before the river stirred again, the hull a-shiver
Beyond the Lough, the remorseless sea called us back
    - from Derry's Quay.

Long ago we sailed the Foyle, back to war's demanding toil;
we'll rest no more by Derry's Quay
    - is there a Quay by Galilee ?

H.M.S. POLYANTHUS was torpedoed by U 952 in position 57.00N 31.10W. at 23.20 on the 20th of September, 1943
    She was south of Greenland.